Nazi Prisons in the British Isles

Nazi Prisons in the British Isles

Political Prisoners during the German Occupation of Jersey and Guernsey, 1940–1945

Gilly Carr

Series Consultant
Nicholas J. Saunders

PEN & SWORD
ARCHAEOLOGY

First published in Great Britain in 2020 by
PEN & SWORD ARCHAEOLOGY
An imprint of
Pen & Sword Books Ltd
Yorkshire - Philadelphia

Copyright © Gilly Carr, 2020

ISBN 978 1 52677 093 6

The right of Gilly Carr to be identified as Author of this work has been asserted by her in accordance with the Copyright, Designs and Patents Act 1988.

A CIP catalogue record for this book is available from the British Library

All rights reserved. No part of this book may be reproduced or transmitted in any form or by any means, electronic or mechanical including photocopying, recording or by any information storage and retrieval system, without permission from the Publisher in writing.

Typeset in Ehrhardt MT & 11/14.5
by Aura Technology and Software Services, India.

Printed and bound in the UK by TJ International Ltd.

Pen & Sword Books Ltd incorporates the imprints of Pen & Sword Archaeology, Atlas, Aviation, Battleground, Discovery, Family History, History, Maritime, Military, Naval, Politics, Social History, Transport, True Crime, Claymore Press, Frontline Books, Praetorian Press, Seaforth Publishing and White Owl

For a complete list of Pen & Sword titles please contact

PEN & SWORD BOOKS LTD
47 Church Street, Barnsley, South Yorkshire, S70 2AS, England
E-mail: enquiries@pen-and-sword.co.uk
Website: www.pen-and-sword.co.uk

Or

PEN & SWORD BOOKS
1950 Lawrence Rd, Havertown, PA 19083, USA
E-mail: Uspen-and-sword@casematepublishers.com
Website: www.penandswordbooks.com

Contents

Acknowledgements	ix
List of Illustrations	xi
Modern Conflict Archaeology	xv
Preface	xix
Prologue – The Sexton's Tale	1

Part I – Jersey Prison

Chapter 1 – Introduction and Sources	7
Chapter 2 – The Geography of Jersey Prison	19
Chapter 3 – Who were the Political Prisoners?	41
Chapter 4 – Interrogation, Incarceration and Solitary Confinement	45
Chapter 5 – 'Rather a Mixed Crowd': The Prisoners and the Guards	53
Chapter 6 – Solidarity, Legitimacy and Resistance	63
Chapter 7 – 'The 'Calendars . . . of Previous Prisoners': Graffiti and Interior Decoration	79
Chapter 8 – 'Yielding to so Rare a Pleasure': Autograph Books and Artwork	83
Chapter 9 – 'Any Time Now!' The End is Nigh?	99

Part II – Guernsey Prison

Chapter 10 – Introduction and Sources	109
Chapter 11 – The Changing Geography of Guernsey Prison	119
Chapter 12 – The Names and Numbers of Prisoners	131

Chapter 13 – Daily Life in the German Side of the Prison   139
Chapter 14 – Forced Labour   153
Chapter 15 – Interrogation and Trial   157
Chapter 16 – Violence and the Case of the Guernsey Police   163
Chapter 17 – Conclusion: A Comparison of the Prisons in the
             Channel Islands with the Nazi-Controlled Prisons
             in Europe   175
Postscript: The 1946 Hilton Report   183

Notes   187
Bibliography   205
Index   207

Any Time Now!

The political prisoners' poem, composed in Jersey Prison in 1943 by Joseph Tierney, one of the Jersey 21

At our hotel in Gloucester Street
When we all get together,
And talk of soup that's green, and bread
That's tough as any leather.
A chum of ours chants this refrain
In every kind of weather: 'Any time now!'

We talk in whispers low, in case
The Boche should overhear us,
We peep round every corner, for
The Guv'nor might be near us,
And when we plan our getaway
We have this thought to cheer us: 'Any time now!'

We ask 'When does invasion send
Our armies o'er the waters?
When shall we drive the Huns right out
And free our sons and daughters?
And, all old soldiers have their fill
Of beer and ales and porters? Any time now!'

How soon will profiteers be made
To walk the line and dither?
Black-marketeers in harbour mud
Be pummelled hither-thither?
And States officials all sent to – Well
To play upon the zither? 'Any time now!'

And should we say, how soon the day
Will come for our returning –
And how long will it be before
The home-fires we'll be burning?
The answer still is just the same
It needs but little learning:
'ANY TIME NOW!'

Acknowledgements

The author would like to acknowledge the help of a number of people during the research for this book. In Jersey, I would like to thank most especially the staff at Jersey Heritage, Jersey Archives, the Lord Coutanche Library at the Société Jersiaise, Jersey War Tunnels and at St Helier public library. I have also received help from several former political prisoners, including Francis Harris, who answered many letters from me in 2010, and Peter Gray, who lent me his unpublished manuscript in 2012, and which I tried to get published; it was not to be. My thanks to Micky Neil, who gave me an interview during the research for *Protest, Defiance and Resistance in the Channel Islands: German Occupation 1940–45*. He also let me view George Le Marquand's diary. Pauline Hacquoil let me photograph her aunt's letter; it is from her that I got Dora Hacquoil's wonderful description of her cell. Barbara Greene, daughter of the indomitable Belza Turner, made contact with me more than five years after I put out a call in the *Jersey Evening Post* for her to get in touch. Like a note in a bottle flung into the ocean, that message eventually arrived in Toronto and she has kindly shared many documents from her mother's collection with me. Richard Ahier and Victor Webb kindly allowed me to photograph their political prisoner certificates.

I passed an idyllic Jersey summer afternoon with Paulette de la Haye (who must have the most glorious view in the Island from her back garden) while she showed me her mother and grandfather's political prisoner autograph book. Angela O'Connor told me about her father's experience as a prison warder during the Occupation, and Wendy Janvrin-Tipping generously permitted me to photograph her mother and aunt's beautiful political prisoner autograph books and preserved painted egg, which readers can now see in Wendy's own book, *Any Day Now*. I owe her my sincere thanks for allowing some of the images to be reproduced in this book. Mick Mière, son of Joe Mière, allowed me to take boxes of his father's papers back to my hotel to read each evening – I thank him for his trust in lending such precious papers. My thanks also to Brian Le Cornu, who lent me his glass slides of images of the inside of Jersey Prison, taken before it was demolished. I was able to scan these for this book. Alex Stuart from the department of Modern and Mediaeval Languages at the University of Cambridge translated the pages of the works of Claude Cahun, whose voice is so eloquent and important in understanding Jersey Prison.

In Guernsey, the staff of the Island Archives, especially Nathan Coyde and Darryl Ogier, were extremely kind and helpful, always putting up with my endless requests for further documents and permissions to see them. I would like to thank Museum of London Archaeology (MOLA) for allowing me to use the images of the demolished Guernsey Prison, currently kept at the Island Archives. Susan Ilie has been my invaluable eyes and hands at the archives in Guernsey in between my research visits, helping me winkle out information and images from the archives, and many times thinking up new ways to get the information I needed. My thanks to her for also taking several photos for this book. At the Priaulx Library, Sue Laker kindly helped me find papers connected to the prison. My greatest thanks in Guernsey must go to the families who let me study and quote from their family member's diaries, unpublished memoirs and letters: the families of Frank Falla, Gerald Domaille, Hubert Lanyon, Henry Marquand and Cecil Duquemin. My thanks to Bill Ozanne, for generously letting me quote from Marie Ozanne's diary. Olive Frampton also kindly spoke to me on the phone almost a decade ago about her time in Guernsey Prison. In London, further research was carried out at the Imperial War Museum and The National Archives; precious gems were extracted from documents kept at these institutions, even the wartime report marked 'DESTROYED'.

Susanne Carr kindly proofread Part I, on Jersey Prison, and I thank her for saving me from howlers. Nick Saunders, my mentor of the last decade and a half, also read through the manuscript and made suggestions. I am very grateful to him for his wonderful preface and for inviting me to publish this book in his series. Finally, I would like to thank Pat Fisher for showing me the precious papers belonging to her father, Joseph Tierney. I hope that she likes his voice at the start of this book.

List of Illustrations

Portrait of Joe Mière by Andrew Tift
The exercise yard of Naumburg Prison today
The Frank Falla Archive homepage, www.frankfallaarchive.org
Part of Frank Falla's personal archive
Former political prisoner Richard Ahier after interview by the author
Political Prisoner logbook
Dr Philip Bentlif
Location of Jersey Prison within St Helier, Ordnance Survey Map 1935
The 1812 prison block (A-Block) before its demolition
A corridor in Jersey Prison in the 1960s or 1970s
A cell in A-Block
The prison chapel
Jersey Prison
The stone yard, later on renamed the wood yard after prisoners used it for cutting wood
Prison cell in B-Block
Peep-hole or 'judas-hole' in a prison cell door
A typical prison door, today preserved in Jersey Museum
The prison chapel
Exercise yard with the Prison Governor's house in the background
The prison library in the 1970s
The Viscount (Charles Le Gros) and the Receiver-General (Major John Giffard), two members of the Prison Board
George Le Marquand
George Le Marquand's prison card
Silvertide today
The Folie Inn today
Wölfle, Lohse and Bode of the *Geheime Feldpolizei*
Avondale, Lower King's Cliff today
Peter Gray
Ernest Briard (Prison Governor) and Dina Briard (Prison Matron)

Ernest Briard's signature in Pauline Lamy's autograph book
Page of a library book pricked with a pin by François Scornet to create words of defiance
Nurse Renée Griffin's autograph book
Page from Nurse Renée Griffin's autograph book signed by Peter Gray
Page from Peter Gray's autograph book signed by Harry Durtnall
Example of patriotic artwork in autograph book belonging to Evelyn Janvrin
Belza Turner's political prisoner certificate
Belza Turner
Image of Britannia in Muriel Costard's autograph book
Image of Peter Gray in Nurse Renée Griffin's autograph book
Victor Webb's entry in Nurse Renée Griffin's autograph book
Bernard Hassall's entry in Peter Gray's autograph book
George Le Marquand's entry in Nurse Renée Griffin's autograph book
Edward Rutherford's entry in Nurse Renée Griffin's autograph book
Siebe Koster's entry in Nurse Renée Griffin's autograph book
Frank Keiller's entry in Nurse Renée Griffin's autograph book
Prison artwork by Allan Costard
Image of the demolition of Jersey Prison
The remains of the stones of the 1812 block of Jersey Prison today
Philip Bailhache unveiling the Political Prisoner Memorial, April 1995
Location of Guernsey Prison, St Peter Port, 1939 Ordnance Survey Map
Frank Falla's book, *The Silent War*
Occupation registration card photographs of Frank Falla and John Hayes
Occupation registration card photographs of Hubert Lanyon and Cecil Duquemin
Marie Ozanne and Olive Frampton
Main building of Guernsey Prison
Reconstructed facade inside Magistrate's Court, Guernsey
Plan of Guernsey Prison
Occupation registration card photograph of Harold Blampied
Occupation registration card photo of Albert Pike and William Ferbrache
Prison building used for the incarceration of male civil prisoners during the Occupation
The Gaoler's house
Entry in prison logbook
Frank Falla's prison diary
Sketch of his prison cell by Norman Dexter, 9 September 1943

Photograph of prison cell taken in 2003
Marie Ozanne's diary on display in Guernsey Museum
'The Terres' (*GFP* headquarters in use 1944), as it looks today
The Magistrate's Court today
Occupation registration card photographs of Kingston Bailey and Frank Tuck
Grange Lodge, headquarters of the *GFP* in 1942
The entrance to Fort George today
The remains of the exercise yard of the former prison today
Cell door keys from Jersey Prison

Modern Conflict Archaeology

THE SERIES

Modern Conflict Archaeology is a new and interdisciplinary approach to the study of twentieth and twenty-first century conflicts. It focuses on the innumerable ways in which humans interact with, and are changed by, the intense material realities of war. These can be traditional wars between nation states, civil wars, religious and ethnic conflicts, terrorism, and even proxy wars where hostilities have not been declared yet nevertheless exist. The material realities can be as small as a machine-gun, as intermediate as a war memorial or an aeroplane, or as large as a whole battle-zone landscape. As well as technologies, they can be more intimately personal – conflict-related photographs and diaries, films, uniforms, the war-maimed, and 'the missing'. All are the consequences of conflict, as none would exist without it.

Modern Conflict Archaeology (MCA) is a handy title, but is really shorthand for a more powerful and hybrid agenda. It draws not only on modern scientific archaeology, but on the anthropology of material culture, landscape, and identity, as well as aspects of military and cultural history, geography, and museum, heritage, and tourism studies. All or some of these can inform different aspects of research, but none are overly privileged. The challenge posed by modern conflict demands a coherent, integrated, sensitised yet muscular response in order to capture as many different kinds of information and insight as possible by exploring the 'social lives' of war objects through the changing values and attitudes attached to them over time.

This series originates in this new engagement with modern conflict, and seeks to bring the extraordinary range of latest research to a passionate and informed general readership. The aim is to investigate and understand arguably the most powerful force to have shaped our world during the last century – modern industrialised conflict in its myriad shapes and guises, and in its enduring and volatile legacies

THIS BOOK

An integral part of Modern Conflict Archaeology is the anthropology of material culture. While large-scale and visually impressive objects often command our attention, it can be smaller more personal items which carry a greater emotional charge, and sometimes preserve information that would otherwise be lost. In both world wars, handwritten letters and documents are arguably some of the most powerfully evocative and informative kinds of such material culture, providing insights into the social, physical, and psychological lives of those who produced them. Counter-intuitively, such fragile objects often survive where larger more overtly robust objects do not. During, and beyond, the Second World War, documents produced by those incarcerated in Jersey and Guernsey provide a wealth of data, and in a philosophical sense stand in for those individuals who are no longer here.

Gilly Carr's research over the last fourteen years has transformed our knowledge and understanding of the Nazi Occupation of the Channel Islands during the Second World War and its many legacies. Her indefatigable investigations are a benchmark for such interdisciplinary work, and her publications are mileposts recording her and our progress in understanding what occupation and resistance mean, how they can be assessed, and what they can teach us for the future. Her research, therefore, is a unique contribution to the study of the Channel Islands, and to the nature and consequences of imprisonment and occupation.

In this book, Gilly has written an erudite and highly accessible account of the experiences of political prisoners in Jersey and Guernsey during the Second World War. Her encyclopedic knowledge of public and private sources as well as her relationships with individual descendants allows her to get as close as we will probably ever get to knowing about and understanding what these men and women experienced. She draws on the available documents – memoirs, diaries, autograph books, paintings, as well as official records – to bring the story alive; it reads like, and indeed is, an account of war experiences of incarceration in the prisoners' own words. In this way it is an ethnography, a contribution of detail and value to the endeavour of modern conflict archaeology's aim of capturing and presenting as much information as possible about a particular conflict.

This book is neither military history nor an avowedly theoretical text. Yet it is deeply anthropological in the stories it tells and thereby preserves. It penetrates deep into the human experience of physical and psychological constraint and suffering at many different levels. For example, while torture on the Channel

Islands didn't reach the levels of Nazi prisons and camps on mainland Europe, it is still shocking to read what did occur, and disturbing to be told how a prisoner's eyes watered in reaction to the everyday stench of the toilet bucket in his cell. Carr pulls no punches, yet navigates skilfully between the terrible, the bad, the not so bad, and the occasionally uplifting.

Importantly, we see too how memoirs and diaries are not just the record of events, but multi-dimensional objects in their own right, with trajectories and unintended consequences of their own. We are shown how they can be mined for rich contextual details – occasional references that give clues to issues not otherwise dealt with in an obvious way. We are told how the production of certain documents and activities created a 'political prisoner consciousness' – which, as Carr herself writes, was 'a mindset and bonds of friendship' which 'stayed with them all their lives, and was likely to be a common motivating factor in encouraging them to write their memoirs'. Here we see plainly how an aspect of group identity can be created at the time of collective suffering and how, much later, it can in turn lead to new kinds of material culture – the memoirs written after the war.

It is both interesting and insightful to see how different were the attitudes towards the prisons in Jersey and Guernsey, though both are now demolished. While Jersey's can be regarded as a site of martyrdom, suffering, and the location for the production of political prisoner consciousness, in Guernsey the old prison evoked little local affection and no sense of commemorative value. As Carr tells us this is likely because Guernsey's prisoners focused their attention on the Nazi prisons and camps on continental Europe where many were subsequently taken. Two islands, two prisons, and two sets of prisoners all under Nazi occupation, yet two very different legacies today.

This is an important book which tells a universal human story of incarceration, albeit focused on the author's richly detailed knowledge of the Channel Islands during the Second World War. Ultimately it shows how human lives are invested in objects, and how these objects convey those lives across time and space.

Nicholas J. Saunders
University of Bristol
March 2020

Preface

I write this foreword after returning from a research trip to the Baltic cities of Vilnius, Riga and Tallinn, where I explored the former KGB prison cells now presented to the public as heritage sites. Jersey and Guernsey prisons were very much in my mind. The prisons in all three Baltic cities are visually very similar, although presented to the public in different ways. In Vilnius I was shown round by a tour guide, but in Riga a former political prisoner guided me round the cells. His testimony was a powerful one, and the resulting tour had a greater emotional impact on me as he was able to relate his experiences to the surviving fabric of the prison. In Tallinn, the wealthiest of the three cities today, the stories of those who were interrogated and imprisoned by the KGB was mediated through art installations, films of oral testimony, prisoners' quotes on the wall, projected images of watching eyes and by transcripts of interrogations.

All of these made me wonder: if Jersey's Occupation-era prison in Gloucester Street, for example, still stood today, what would it be used for? What narratives would be associated with it? Would it still function as a prison, as is the case today for many former Nazi prisons throughout Europe, or would it be a heritage site? If so, at what point would it have made this transformation? Would its very presence have meant that Jersey would have begun to recognise political prisoners as people who 'did the right thing' at an earlier date? This seems unlikely, given that the guardian of memory of political prisoners, the late Joe Mière, had a fight on his hands to get a memorial erected outside the site of the prison even in 1995.

If political prisoners had been recognised as heroes after the Occupation, would the prison – or some of it – have been retained as a heritage site? Would former political prisoners have given guided tours and testified to their treatment during arrest, interrogation and imprisonment? If Jersey Heritage owned the prison today, or had preserved some of the cells (in addition to the cell door that it owns and displays in Jersey Museum), how would it be presented to the public? How would this have changed through the years since the Occupation? Now that we are on the very edge of living memory of former political prisoners, their story could no longer be related by the men and women who survived Jersey or Guernsey prisons.

But I would like to think that enough information survives in their memoirs, their autograph books, paintings and diaries to tell their story in their own words.

Jersey Prison was demolished in 1975 while Guernsey Prison was knocked down only in 2003. We can visit these places today only in the imagination. I hope that this book will provide enough information to enable future generations to visualise and understand the prisons and their system of operation during the Occupation. I also hope that, should such dark times ever descend on us again, the political prisoners have provided us with enough good advice about how to circumvent the circumstances of the incarceration, and how to survive to ensure that the voices of the imprisoned will not be forgotten.

Gilly Carr
University of Cambridge
March 2020

Prologue – The Sexton's Tale

'We must keep smiling and not let Jerry get us down!'

These words, written in black ink on yellowing paper, in a letter from husband to wife during the Second World War, seem a symbolic – even clichéd – evocation of the British war mentality. They are almost stereotypical of the period and could have been written by any British person, such as a prisoner of war, or perhaps a Londoner exhibiting the 'Blitz spirit'. They were, in fact, written by a Briton in a prison under Nazi control. That prison was on British soil.

The 31-year-old sexton of St Saviour's Parish Church in Jersey, Joseph Tierney, had been incarcerated in Jersey Prison, in St Helier, since 3 March 1943. His wife, Eileen, four months pregnant with the couple's first child, was left at home to worry about her husband's fate, although the couple were able to smuggle letters to each other. Tierney was part of what we might now recognise as a resistance group in the German-occupied Channel Islands. Certainly the men involved with him were united in their defiance of the occupiers, but they probably saw themselves as doing nothing more than making sure the BBC news – free of Nazi propaganda – was passed to their friends and other Islanders further afield. However, since radios had been banned and confiscated by the occupiers in June 1942, anybody caught listening to a hidden wireless or writing down the BBC news and circulating it (as Tierney had) was in grave danger of arrest, imprisonment and deportation to the continent. All Tierney could do was to wait in a prison cell with his friends. One by one, they were deported, but Tierney remained – for a while.

A prominent figure in the 'St Saviour's wireless case', as it was termed in Jersey at the time of the trial of those involved, Tierney had written out the news he received every morning from his friend John Nicolle and Nicolle's father, who had retained a radio set. Tierney and another friend produced news-sheets, which were then taken to Canon Clifford Cohu, the acting rector at St Saviour's Church. Cohu would then spread the news in St Helier, the Island's capital, most particularly in the General Hospital, where he was also chaplain.[1]

Quite how many people were involved in this group is unknown, but Joseph Tierney was the first to be caught. Although a total of eighteen people were tried, more were interrogated.² The trial – which became a show-trial to dissuade the rest of the population from illegally listening to the radio and spreading the news – took place on 9 April 1943 and large crowds gathered outside the court house in Royal Square in St Helier, eagerly awaiting the result. Joseph Tierney was, like the others, convicted by German military court martial. He received a sentence of two years for 'manufacturing and distributing leaflets'.

At the beginning of his experience at the hands of his interrogators, Tierney was placed by the *Geheime Feldpolizei* (Secret Field Police, known locally to Islanders as the 'Gestapo'; hereafter *GFP*) in solitary confinement in Jersey Prison. Eileen Tierney later wrote that:

> He went through many nights of mental torture. The Germans then took me to the prison where they used me as the final weapon in their foul endeavours to make my husband talk and confess to what they already knew. They threatened me, pregnant at the time, with a concentration camp in front of my husband. After a whole day's questioning they allowed me to go home. After this experience I was always terrified whenever I saw a member of the Gestapo . . . Before he was questioned my husband told me that the Gestapo had said 'You know you can be shot for what you've done'.³

Eileen's words, written twenty years later in a compensation testimony, give us a unique insight into the methods and regime within this Nazi-controlled prison on British soil, as will be discussed later.

Tierney was not, in the end, shot, but neither did he survive the war. What has survived are his prison letters, kept by his daughter Patricia, whose baptism he was allowed to attend on 29 August 1943 before his deportation three weeks later. Such letters are extremely rare, and all the more so because they belonged to a member of a group known in the Island as the 'Jersey 21'; those who were deported for an act of protest, defiance or resistance and did not return after the war.

Tierney's letters give us a small insight into life in Jersey Prison; they also name some of the other men with whom he was imprisoned, and describe methods of smuggling letters in to the prison. As many of the German records relating to Jersey Prison were destroyed at the end of the war, and yet more in the 1970s, when the prison building was demolished, our knowledge of who was held when is incomplete. Our knowledge of who shared cells with whom is also sketchy. The trajectory of these British men and women through prisons on the continent is similarly imperfect, so the testimony of former prisoners about their conditions of internment is all the more valuable.

Tierney was deported to two prisons in France, followed by four in Germany, and a Czech forced labour camp. Sometimes he was in the company of other Channel Islanders in his places of incarceration. They were able to later testify to his presence; such testimonies are of the greatest importance to us when trying to reconstruct journeys across prisons in occupied territories. Those who survived tell us that Tierney constantly worried about his wife and daughter and counted the days until he could be reunited with them.

The last Channel Islander to see Joseph Tierney alive was Guernseyman Frank Falla, a fellow prisoner in Naumburg Prison, and a later campaigner for compensation for Islanders who had experienced Nazi prisons and camps. Falla's writings were not the last to record Tierney's presence; that sad duty fell to two Belgians. One, Albert Sauvage, was in Zöschen labour camp with Tierney, and recorded the escape attempt made by the two of them from the forced march on which they were placed as they left the camp in early April 1945. The other, Albert Koch, was in the cattle truck in which Tierney had been thrown after he was caught. Joseph Tierney died in Koch's arms in early May 1945. There was, wrote Koch, 'a sincere and spontaneous friendship which grew during the atrocious agony which we had to endure which alas ended with the death of the person who died in my arms and will remain for me a model of courage, bravery and self-sacrifice'.[4]

The letters written by Koch and Sauvage, kept to this day despite their ragged and torn state, were treasured by Eileen Tierney as a last link to her husband. These letters also provided crucial evidence, in 2016, to find the body of Joseph Tierney. Koch and Sauvage had given information about the route of the cattle truck, and its final intended destination of Theresienstadt concentration camp. Thanks to these two Belgian men, the location of the village of the mass grave in which Tierney's body was thrown by the SS was identified as Kaštice in the Czech Republic. Archives in Prague confirmed that Tierney and those in the grave with him were exhumed from July to August 1945 and their bodies transferred to a Catholic cemetery in the nearby hamlet of Pšov.[5]

In March 2016, I travelled with Patricia, Joseph Tierney's daughter, to visit her father's grave. She carried with her some ash from her mother's cremated remains and scattered them on his place of burial, reuniting her parents once again. We were accompanied by the BBC, who made a documentary of our extraordinary journey.

Also on this pilgrimage across Europe was Jean, the daughter of another Channel Islander. Joseph Gillingham from Guernsey had been in a number of the same prisons as Tierney. He, too, had been involved in disseminating the BBC news; like Tierney, he did not survive the war. Thanks to documents still surviving in archives in Halle, Germany, Gillingham's final resting place was also located. For the first time in over seventy years, Gillingham's daughter was reunited with her father.

Prison-related records surviving from the Second World War, whether official archival records, memoirs or letters, or many of the other forms of testimony that will be discussed here, can still be of crucial importance to families today. These records can be pieced together to reconstruct the lives of those long gone. Now, seventy-five years after the end of the war, they can still be used to track the trajectories and find the bodies of former political prisoners who defied the Nazi regime, including those imprisoned on British soil.

In this sense, of course, the study of such documents is an integral part of the interdisciplinary study of modern conflict, where, as material culture, they enable the partial reconstruction of the experiences and lives of those who were imprisoned during the Nazi Occupation of the Channel Islands. The biographies of these various documents incorporate the lives of their creators as well as of those who came into contact with them after 1945. Their significance is all the more valuable as the large-scale material culture of the events – Jersey and Guernsey prisons – are no longer available to study, having been demolished in 1975 and 2003 respectively. Conflict has unpredictable consequences, and it is indeed ironic yet fortunate that fragile paper records have survived where large stone-built structures have not.

Part I
JERSEY PRISON

Chapter 1
Introduction and Sources

His Majesty's Prison, Jersey (often referred to as Gloucester Street Prison or Newgate Street Prison – both streets bordered the prison compound, although the main entrance was in Gloucester Street) has emerged as a special place in the memory of many people from Jersey, for it was here that 'political prisoner consciousness' was formed. Despite attempts on behalf of the occupiers at dividing prisoners, putting them in solitary confinement, mixing up nationalities, moving prisoners between different cells, and between different prison blocks at various stages in their prison career, many young (and not so young) men and women were able to communicate with each other to solidify their patriotic ideology and resistance against the occupiers. Many in this group were to grow to maturity – and even old age – without letting go of their pride in their wartime activities and their patriotic stance. Most importantly, they never lost their conviction that their resistant and defiant actions were not only legitimate, but the *only* legitimate stance to take against the occupiers. We must acknowledge most particularly the role of former political prisoner Joe Mière, later a curator of an occupation museum once known as the Underground Hospital, the former name for what is known today as Jersey War Tunnels. Joe made it his life's work to preserve the memory of Jersey's political prisoners and their stories. His notes about the prison and annotations of a plan of the prison are split today between Jersey Archives and Jersey War Tunnels.

Our knowledge of the activities of political prisoners in Jersey Prison during the German Occupation is scattered across a variety of sources. The bringing together and critical analysis of all available records has never before been carried out, although attempts have been made in the past, which have sometimes been partial, brief, poorly referenced or unreferenced altogether, which – for the serious researcher – is a handicap. For when the sources of research notes or short articles are not properly referenced, it is impossible to tell whether the information came directly from the mouth of a former political prisoner in 1945, or from a prisoner's grandchild in the present (with all that this entails regarding loss of detail and the addition of confusion over time), or from a diary, a memoir or from contemporary archival sources. It also means that we lose the nuance of whether the information is from a man or woman, what year they were in prison and for what offence.

Portrait of Joe Mière by Andrew Tift. (Jersey Heritage Collections, Copyright Andrew Tift)

Without this knowledge, assessing either the veracity or the reliability of the information is impossible. Neither is it possible to factor in the weaknesses inherent in certain types of sources, or the knowledge of whether the perspective is unusual, typical, or time- or gender-specific. This book attempts to address these issues. While these shorter or unreferenced secondary accounts have been read by the author, they have not been drawn upon or quoted in this research as their authenticity cannot be guaranteed. Wherever possible, this book relies upon primary sources alone.

This book does not purport to present a chronological overview of the experience of political prisoners from 1940 to 1945. The archival resources are simply not fine-grained enough to allow this. However, it is written in order to provide an insight into prison geography and the prisons' regimes, and to build an idea of the typical experience of a prisoner who passed through the system during the Occupation, and how they circumvented the prison system for their own ends.

It is worth pausing at the outset to consider the Jersey 21 in particular: most of these people were, before their deportation to prisons and camps on the continent, political prisoners in HMP Jersey. Their experiences and their voices are now almost entirely lost to us because they did not survive. However, a few letters to their families have survived, written while in Jersey Prison. It is in acknowledgement of their experience, and a desire to bring them into the story, that I have included at the start of this book a poem about Jersey Prison composed by Joseph Tierney in 1943, before his deportation. His sentiments echo that of political prisoners of 1944 and 1945, leading us to observe that the foundations of political prisoner consciousness were already present and thriving at this date.

One of the curiosities of the testimonies, diaries, memoirs and autograph books which detail the experience of internment in Guernsey and Jersey's prisons during the German Occupation is that they are very heavily skewed towards Jersey. We can even speak in terms of a genre of Occupation prison literature from Jersey, but not from Guernsey. In fact, to learn anything at all about Guernsey Prison during the Occupation in the words of those who were imprisoned there is very difficult indeed. Such information can usually only be gleaned from the few testimonies which have continental Nazi prisons and concentration camps as their focus and Guernsey Prison as their first step. Even then, the evidence is scant and glossed over. There are also a tiny number of short unpublished memoirs to draw upon, which I have done here.

While this gap seems, on the face of it, puzzling, the explanation lies in the prisoners themselves, the offences for which they were imprisoned, and the reasons why they chose to write about their experiences. At the heart of this lies the status of 'political prisoner', an epithet claimed by people from both Islands but, crucially, was a title applied in different circumstances. For those from Guernsey who were deported to continental prisons and camps, their political prisoner consciousness was forged in the squalid, unsanitary, lice-infested cells of continental Nazi prisons, where they were kept with people from other parts of Europe who had committed acts of resistance. These political prisoners inspired those from Guernsey to see themselves in similar terms. In Jersey, despite the similar experience of people from that Island in continental prisons, the term 'political prisoner' was used to denote those who spent time in Jersey Prison. Further, it was a title claimed by a very particular group of young men and women imprisoned from the late summer of 1944. The deportation vessels containing prisoners stopped travelling to Granville or St Malo in July 1944 in the wake of the D-Day landings in Normandy and the subsequent piecemeal liberation of France in the months that followed.

What united groups in Guernsey and Jersey was that the title of political prisoner was not only politically motivated, but had to be earned through suffering in prison *for specific offences*. Those offences had to be patriotically motivated acts of resistance against the Germans. While not everyone from Guernsey who was deported to Nazi prisons and camps seems to have described or thought of themselves in this way, it is clear that people like Frank Falla (a member of the Guernsey Underground News Service) did, as did those Islanders who kept him company in Frankfurt Preungesheim and Naumburg prisons which held a number of Channel Islanders at the same time. These men who knew each other in prison described themselves and their suffering in *political* terms, believing that the injustices suffered by people who had committed no *criminal* act would increase their chances of compensation during the mid-1960s compensation claims for victims of Nazism.

There are a number of different extant sources, which each give us a different insight into Jersey Prison and its workings during the Occupation. First and foremost, there are a small number of memoirs,[1] all written by men and mostly by those who were caught trying to escape from the Island or who were convicted for stealing or stockpiling weapons and belonging to small resistance groups. Most of the people who indulged in either of these offences were (during the Occupation)

The exercise yard of Naumburg Prison today. (Copyright Gilly Carr)

young people in their late teens and early twenties. They were strongly patriotically motivated,[2] found more like-minded friends in prison and together developed a 'political prisoner consciousness'. This mind-set and bonds of friendship stayed with them all their lives, and was likely to be a common motivating factor in encouraging them to write their memoirs. They were also motivated to legitimise their actions to their fellow Islanders who might have considered them to be 'trouble-makers'. A third motivation might have been to correct the popular opinion outside the Channel Islands that Islanders collaborated during the Occupation. This group was united by its patriotism and its desire to legitimise acts committed by their younger selves. It is not surprising that most of these memoirs were published after the erection of a memorial to political prisoners in St Helier in 1995. This memorial gave them a voice and reminded them of a past (and, for some, present) identity. The unveiling provided an opportunity for them to meet up again, talk about the past, and perhaps prompted some to write their wartime stories.

To these, we can add the very small number of memoirs published by higher profile publishers and written by more controversial figures (some of whom were English and came to Jersey just before the Occupation). Among these we include Eric Pleasants[3] and Eddie Chapman.[4] Other memoirs were written by people who went on to experience the full horror of Nazi concentration camps, namely Jerseyman Anthony Faramus.[5] While these books speak to an audience beyond that of other political prisoners in Jersey, with whom they did not feel any great affiliation, their insights into Jersey Prison in the early years of the Occupation are valuable. The unpublished memoir of Peter Hassall, a Jerseyman who survived horrific treatment in Nazi concentration camps as a *Nacht und Nebel* prisoner,[6] also gives us an insight into the treatment of prisoners in Jersey Prison who committed serious offences.[7]

These categories of political prisoner memoir are supplemented by a veritable cottage industry of general Occupation memoirs and diaries, published and unpublished. A small number of these mention the prison,[8] and one of the diaries drawn upon in this book was written by a local politician, Deputy Edward Le Quesne, who spent a brief period in prison for possession of a radio. As an older adult and a person in a position of authority, he was able to plead with some success for a number of concessions for the other prisoners. It seems that there was mutual benefit to his period of incarceration. Just as his diary suggests evidence that he became more politicised (or supportive of political prisoners and their cause) by his brief time in prison, so the other prisoners learned negotiation skills from him which they could use to improve their conditions.

Letters between incarcerated prisoners, between prisoners and their families, and between prisoners after the Occupation are another important source of insight into prison life. As they were private, they can often shed light on real emotions behind the bravado put on for a wider audience. As most of the prisoners were either in solitary confinement, or else in overcrowded cells, that 'wider audience' was the wider group of political prisoners, who communicated with each other through autograph books and artwork which was passed from cell to cell and slid under doors.

One of the most detailed and complete insights into Jersey Prison was written in a series of letters by Claude Cahun, the nom de plume of Lucy Schwob, who, with her step-sister and life partner, Suzanne Malherbe, settled in Jersey from France shortly before the war. These have been drawn on extensively for the richness of their content and commentary on important details which others have glossed over or forgotten in the half-century which lay between the events and putting them down on paper. As educated women and, by their own admission, outsiders, these women offer us a different perspective to that of the teenage schoolboys and young people who filled the prison in the last year of the end of the Occupation. They also give us an insight into the female experience.

We are also fortunate to have at our disposal a new source of information: the recently opened testimonies of Nazi persecution written for compensation in the mid-1960s and available at The National Archives (TNA) in London since 2016. The author was responsible for getting these documents transferred to TNA and opened to the public after four years of pressure on the Foreign Office to release documents relating to Channel Islanders. The author has had access to

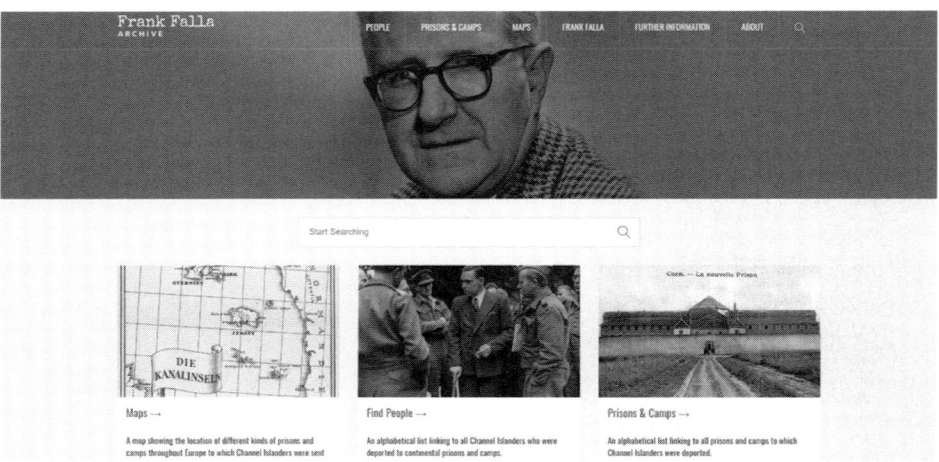

The Frank Falla Archive homepage, www.frankfallaarchive.org. (Copyright Gilly Carr)

these documents since 2012 after providing proof of death of those Islanders who applied for compensation, which itself was produced after a period of archival research and the help of the archive services in Guernsey and Jersey. Copies of all these testimonies are available on a website written by the author, the Frank Falla Archive (www.frankfallaarchive.org), hosted by Jersey Heritage.

The website is named after Guernseyman Frank Falla because he was the Channel Islander who made it his personal responsibility, in the absence of any official help from the governments of Guernsey or Jersey, to help Islanders claim compensation for deportation to Nazi prisons and concentration camps. He collected copies of the testimonies he helped to write and they were present in his personal archives which were given to the author by Falla's daughter in 2010. These ultimately provided the clue to the vast wealth of closed testimonies still held by the Foreign Office at that time. The reader is invited to browse this website to find out more about the experiences of Islanders in continental prisons and camps.

In addition to memoirs and testimonies, some oral testimony collection has also been possible, although very few political prisoners are still alive today.

Part of Frank Falla's personal archive. (Copyright Gilly Carr)

The memories of these men[9] are hampered by the passage of seventy years or more since their period of incarceration. Further, they only saw and understood things from their own experience and had little knowledge of the wider prison system, or of the trajectory of other kinds of prisoners, or of what went on in other prison blocks that they had not visited personally.

To the perspective of prisoners we can add the archival records of officialdom. These comprise correspondence – relating to prisoners and prison conditions – between the Germans and the local authorities, and between prisoners and the Prison Board. These are important for giving us alternative perspectives on the prison and for allowing us an insight into the position of the Bailiff[10] and other members of the Prison Board who had to avoid provoking the Germans while at the same time looking after Jersey prisoners. Unfortunately, many of these archival records have been lost, perhaps thrown away at the time of the demolition of the prison. This means that we lack many key records kept by the prison governor or warders, or the Prison Board. Our sources are thus partial and biased towards the prisoners.

Former political prisoner Richard Ahier after interview by the author.
(Copyright Gilly Carr)

Introduction and Sources   15

The prison ledger for the German side of Jersey Prison would – if it existed – be a key archival source. The closest alternatives, kept by Jersey Archives today, are two books. The first is a record of the sentences of Islanders who passed through Jersey Prison[11], and the second is a record of sentences of just the political prisoners.[12] While this may sound ideal, it does not list those put in prison and not yet sentenced. This group were kept on the military side of the prison and guarded by Germans. Whether the original prison ledger recorded the entry of all into the prison, or whether the Germans kept their own records of their prisoners, we do not know as no such records survive. All we can observe is that not all 'known' prisoners are recorded in official records and, indeed, not all sentenced prisoners are recorded in official records. This is why autograph books are so important in adding extra names to our list. While we are all too painfully aware of the theft of records from a government building in Jersey in 1991 (5 per cent of which are still missing[13]), before the Island's archives service came into existence, we cannot say for sure whether any prison records were among this number. Nor can we say whether any prison records are still in the hands of private collectors in Jersey, nor whether any of these have been sold abroad to America, as has been rumoured.

It is important to stress at the outset, therefore, that all of the extant, available sources combined do not produce a complete picture. Some gaps in knowledge

Political Prisoner logbook. (Copyright Jersey Heritage Collections/Gilly Carr)

inevitably remain, and not just because the prison itself no longer stands. German records relating to the prison are lost or unavailable and, without a number of detailed prison diaries for every day of the war and for each prison block, we cannot reproduce accurately the change in prison regime over time. This account of prison life has inevitably largely been built from published and unpublished memoirs, most of which were written (or at least published) many decades after the war. Although they have been tempered, nuanced or corrected with reference by their authors to contemporary diaries and letters written at the time or a few years after the war, without sufficient archival records from the guards this cannot be taken as a full, balanced or even wholly accurate account. However, I have endeavoured to present a picture of what the prison was like most especially in the last year of the war given that the evidence for this period is the most abundant. This is when political prisoner consciousness was formed, and was when the political prisoners who later wrote memoirs were incarcerated.

Unfortunately, no single archival document exists which details the negotiation between the Germans and local authorities regarding how the prison was initially to be used and divided up between them during the Occupation. However, the short memoirs of the prison medical officer, Dr Philip Bentlif, indicate that the Germans took over the prison in July 1940, and that at some time before that, he remembered arriving one morning 'to find three Germans looking over the prison. They were very surprised that there were no political prisoners in detention, and were also struck by the cleanliness of the buildings compared with the French prisons.'[14] It appears, therefore, that there was no negotiation over use of space; the Germans simply took what they wanted.

Although we have some idea of the way the prison was used both before and after the Occupation, things were not the same between 1940 and 1945. As more acts became illegal, so the prison rapidly filled up and it became necessary to differentiate between those offences which were ordinarily punishable under Jersey law and those which the German authorities deemed criminal and to be tried by court martial. There were also those offences which would have been (and were) punished under both systems. We must bear in mind the motives behind those who committed such acts. Political prisoners would not have been motivated into 'illegal' activity had the Island not been occupied, and so the very system of occupation was a trigger for offences and the cause of the prison population rising. Of course, these 'offences' were entirely legitimate actions in the eyes of those who committed them and this is why the resulting consequences of their actions, i.e. imprisonment, plays a large part in the memoirs of political prisoners. It was the

Dr Philip Bentlif. (Copyright Jersey Heritage Collections ref. D/S/A/5/A70)

act of imprisonment, just as much as the offence, which gave political prisoners their identity and badge of honour.

Our source material about the prison regime is thus largely limited to descriptions in memoirs of what was observed by those imprisoned who did not necessarily have access to an understanding of the prison system as a whole. Instead they had only their own experience of their own journey on which to rely. An added complication is that most memoirists were in prison towards the end of the Occupation, as already stated, and thus give an insight into the prison workings only during this period. We have little information about the earlier period and assumptions of continuity of the pre-war system may be deceptive. Prison memoirs can mislead the researcher because of the problem of certain prisoners being treated in a non-standard manner both because of their status (or lack of it) and their offences, and because of their behaviour towards the jailers and the *GFP*, who continued to question them once inside and before their court martial, and which may also have been non-standard.

Coupled with memoirs, we have some limited archival information relating to subjects such as the requisitioning of prison buildings by the German authorities, and details of requests for new buildings because of prison overcrowding. We cannot always tell whether requests were carried out, when and to what extent. Sources are sometimes contradictory, especially those written down many years after the event.

Chapter 2

The Geography of Jersey Prison

Jersey Prison, situated on the 'wrong side of Gloucester Street' according to former prisoner Anthony Faramus,[1] was demolished in the mid-1970s. A new prison, La Moye, was built in the parish of St Brelade, and a new hospital was built on the site of the old prison. While photos and even a plan of the old prison survive, the clearest description of the building can be found within the testimonies and memoirs of those who were imprisoned within it.

Jersey Prison was built in 1812 in St Helier on a piece of land owned and overlooked by the General Hospital, a location that proved to be advantageous for those imprisoned during the Occupation. After reforms dating to the mid-1830s, a Prison Board was formed, a committee that was still in place during the Occupation. Members included the Bailiff himself, the Lieutenant-Governor (who evacuated just before the Occupation) and the Viscount.[2] Within their remit was the direction of all matters relating to the alteration, repair and discipline of the prison.

The 1812 prison block was a two-storey granite building with grilles on the windows, the bottom cells looking out onto a vaulted arcade which was used as a place of exercise by the prisoners. On the middle arch of the arcade, the date 1812 was surmounted by a coat of arms, and directly above this was the prison chapel. The upper part of the building constituted the debtors' cells and it was here where political prisoners who had been charged were placed during the Occupation.[3]

A newspaper article about the prison was published about a decade before it was demolished, which is valuable in highlighting to us how little it had changed since the Occupation twenty years earlier.[4] This was also the first time that photos of the interior had ever been published. A journalist from the *Jersey Evening Post*, along with a party of local politicians, was shown round by the president of the Prison Board, the Prison Governor and the Chief Warder. The article took readers on a tour of the central courtyard, where prisoners on remand took their twice-daily exercise. 'Encircling the prison grounds', wrote the journalist, 'are the claustrophobic-high perimeter walls overtopped by the Hospital, the nurses' quarters and a number of private properties which lie close by. To one side of the

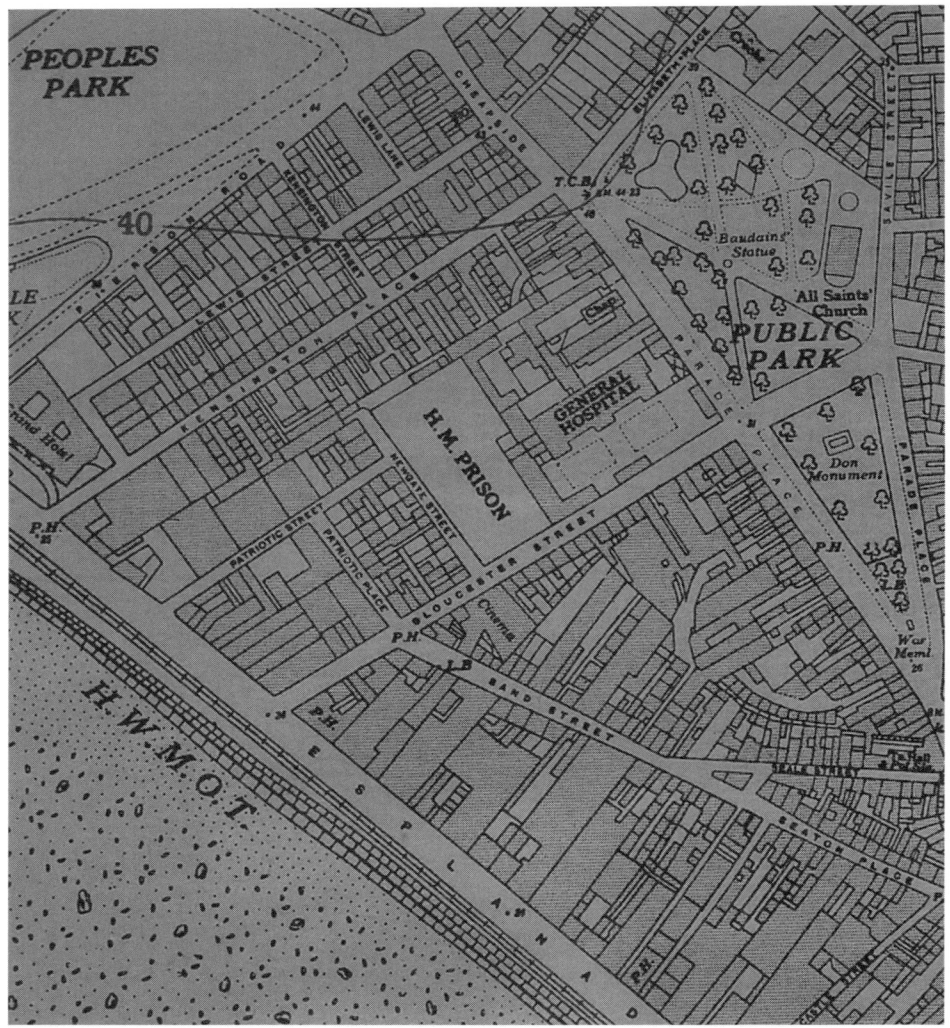

Location of Jersey Prison within St Helier, Ordnance Survey Map 1935. (Copyright expired, courtesy Jersey Heritage Collections ref. D/Z/L/8/2)

courtyard is the solid block of what must have been one of the original buildings with a date – 1812 – and a brightly-painted coat of arms on it.' However, after extolling the virtues of the facade of the building, the journalist went on to paint a grimmer picture of the fourteen single cells which lay behind the walk on the ground floor. 'Even with the spotless whitewash and green paint which greeted us everywhere we went, [the cells] are grim indeed. Arched brick ceilings, small windows set high up, stone floors and massive nail-studded wooden doors we found

The Geography of Jersey Prison

Above: *The 1812 prison block (A-Block) before its demolition.* (Copyright Brian Le Cornu)

Right: *A corridor in Jersey Prison in the 1960s or 1970s.* (Copyright Brian Le Cornu)

were common to nearly all the prison cells, but there seemed to be an especial coldness.' This block was known as 'A-Block' and was used for convicted prisoners during the Occupation, with political prisoners on the first or upper floor.

The upper floor was described by the journalist as being in a poor state of repair. By the mid-1960s, it had been turned into ten four-berth cells complete with double bunk beds. The cells also each had their own fireplace. On the same floor was the small prison chapel, divided by screens to segregate the male and female prisoners. A small room for sick prisoners and a library were located on the same floor. At the top of the yard, set into the prison walls, was the home of the prison governor. Although the prison conditions were poor during the Occupation, twenty years later the situation was even worse. The reception block was described as 'miserable', the bathing facilities 'inadequate', the washing and sanitary arrangements were 'primitive'.

A cell in A-Block. (Copyright Brian Le Cornu)

The prison chapel. (Copyright Brian Le Cornu)

HMP Jersey was divided into three two-storey blocks, named A, B and C, built in 1812, 1839 and the 1880s respectively. Blocks B and C were requisitioned by the Germans in 1941 and 1942, leaving only A-Block under the control of the Jersey Prison Board.[5] Eddie Chapman, a criminal on the run and, later in the war, a spy, came to Jersey in April 1939 where he was promptly arrested. In prison until October 1941, he gives us an insight into what it was like for the Jersey prison warders before the requisitioning of the prison blocks:

> At one period, the enemy occupation forces started sending in their soldiers who were convicted of minor offences. What partly reconciled us of the regular prison population to the newcomers was the trouble they caused the prison authorities. They cussed their British jailers soundly in German. 'Scheiss Engländer' they would yell, 'Sie konnen mich am Arsch lecken.' (Cursed Englishmen – you can kiss my backside.) They refused to be locked up; they walked about the prison doing just as they liked. The entire staff was terrified of them. At last a German military guard was put into the prison to keep discipline and protect the warders.[6]

Any dismay by the Prison Board over lost prison blocks was probably, at the same time, welcomed by the Jersey warders.

24   Nazi Prisons in the British Isles

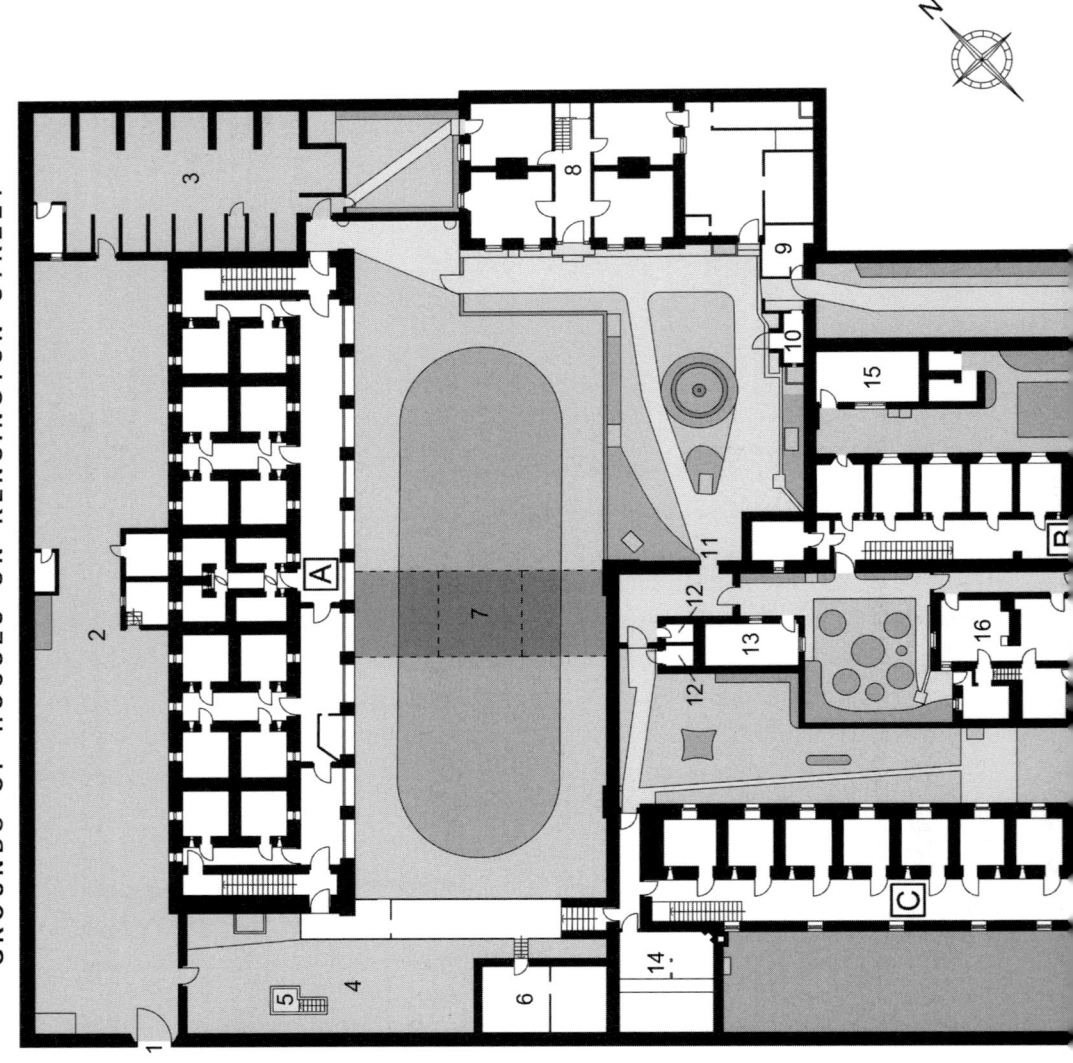

The Geography of Jersey Prison

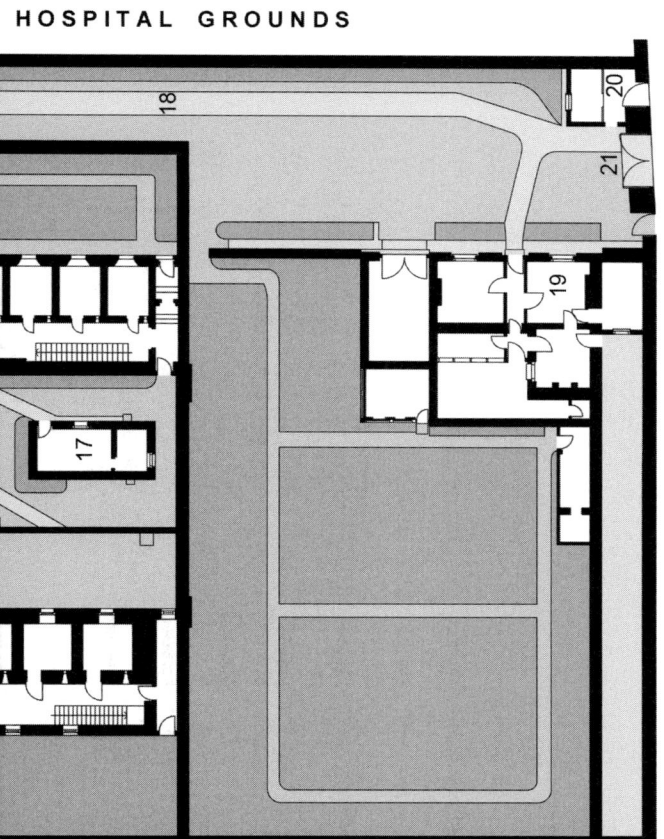

Legend

- Ⓐ Block A
- Ⓑ Block B
- Ⓒ Block C

1. Newgate Street gate
2. Stone breakers yard
3. Stone yard
4. Bradley's yard
5. Scaffold
6. German guards' quarters and store
7. Location of bungalow
8. Governer's house
9. Warders' lobby
10. Visitors' room
11. Entrance to German side of prison
12. WC
13. Store
14. Location of former treadmill
15. Old laundery
16. Germans' guard room
17. Guards and store
18. Path from main entrance
19. Chief warder's house
20. Entrance lobby
21. Main entrance

Jersey Prison. (Drawn by Ian Taylor, copyright Gilly Carr)

A-Block was rarely, if ever, mentioned by that name by political prisoners in their accounts; instead they called it the 'civil' or 'civilian side', and it was used for prisoners who had been charged. An annotated map in Joe Mière's files indicates that there were civil (i.e. non-political) prisoners on the ground floor (comprising sixteen cells) and political prisoners on the first floor, squeezed into twelve cells.[7] Blocks B and C were on the 'military side' and guarded by Germans. B-Block, the old female prison, was used for male and female political prisoners and comprised eighteen cells in total, nine on each floor. C-Block, larger than B, had twenty cells spread over two floors and was used for German servicemen and some political prisoners in solitary confinement. The military side of the prison was called, according to the official inscription on the door, *Kriegswehrmachthaftanstalt* (KWHA or 'war army prison facility').[8] In March 1945, the name changed to *Standortarrestanstalt* (garrison prison facility).[9] Political prisoners could be found in all three blocks of the prison at various stages of their confinement.

The presence of political prisoners in the block for German military offenders, and vice versa, was a special practice designed to isolate male prisoners by dividing groups and friends, and mixing up nationalities.[10] Four of the cells in C-Block were marked with the letter 'E' (*Einzelhaft*) for solitary confinement, used for prisoners who had misbehaved or who had just entered the prison and needed to be kept separate for questioning. Even worse than this were the cells marked with an 'S' for *Streng*, or hard punishment. This regime involved no mattress or pillow, no blanket, no evening meal, midday soup provided only every other day and no parcels or packages allowed from outside the prison.[11]

Generally speaking, political prisoners who were incarcerated but not yet court-martialled or who were still being questioned were kept in B-Block or, more rarely, C-Block. They were kept in solitary confinement, although the pressure on cells meant that this was not always possible. After sentencing, they were transferred to the 'civilian side', to A-Block. Blocks B and C were guarded by uniformed German prison warders while A-Block had civilian Jersey warders, something that the political prisoners greatly resented because they considered it unjust that they should be guarded by their 'own people' for German offences. A-Block was considered to be more comfortable than the military side of the prison, and the regulations were less stringent. Although men and women were kept on the same floor, they were separated by a thick door, and female warders attended the female prisoners.[12]

In addition to the three prison blocks, there was also the hut or 'bungalow'. By the late summer of 1944, when the French coast had been cut off because of the

Allied advance, the size of the prison population had become a serious problem. Thus, at around this time, a three-roomed single-storey building was constructed for political prisoners in the prison grounds. Former prisoner Frank Keiller described it in the following terms:

> By the middle of 1944, the prison was so overcrowded that the authorities were forced to build a wooden hut between the main cellblock and the internal wall of the German side, to house the excess population of wrongdoers. It abutted against a square stone building with a flat roof which itself reached to the outer wall of the prison.[13]

Joe Mière noted on his map that it held twenty-two prisoners, adding elsewhere that the first and second rooms held six beds and the third, ten beds, and that this hut, which had sealed windows, was on the civilian side of the prison, and was run by Jersey Prison Board.[14] Former prisoner Mickey Neil testified that those in the bungalow were given the freedom to go in and out of it, into the prison garden and around the yard. It was possible for them to receive things through the railings from visitors if nobody was looking.[15] However, from December 1944, new restrictions were brought in and they were supposed to be locked in all day apart from at exercise time, although it seems that this new order was not carried out until February 1945.[16]

Jersey's Victorian prison was not a modern, comfortable place. It was described by its inmates as 'mediaeval' and as a place of 'stark, almost brutal, rigours, worsened by the Occupation'.[17] While the only labour imposed upon political prisoners was keeping their living quarters clean, civil prisoners wore white institutional cotton uniforms and could sometimes be given a sentence which involved hard labour – at least, in the early years of the Occupation. This comprised stone-breaking in the stone-yard or in the cell if they were sentenced to solitary confinement.[18] Such work was described in his memoir *Journey into Darkness* by Anthony Faramus, who was in prison in the autumn of 1940:

> For five and a half days a week I was condemned to the notorious stone yard, a narrow quadrangle of walled cages each equipped with a saddle-stool, wire eye-protectors, a short-handled hammer and the material – granite boulders – which one had to reduce to chippings. Normally in demand for repairing roads and laying out driveways to hotels and large country houses, now they were claimed for German military uses.

Squatting all day without exercise on a growing mound of chippings, limbs ached and contracted, ears buzzed, heads drummed and the palms of one's hands burned with huge bursting blisters. Scabbed backsides, like every other lesion, went untreated. The rules were strictly enforced by the governor and his warders, men, English and local-born, who had seen military service . . . No speaking, no togetherness, one eked out one's time in complete silence and solitude.[19]

The prison's cells were very simple. In B-Block, they were around 10 by 12ft in size[20] with whitewashed stone walls, now 'scrofulous' according to at least one memoirist, and covered in graffiti. There was also a wooden floor, and a small, arched steel-grilled window high up on the outside wall. The door was also made of steel, painted grey, and had a peep-hole or 'judas-hole' through which warders

The stone yard, later on renamed the wood yard after prisoners used it for cutting wood. (Copyright **Brian Le Cornu**)

could look in and prisoners could look out. The furniture comprised a low wooden bed made of plywood with a boxed plywood headrest. The mattress was of dirty, heavy cloth stuffed with straw, coconut or horsehair (accounts differ), and one or two dirty blankets were provided. The mattress was so scratchy that it caused little cuts along prisoners' spines and scalps; the congealed blood made their hair stick to their scalps.[21] In the cell there was also a chamber pot (an old rusty jam tin) in one corner, and a little table in the other, next to the entrance, on which light shone through a hole in the wall.[22] Lucy Schwob paints a thoroughly miserable picture of her cell in B-Block during the last winter of the war:

> The cells were small, with little light from a 'window' touching a fairly high ceiling, and oriented north-east. There were pipes running along the stone white-washed walls but, throughout the winter of 1944/45, there was never any heat at all. The only furniture was a plank, a dirty straw mattress, two ultra-thin rags called 'blankets', a wooden stool. There was also a rusty enamelled basin, a drinking pot, and a chamber pot. A multitude of fleas, a few mice, and a familiar kitten provided entertainment. Dysentery was frequent.[23]

Prison cell in B-Block.
(Copyright Société Jersiaise ref. SJPA / 007779)

Peep-hole or 'judas-hole' in a prison cell door. (Copyright Gilly Carr)

In C-Block, occupied mostly by German servicemen, the cells were 9 by 9ft[24] and the doors were of black steel. As the building and the floors were of granite, the walls were much thicker than in B-Block, and the windows thus appeared smaller to the inmates. These rooms were equipped with a bed and several blankets, table and chair.[25] The building faced north and so the cells were always cold and didn't receive sunlight.[26]

In A-Block the cells were in a very dilapidated state and were verminous. The prisoners would sometimes pass their time trying to catch the mice.[27] The cells had been condemned before the war but re-opened when the Germans requisitioned the other blocks. The cells of 10 by 10ft had arched brick ceilings, whitewashed walls, stone floors and nail-studded wooden doors. There was a small Victorian fireplace in one corner which prisoners could use to cook food or burn wood. The windows were relatively large compared with the other blocks, heavily barred and opaque, although there were places where the prisoners could see out. The rooms also had mantelpieces, on which prisoners could place possessions.[28] Although these cells were more crowded because they were larger, conditions were better as prisoners were allowed visitors who could bring in parcels of food.[29] These cells

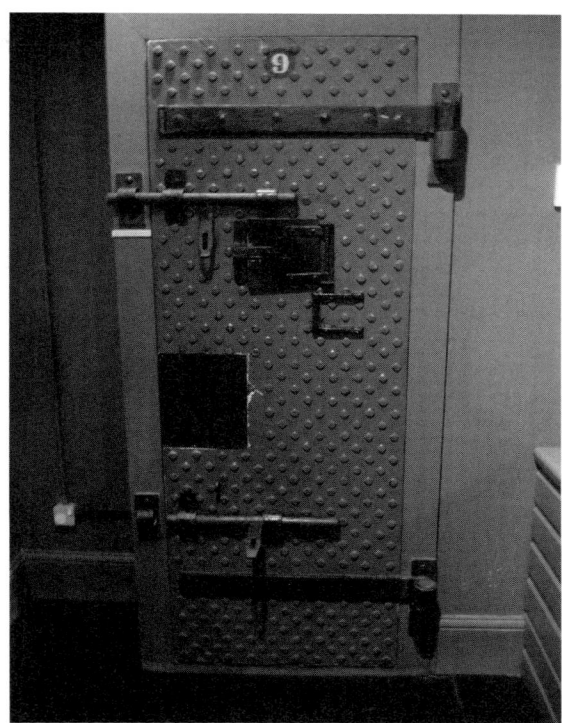

A typical prison door, today preserved in Jersey Museum.
(Copyright Gilly Carr)

were inhabited by as many as five people at a time.³⁰ The beds, as in other blocks, were wooden, with a mattress, cushion or pillow and an army blanket.

Such prison conditions, comprising overcrowded austere cells, vermin, fleas, illness, hunger and cold – and the risk of deportation if a person's sentence was of three months or longer – was not so very different to many prisons in occupied France or further afield. Eric Pleasants, who experienced many Nazi prisons and even a Russian Gulag, wrote in his memoirs an assessment of Jersey Prison in late 1941:

> I have been in many prisons in my time, but conditions in Gloucester Street Prison were among the worst I have experienced, not merely from a physical point of view – the mediaeval cells, the meagre and disgusting food – but also because of the attitude of the warders in general. Most of them exhibited an absolute disregard for the human dignity and feelings of the prisoners in their charge that was unique in my experience.³¹

At least one (and quite possibly many more) former political prisoners suffered from symptoms of post-traumatic stress disorder as a result of their experiences.

On 11 January 1944, 21-year-old cinema operator Stanley Coombs was given an eighteen-month sentence for 'prohibited reception of wireless stations, failure to surrender a wireless receiving set and dissemination of anti-German information'. He was kept in Jersey Prison for the length of his sentence. In 1964 he submitted a testimony for compensation for Nazi persecution (the only person to do so based on imprisonment solely in Jersey Prison), which is worth quoting at length:

> The general prison regime was extremely cruel and I lived in constant fear of my life. My cell was permanently lit by electric light so that the guard could continuously view me through the spy hole. This resulted in never having any rest or sleep of any kind. After my detention I was taken for three months daily to 'Silvertide', Havre de Pas, Jersey, for interrogation. These interrogations sometimes took place during the day or at night. They lasted from three to six hours without food and drink . . . About three months after my incarceration I was tried with 12 other defendants . . . by that time my health had already deteriorated. In addition to my solitary confinement I would like to state that I had no contact with my sisters or anybody else . . . After a while I contracted inflammation of the lungs which reduced my resistance considerably. It was also very painful for me to listen to the screams and beatings inflicted upon my fellow prisoners. To enhance these mental tortures I could see daily prisoners to be taken into the yard to face the firing squad.[32] In addition I had been informed that I had been selected for deportation to a German concentration camp. After about 6 months solitary confinement I could not stand the stress and strain any longer and I had a nervous breakdown. I was transferred to another block of the prison and could mingle with the other political prisoners. I was forced in my weak condition to chop and saw wood . . . After about 12 months I was physically and mentally exhausted on account of this diabolical treatment. I had a further nervous breakdown accompanied by a mental black-out – I was discharged for being unfit for further detention before the termination of my sentence.[33]

After the war, Coombs saw various mental health specialists in London who were unable to cure his 'nervous disease'. This was followed by years of ill-health and breakdowns, and an inability to hold down a job for long. He wrote 'For the last 20 years I have suffered indescribable pain and mental agonies due to the irreparable damage done to my health since I became a victim of Nazi persecution.' Coombs was not awarded compensation on the grounds that Jersey Prison was not comparable with a concentration camp, and that his treatment did not amount to 'Nazi persecution'. Despite this, it is instructive to read about the long-term impact and damage done to at least one vulnerable young man because of imprisonment. It is possible that Coombs' experience speaks for many, and such trauma and bad experiences may be at least one motive for putting pen to paper for many of the political prisoner memoirists.

The experience of being a political prisoner in A-Block could not have been more different for some. If you had friends in high places (most especially if you were friends of the prison governor), or who lived on a farm or who were wealthy enough to be able to afford to buy food on the black market, then the experience could be quite comfortable. Headmistress Dora Hacquoil was imprisoned from 3 July to 29 August 1944 with two other women (Ivy Forster and Alice Gavey) for their part in helping Louisa Gould (who died in Ravensbrück) to conceal an escaped Russian forced labourer. Tellingly, Hacquoil seemed to be friendly with the prison governor, Mr Briard, who was head warder before the Occupation. In a letter written to her mother after the war, she described her cell as follows:

> Everybody was very kind: Mr and Mrs Briard did their best for Ivy, Alice and me. We brought our own sheets and she lent me some of her own blankets. We brought in our own comfortable beds and a sideboard to keep our food and our crockery in and the three of us shared one cell. We played cards, read books, talked, exercised and ate and ate for the kind farmers and friends brought us the best of everything. Never have I fared so well, I gained 6lb in my 2 months. People brought us flowers and our cell was well decorated I assure you. Really a political prisoner's life in Jersey is a farce.[34]

Prisoner Laura Brideaux, given a sentence of four months in January 1945 for black-market activities (in reality, the gift of some butter to a diabetic neighbour), also benefitted from the Briards' kindness on account of her previous friendship with Dina Briard. Her daughter was interviewed by Wendy Janvrin-Tipping about her mother's experience:

> My mother's silver wedding was, I think, 22 April 1945. She had got married 22 April 1920. I had made a cake and we had a little party with Mr and Mrs Briard who were the governor and matron of the prison. We went to her sitting room and there we had a cup of tea and the cake. I had brought some tea with me because we had our Red Cross parcels and my father and I went to meet mum; she came down from her little cubbyhole and we had a little get together there. That was her Silver Wedding. Fancy spending your Silver Wedding in prison![35]

It seems likely that Hacquoil's and Brideaux's experiences were unusual and no other records have been found of such a comfortable incarceration or favours bestowed upon prisoners. The description of cells by Lucy Schwob, Stanley Coombs and Dora Hacquoil in different blocks of the prison could not be more different. Even if we consider the account by Deputy Edward Le Quesne, a local politician, well-connected and highly thought of, he was one of five in his cell, which he describes as 'no Savoy accommodation'. He noted that the room accumulated vast amounts of dust and dirt as it had to function as 'bedroom, dining room, kitchen, scullery, parlour and wash-house as well as lavatory and bathroom'. However, Le Quesne's account of his time in prison conveys the impression that he had a thoroughly enjoyable two weeks in prison in October 1944. In one entry, not un-reminiscent of Hacquoil's account, he wrote: 'Today the head warder had dinner with us in our cell and we put up a five course meal, i.e. soup, fish cakes, stewed rabbit, apple pie, cheese and fruit, added to this were potatoes and cauliflower. Our chef excelled himself and few of us had had such a meal for months past.'[36] Such a feast seems incredible at this date in the war, and shows the importance of friends on the outside who could deliver food into the prison for those in A-Block. It can be violently contrasted with what was happening elsewhere in the prison around a month earlier, where Frank Keiller, in solitary confinement, was standing in the middle of his freezing cell and crying with hunger.[37]

Prisoners did not rely solely on food from outside; there were, of course, prison rations which diminished during the Occupation as they did for those on the outside. However, from prisoner accounts it seems that the rations in the prison seemed little changed between 1942 and 1944, an indication of how low rations were to begin with. There are indications that prison rations on the civilian side seem to have been brought to political prisoners by the civil prisoners in A-Block who were made to wait on them. On the 'military side', soup and ersatz coffee were taken to cell occupants by fellow political prisoners Jimmy Thelland and Ron Bouchere in the later months of the war. The young men also passed on the news while on their rounds.[38]

For those in solitary confinement during the autumn of 1944, prisoners were given a mug of ersatz coffee and a thin slice of bread or a small mug of watery porridge for breakfast. At midday they received thin cabbage soup with the odd piece of offal floating on top and sometimes a few often-rotten potatoes in a small zinc mug. In the evening there was a crust of bread, a tiny bit of margarine and more ersatz coffee.[39] For those in A-Block at the same time, the ration seems to have been marginally better in quality, comprising a pint of tea and a piece of bread for breakfast, a piece of bread and a pint of 'quite palatable' soup at midday and a pint of tea and a pint of thin meat broth in the evening.[40] The 'meat' broth in B-Block could sometimes contain nasty surprises, such as a piece of cow or horse jawbone still containing rotten green-black teeth.[41] Kevin Le Cocq recorded that he lost 7lb in weight in two weeks.[42] Edward Le Quesne, whose diet was well supplemented from those outside the prison, put on weight during the two weeks of his sentence.[43] By January 1945, bread and potatoes disappeared entirely from the menu, although by then Red Cross parcels were brought monthly to the Channel Islands by ship, the SS *Vega*, and were also distributed to political prisoners.[44] German soldiers on the military side were not allowed parcels and would beg for additional food from the political prisoners.[45]

A-Block also had other attractions beyond the possibility of food parcels. In the middle of the first floor was a chapel, presided over by the Reverend Quarrie, which political prisoners visited on Sunday. Space was strictly divided up in this room, with male political prisoners in the front pews on one side, and the female political and civil prisoners behind them. It is not known whether the male political prisoners themselves decided to commandeer the front seats or whether this was dictated by the warders in recognition of the status of the political prisoners. The room was divided by a glass partition with a door in it, and this door was closed on the political prisoners and female civilian prisoners before the male civilian prisoners filled the other side of the room.[46]

Prisoners in A-Block were usually expected to shave and wash in their cells, or to use the communal sinks on the ground floor.[47] Communal baths in a large wooden tub, heated by a copper boiler (when the fuel was still available), and using a piece of coarse soap (when that, too, was available), were possible now and again,[48] presumably weekly, but in groups of four prisoners at a time. If one wanted to bathe in solitude in B-Block, then one had to decline morning exercise when everyone else would be outside. The system was not as luxurious as in A-Block and involved, by the winter of 1944, a bucket of cold water and a piece of cloth with which to mop oneself down.[49] The water in this bucket was both for drinking and washing, so choices had to be made. When the temperature dropped, the choice was easy: the water froze in the bucket making washing the less attractive option.[50]

In addition to the chamber pots available in the cells, prisoners were also allowed to ring the bell to be allowed access to the toilets at the end of the corridors. In September 1942, in A-Block, old newspapers dating to the last century were being used as toilet paper (quite where these had come from is not recorded; one hopes

The prison chapel. (Copyright Société Jersiaise ref. SJPA 007782)

that archived copies were not being plundered).[51] No evidence survives to suggest what, if anything, was being used in the last year of the war. It seems probable that letters from outside were used, making the survival of any into the present a rare commodity.

On the civilian side, political prisoners were allowed out of their cells for most of the day but were locked in at 6pm. This meant that they could visit friends in other cells in their corridor. They were also allowed to exercise in the yard for an hour in the morning and an hour in the afternoon every day, weather and circumstances permitting. Those on the military side exercised in a different, high-walled internal yard at different times to those on the civil side. If the weather was bad, they walked in the corridor, isolated or in groups. On both sides of the prison, exercise involved walking round and round in single file while the guards prevented any talking.[52] Some accounts suggest that the rules were more lax on the civilian side and people could talk occasionally to each other (if the opportunity presented itself) or even play handball.[53] Those in solitary confinement spent 15 to 20 minutes twice a day walking round the courtyard with a guard.[54] Not all of those in solitary confinement were allowed exercise:

Exercise yard with the Prison Governor's house in the background. (Copyright Brian Le Cornu)

Francis Harris found an unusual way to exercise in his cell, which was close to the exercise yard used by German prisoners:

> The German prisoners . . . marched round and round, accompanied by 'helpful' orders and commands by a drill sergeant. I could not see them but an inverted image appeared high up on the wall and ceiling of my cell of the men in their fatigue whites and black boots marching round . . . I was really in a box camera! The small window (aperture) being the lens – sometimes I had to march with them (20 minutes silent exercise).[55]

When they were in their cells, prisoners on the civilian side passed the time in reading books from the prison's small library, playing darts, cards or draughts, holding debates, chatting and telling stories, cleaning their cell or just getting very bored.[56] They would also sometimes wrestle, box, engage in 'bouts of mayhem' or learn self-defence manoeuvres from each other to keep warm.[57] As most of these activities were communal, they were not available for those on the military side in solitary confinement. For these prisoners, paper and pencils were strictly forbidden and books or magazines were a luxury and unavailable unless given to them by another prisoner or a friendly German guard.[58] Such prisoners were also not allowed visitors or letters.[59]

The prison library in the 1970s.
(Copyright Brian Le Cornu)

Jersey men and women and the Germans were not the only people in the prison. The Germans had young Ukrainian or Russian servants in the military side of the prison who were given partial access to various places in order to carry out tasks demanded of them, namely sweeping the cells and corridors and keeping the military side of the prison clean. They also emptied the chamber pots for those in solitary confinement, fetched hot water for some of the prisoners and carried out administrative tasks for the guards. These men were chosen from among the forced labourer population, and the names of those recorded by political prisoners include 'Wassili', who was replaced by 'Mikail' and then 'Karlschen'.[60] These men slept in cells with other prisoners, sometimes on the floor, or in the prison library.[61] While Lucy Schwob and Suzanne Malherbe were kind to these men, they observed that the other political prisoners ignored the Russians, commenting that 'they didn't see the situation of these two men, exiles, in rags, hated by the jailers, without family contacts, deprived of distractions and the food supplements that their contacts brought them . . . too proud to ask for anything'.[62]

Imprisoned German soldiers were put into cells in C-Block and sometimes even B-Block. The ones who aroused the interest and even sympathy of the political prisoners were those who had tried to desert – or had even spoken of desertion – from the army. These men were destined to be executed by firing squad, usually on the parade ground at Fort Regent in St Helier. They included 23-year-old Nikolaus Schmitz, who had deserted and then hidden with his Jersey girlfriend in the closing stages of the war.[63] He swallowed some nails to delay his trial, or perhaps to commit suicide, but he was not sent to hospital and his execution went ahead as planned.[64] It was extremely distressing for the political prisoners to hear him cry the night before his execution and to see him led away. They feared the same fate for themselves.

Chapter 3
Who were the Political Prisoners?

As Peter Le Sauteur remarked in his Occupation memoirs for mid-February 1943, life under the Germans meant that one could be deported for 'breathing in when one should be breathing out'.[1] This meant that the prison population at any one time could encompass people arrested for many different types of offences, but there was a sub-group in prison who sought to mark themselves out as political prisoners. Because they were housed separately from those they called 'civil' or 'criminal prisoners' (i.e. those convicted for ordinary crimes such as burglary), this helped to define and consolidate their identity. However, there were other ways in which their identity was marked, as discussed later.

For the most part, we can identify precisely who was in the group which formed a 'political prisoner consciousness'. They were the young men and women who filled the prison and remained there from July 1944 onwards, after the last group of convicted Islanders were deported to France on 30 June 1944.[2] As the Allied invasion of France meant that nobody could be transferred across to France soon after this date, the prison slowly filled up. The number of convictions broadly increased from this time onwards,[3] probably perhaps because it was clear that the tide of war was turning and that deportations were no longer possible.[4] People were also growing more desperate. The prison became increasingly overcrowded and there was even a waiting list to enter in early 1945.[5] Frank Keiller describes the prison as 'overflowing' in late 1944, commenting that new offenders in early 1945 either had to take their beds in with them or sleep on the floor of their cells.[6]

If we examine the constituents of the political prisoner block of this time, we can get an idea of the demographic. It is difficult to calculate who made up the 'hard core' of the political prisoner group, not only because those charged with minor offences would often be let out early in order to ease overcrowding,[7] but also because the last entry in the political prisoner logbook is dated to July 1944. However, we have a second record of offenders in the form of loose pages of German notifications relating to prosecutions by the Field Command and Troop Courts, which continue until the end of the Occupation (records which are likely

The Viscount (Charles Le Gros) and the Receiver-General (Major John Giffard), two members of the Prison Board. (Jersey Heritage Collections ref. D/S/A/1/A546 and D/S/A/4/A4707)

to have been the source of information of the large ledger in Jersey Archives[8] which lists the convictions of Islanders), and we can usually tell from this ledger who had already been let out.

On 4 April 1945, two members of the Prison Board, the Viscount (Charles Sidney Le Gros) and the Receiver General (Major John Giffard), met with the Germans to discuss overcrowding in the prison, and a 'full list' was drawn up so that a 'possible remission of sentences' could be considered.[9] That list, headed 'list of political prisoners' (indicating that it was this wing of the prison that was bursting at the seams) contains thirty-eight names. This is likely to have been the already convicted people, namely, political prisoners in A-Block who were squeezed into twelve cells. We know that this cannot be a full list of all political prisoners, as claimed, as it omits the names of Lucy Schwob and Suzanne Malherbe, sentenced to death for 'inciting the troops through propaganda' in November 1944, reprieved in February 1945 and freed from prison on 8 May 1945. Similarly, Francis Harris appears in most autograph books but he was not on the list because he had not yet been sentenced.

One possible alternative clue to some of these omissions lies in the last column in the list produced for review by the Germans, which indicated the conduct of the prisoner concerned. Nearly every person on the list is described as having good or very good conduct, with the behaviour of only one man described as fair. Perhaps those who had a record of bad behaviour were omitted or listed elsewhere. Additionally, the inclusion of Malherbe and Schwob on a list for remission of sentence, women so recently reprieved from a death sentence following an appeal by Bailiff Alexander Coutanche,[10] might have been seen as pushing luck, and may even have jeopardised the chances of others on the same list if the ire of the Germans had been roused by such as request. Either way, the number of political prisoners at this time was certainly higher than 38; indeed, the number of people sentenced by the Field Command and Troop Courts between January and April 1945 alone was 120,[11] although they could not all have fitted into the political prisoner wing at the same time.

Of the thirty-eight listed, then, three or nearly 8 per cent were female. The ages of all prisoners ranged from 17 to 64, with the majority (68 per cent or twenty-six people) under 25. The young people were convicted of crimes such as attempting to escape (eighteen people or 47 per cent), insulting the occupying authority (four people or 11 per cent) and being in possession of arms (three people or 8 per cent). The older adults' offences included those related to the black market (four people or 11 per cent) and listening to the BBC on illicit radio sets (four people or 11 per cent).

There is also a second list, kept in his diary by George Le Marquand, who was in prison from 11 October 1944 until 7 May 1945. We do not know how complete it is and whether it included people from both the military and civilian side of the prison. Le Marquand's diary started only upon his arrival on the civilian side on 2 November 1944. His list is titled simply 'Political Prisoners during my stay in Gloucester Street'. He gives the names and offences of sixty people but, as the first names are given by initial, only cross reference with the court-martial records would allow one to count the number of female prisoners. Suzanne Malherbe and Lucy Schwob are not listed, perhaps indicating that his list concerned only those on the civilian side. Of the sixty people listed, twenty-two or 37 per cent were in prison for attempting to escape from the Island; only two are listed as being imprisoned for firearms offences; and thirteen or 22 per cent had been imprisoned for illegally listening to the radio. Although these figures are not the same as the April 1945 list, they give a broader perspective on the profile of political prisoners during the period when political prisoner consciousness was formed. We can see that in both lists, escapees dominate to the extent that we might suggest that their concept of what a political prisoner was and should be might have had more weight.

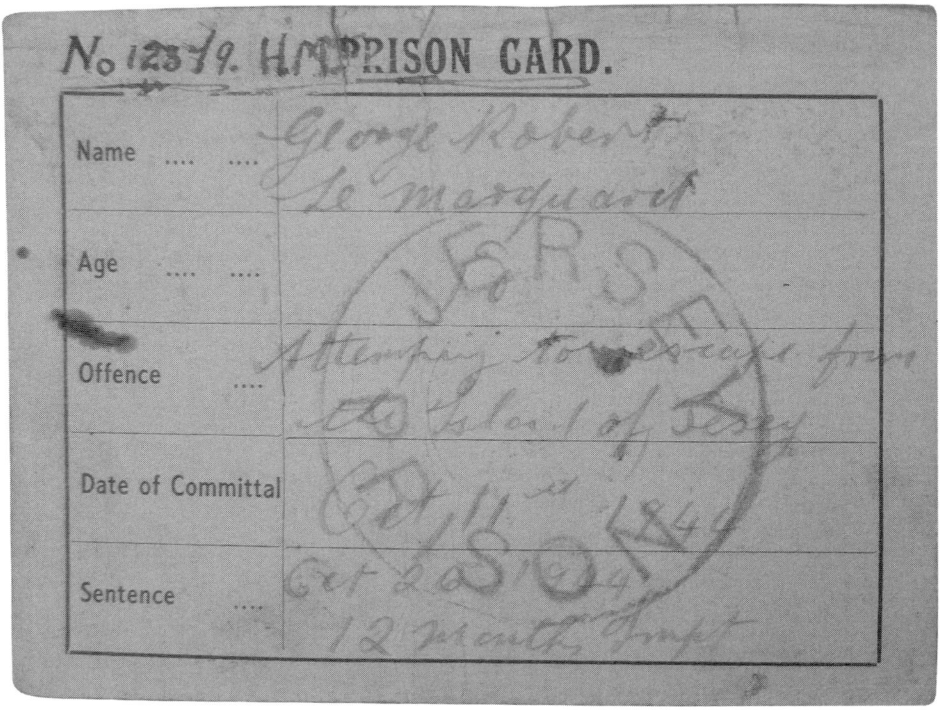

No 12379. H.M. PRISON CARD.

Name	George Robert Le Marquand
Age	
Offence	Attempting to escape from the Island of Jersey
Date of Committal	Oct 11th 1944
Sentence	Oct 20 1944 12 months Impt

JERSEY PRISON

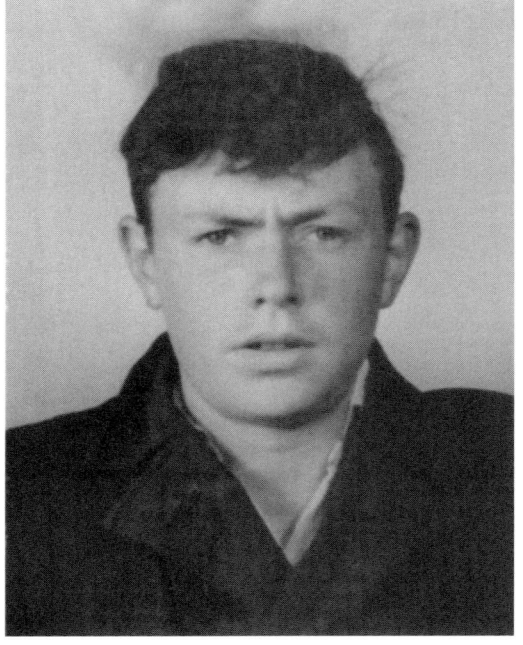

Above: *George Le Marquand's prison card.* (Courtesy of Tony and Anne Lewis)

Left: *George Le Marquand.* (Copyright Jersey Heritage Collections ref. D/S/A/2/A1174)

Chapter 4
Interrogation, Incarceration and Solitary Confinement

Of course, attempting to escape from the Island or stealing weapons from the Germans were not the only offences that warranted a prison sentence. We have already seen that those caught for radio offences were imprisoned, but other 'offences' typically committed by those put in Jersey Prison included theft of foodstuffs, building materials or military property from the Germans, black-market activity, insulting or assaulting German soldiers, being caught in possession of a camera or sheltering forced labourers. If given a sentence of more than three months, almost all of those so charged would have been deported to a continental prison in France or Germany. Those put in Jersey Prison after July 1944 were not deported and saved from a much more serious fate. In fact, a study of prison sentences over the course of the Occupation shows that the later in the Occupation a person was sentenced, the more severe the sentence tended to be, and the less chance that person had of surviving the war. Conversely, at the start of the Occupation, until around mid-1942, sentences tended to be lighter and a person was often deported to Caen or Saint-Lô Prison for a few months before their prompt return to the Island.[1]

Most prisoners spent time in Jersey Prison before their deportation. But whether they were deported or destined to spend months in prison, there was a certain procedure which followed their arrest or capture. The political prisoner would either be interrogated straight away or be sent to the military side of the prison, often beginning their stay in solitary confinement. If they had already been sentenced and began their prison career in A-Block, like Edward Le Quesne, the entry to prison was straightforward: 'Commenced my sentence in HM Prison. Entering at 10am accompanied by a German guard I was weighed, inspected and shown to my cell. There I found a happy band of fellows condemned, like myself, for the crime of having listened to the truth.'[2]

Entry to the prison could be either mild, as it was for Le Quesne, or traumatic, especially if the prisoner was entering blocks B or C. Prisoners were searched, weighed and their details were recorded before they were handed a thin blanket, towel and a 'wafer of soap' and led off to their cell.³ However, this could be done in a very intimidating and humiliating way, especially for women – so much so that it was not spoken about until later in life. In a letter to Joe Mière, one of the female prisoners, Belza Turner, a close friend of his who had been caught trying to escape from the Island during the Occupation, ventured to ask whether he knew whether others were strip-searched on their arrival at the prison, saying that she was 'too shy' to have asked before.⁴ She wrote that a female German military guard asked her to undress and, when she refused, was told that there were four men outside the door who would gladly do it for her and that she would have to 'put up with it' if anything happened – i.e. if she was raped. She undressed and was given an internal examination. The guard then laughed at her, and she was taken away to be processed into the prison system and taken to her cell.⁵ Belza was also scared of being raped throughout her time in Jersey prison, a fear emphasised by being kept in solitary confinement. She also refused to go out into the exercise yard in case anything happened to her.⁶

Sexual assault or its threat was not limited to women entering the prison. Although one young male prisoner says that he was 'searched but only in a cursory "patting down" manner', another male prisoner records that he was told to undress and subjected to 'an embarrassing body search', so it is possible that this procedure was not unusual, even if it was not typical, and was reserved for prisoners who the guards wished to intimidate.⁷ As Turner's letter to Mière is the only female account we have of entry to the prison, we have no way of knowing how representative it was for other women. As the majority of political prisoner memoirs were written by men, we have very little insight into the female experience. The letters of Lucy Schwob, comments in autograph books written by women and the letter to Joe Mière are our only source of the female voice, although the male prisoners sometimes recorded events that happened to women.

When prisoners arrived in their cell, other prisoners would 'initiate them into the routine' and tell them what they could and could not do. Rather than the official regulations, which the warder admitting them to the prison would have been sure to impress upon them, these were the unofficial rules that involved advice on how to circumvent the system and outwit the guards, who often tried to catch prisoners in the act of such disobedience.⁸

Entering the prison was only the beginning of the ordeal. Still to come was the interrogation, usually carried out by the *GFP*. The military side of the prison was

Interrogation, Incarceration and Solitary Confinement

Silvertide today. (Copyright Gilly Carr)

a frightening place for many and was an experience that did not improve until after they had been sentenced and were transferred to the civilian side of the prison.

Interrogation was carried out as the first stage in a political prisoner's career. This was carried out at a number of different locations in St Helier, but most commonly, especially for those accused of firearm offences, at No. 1 Silvertide at

Havre-de-Pas in the east of St Helier. From March 1943, this was the headquarters of the *GFP*. The *Hafenüberwachungsstelle* (Harbour Control Service or Harbour police) questioned those who attempted to escape from the Island at the Folie Inn and at the Pomme d'Or Hotel, their headquarters. Other places of questioning included, for the *Feldgendarmerie* (military field police), Bagatelle House and, later, Tudor Lodge on Bagatelle Road, also in St Helier. Prisoners walked under armed guard between the prison and these locations, in full view of other Islanders, probably both as a way of saving rationed petrol and as a warning to others. Islanders who watched the prisoners go past under escort would often shout encouragement or make surreptitious V-signs to indicate their support.[9]

The *Feldgendarmerie* dressed almost identically to the ordinary troops but had the word *Feldgendarmerie* embroidered on their cuffs. They also had the German police insignia of an eagle and swastika emblem, surrounded by an oval laurel wreath, displayed on their left upper arm, and a metal breast-plate suspended on a chain around their neck, also with the word *Feldgendarmerie* engraved on it.[10] The men of the *GFP*, Heinz-Carl Wölfle, Karl Lohse, and head of the *GFP*, *Hauptmann* Bode, appeared both in uniform and in civilian clothing. The methods of the men of all of these police services were similar to those used by the Gestapo,

The Folie Inn today. (Copyright Gilly Carr)

and the vast majority of Islanders referred to them as the Gestapo even though strictly speaking they were not.

In order to extract information from the accused, the *GFP* employed a range of tactics, including threats to shoot prisoners or their family members or send them to a camp in Alderney; long periods of interrogation, sleep deprivation, shouting, and shining a bright light into the eyes; beatings with rifle butts, repeated punching and slapping in the face, being thrown against furniture and kicking. There were also reports of beating with truncheons and prodding with an electric goad. These *GFP* men were also well aware of the power of performance, and often kept the arrested waiting, facing the wall with their hands above their heads for long periods, while soldiers guarding them made a show of loading their guns.[11] The period of taking prisoners in and out of their cells for questioning could go on for weeks, and some were even questioned in their cells.[12]

Ronald Beer, for example, arrested in September 1942, wrote in his 1965 testimony for compensation as a victim of Nazi persecution:

> After my arrest by the Gestapo I was put in the local prison, under German warders, in the wing which they had taken over. For the first seven weeks I was kept in solitary confinement. Wolffe [*sic*] (which I think is the right name) would come in my cell by day and at different times in the nights to try to break me down and name the other people who were in our circle. At times it was not all honey, as you can guess. After the seven weeks was over I was taken to a court martial and was told I would spend the next three years in a German labour camp. After my sentence I was put in another cell and through the bars I was able to see other people who I knew . . .[13]

For 15-year-old Peter Hassall, arrested in May 1942 in the act of escaping from the Island with photographs of German gun positions, his entry into prison was more violent:

> I was taken to the second floor [of the German wing of the prison] by a fat German corporal, who, instead of locking the door, shoved me in the cell then closed the door. He grabbed me by the front of my shirt, then slammed a ham-like fist in my nose. Blood spurted all over the place, even on the man's uniform, but he kept punching and screaming: 'Terrorist Schwein! Du bang bang!', which I took to mean that I was a terrorist pig and would be shot.[14]

Wölfle, Lohse and Bode of the Geheime Feldpolizei. (Copyright The National Archives ref. FO 371/189285; contains public sector information licensed under the Open Government Licence v3.0)

This was the first of three beatings within a few hours of his arrival in prison. The next morning he was able to assess his injuries. In addition to a badly broken nose, he discovered that:

> When I looked in the mirror over the washbowl I was unable to recognise myself. My face was cut, bruised and swollen, like that of a heavy-weight boxer who had taken a terrible pounding in the ring over twelve rounds. My hair was matted and dried blood was caked all over my face and hands.[15]

While Hassall's rough treatment was triggered by the severity of his offence, such violence was by no means unknown to the young men in Jersey Prison. The experience of being thrown in prison and entering solitary confinement, normal among those yet to be tried by court martial, was eloquently described by Frank Keiller:

> My first glance around was not reassuring. The cell was about 10 feet wide and 16 feet long. The floor was bare timber boards and an uncomfortable-looking wooden bed lay along one wall. In the corner by the door there was an old jam tin still half-full of the previous occupant's contributions. There was no other furniture . . .
> The bed was three parallel planks. There was a raised wooden pillow at one end. At night, they gave those of us who were not on punishment, three thin horsehair biscuits to cover the bare boards and a small pillow of the same material. They were hard and uncomfortable even so and sleep didn't come easily. It was so cold and dark that most of us had to get up two or three times a night to pee. At times, mice and rats disturbed our rest.[16]

The military court tribunal for political prisoners, when it came, could take place in a variety of locations in St Helier. Some, like Peter Hassall and Maurice Gould, were questioned in College House, part of the Victoria College (a private boys' school). Others were tried in a large house named Avondale on Lower King's Cliff (a street in St Helier). Family members were not allowed to attend. The court comprised three, four or five senior German officers sitting at a long table, behind which a portrait of Hitler hung on the wall. Little of what took place was translated for the benefit of the accused, although the cross-questioning was interpreted into English.[17] Although the experience was frightening and nerve-wracking for many of the young men who made up the majority of the political prisoner population, it could also be 'an amusing comedy and a day off from prison routine' (or so it seemed when looking back afterwards) for the older and wiser prisoner who could understand German.[18] Once the main proceedings were over, the accused moved into a waiting room while the court decided upon the verdict. The court proceedings could be lengthy, but once it was over, the prisoner was returned to the prison, and to the less harsh regime of A-Block.

Avondale, Lower King's Cliff today. (**Copyright Gilly Carr**)

Chapter 5
'Rather a Mixed Crowd': The Prisoners and the Guards

There were many types of people in prison throughout the Occupation, and it is likely that they reflected the same cross-section of society as resisters in general. Earlier research revealed that resisters came from all social groups in the Islands, and from both English and Island-born inhabitants.[1] However, we do have an eyewitness description of a number of the group who were in prison from the autumn of 1944 onwards. Lucy Schwob and Suzanne Malherbe, who saw themselves by their own admission as outsiders and 'the exception' because they were 'women, foreigners and of bourgeois origin' and also older, observed that the other prisoners were different from them in their 'habits and intellectual interests'.[2] They were 'rather a mixed crowd'.[3] Schwob was able to describe the social classes to which the 'authentic loyalists' belonged, the ardent young patriots who were in prison with them:

> Most of our comrades were young. Most of them belonged to that indeterminate class which takes the place of the proletariat in Jersey. If their parents belonged to the petit bourgeoisie (already a rare thing), they, still at school, were scarcely interested in the world of business and trade. . . . The only active resistance group (which stole arms and munitions from the Germans to help with the English landing . . .) was called The Underground Retaliation Movement. It comprised five members. The youngest was 16 years old. The oldest, 22. All, at least going by their names, were of English origin and were not Norman [i.e. indigenous Islanders]. All 'proletarians' – so it seemed from their accent. A second group, less coherent, comprised members accused of handling stolen weapons and a stolen motorcycle. In this group, two more 'proletarians' (son of a housewife, herself a patriot, helping her son, hiding radios . . . getting away with it beautifully!) and two other boys of the petit bourgeoisie, one of Irish origin, the other of French origin; and a fifth, again a 'proletarian', of English origin, who the Gestapo put on the 'streng' regime for 'verbal impertinence'. All of those people were excellent comrades for us. They had, even in their language, the mannerisms of people who have been brought up well . . .'[4]

This description is the only overview we have of the core band of political prisoners in the last year of the war. What emerges from memoirs is not a focus only on age, sex or class as a *prime* identity marker (although each of these was certainly important within the crowded cell or corridor), but rather the status of 'political prisoner' which united those incarcerated. George Haas, an American POW in Jersey who spent time in the prison late in the Occupation, described the other political prisoners as 'the best people in Jersey . . . for they were the majority of the ones who had been resisting the invaders'. This sentiment would have been widely shared.[5]

However, this unity between the young political prisoners was perhaps perceived to be stronger than it really was by those who fell outside their immediate group (such as the older Malherbe and Schwob, or the American POW, George Haas). A letter sent to his mother by 16-year-old Peter Gray in December 1944, while still on the military side, revealed a conversation that had taken place between himself (convicted for firearms offences) and the escapees:

> They used to say 'Oh, I'm not the same as you.' 'Why?' said I. 'How do you mean?'
> 'Oh, we aren't b— criminals like you' (I didn't know that college boys swear, but have since changed my mind). 'It doesn't matter', said I, 'what you are here for. You have offended the Germans and we are all in the same boat' . . . After that they said no more.[6]

Peter Gray. (Copyright Jersey Heritage Collections ref D/S/A/4/A4975)

This is the only evidence we have of any tension between political prisoners, and we cannot know how widespread these attitudes were. The only other insight we have into the political prisoner groups is a passing comment by Lucy Schwob, who noted how clan and class-oriented the prisoners were, based on friends from school or college. That Peter Gray had also noted that the escapees were 'college boys' backs up Schwob's observation.[7]

The prison letters of Joseph Tierney to his wife Eileen, written between April and September 1943, refer to the group of five men in his cell, all involved in illicitly listening to the radio and sharing the BBC news.

They called themselves 'the radio club'.⁸ This indicates the potential for other smaller groupings of political prisoners based on offence within the larger political prisoner body.

It is thus possible that prison memoirs deliberately present a show of unity and solidarity that was not always present in reality due to class-based attitudes, or attitudes towards different ages and offences. As noted above, escapees were the most numerous of all political prisoners in Jersey Prison during the last year of the Occupation, and thus might have seen themselves as a kind of 'top dog' prisoner. It is possible that some of them looked down on others imprisoned for different offences against the Germans, especially if they came from a different class.

There is virtually no reference made in memoirs to the civil or non-political prisoners. These people were kept absolutely separate from the political prisoners, and the latter perceived them as 'real criminals' in contrast to themselves, who had acted entirely legitimately in their own eyes against the occupier.⁹ The sense of solidarity in adversity (among political prisoners) is one of the strongest themes that emerge from the memoirs and diaries. There are references to 'good fellowship', 'collegiate gaity' and numerous instances of prisoners sharing food, comforting each other and keeping morale high, 'despite the rigours of the cold, the hunger and the threats', primarily through group contravention of prison rules.¹⁰

Although we shall return to this theme later, let us first observe the group against whom the prisoners rebelled and defied: the guards, both local (i.e. Jerseymen) and German. Most prisoners wrote about those who guarded them. For those in solitary confinement, they were the only ones to whom they could speak. Guards could also be persuaded to smuggle goods in and out of the prison, and to other prisoners. Mocking the guards was also a humorous way to pass the time, but there was a limit to how far they could go in the military side of the prison, where solitary confinement and *Streng* could be used as effective deterrents.

We know little about the soldier-guards in C-Block beyond the fact that there were four of them: two young and two old.¹¹ The German prison guards mentioned by the political prisoners in B-Block included Otto von Pluch, Willi Heinrich (identified as Heinrich Ebbers by Janvrin-Tipping¹², although potential for confusion exists) and a man known only as 'Ludwig', all presided over by the head guard, *Chef* ('boss') or 'Cheffy' as he was known; only Heinrich and the *Chef* could speak English. The *Chef*'s name was also Heinrich (although Janvrin-Tipping identifies him as Karl¹³) and so, to distinguish between them, the *Chef* was nick-named '*der Kleine*' and the guard was called '*der Grosse*', as one was small and the other was tall.¹⁴ The *Chef* was probably a *Feldwebel* (a sergeant major, although different accounts suggest that he was a Warrant Officer), had served in the First World War (as had the other guards) and was said to be 'strict but fair', but shouted at prisoners who showed any discourtesy. Although the prisoners were obviously pre-disposed not to like him, they described him variously as a 'little man of mild appearance . . . with no personality and little authority', but also as a 'very kindly man', a 'first class man' who was 'known to share his rations with those whose families hadn't brought in food', or as someone who 'ordered and instructed and strutted'. Whenever members of the *GFP* appeared at the prison, the *Chef* was anxious to give them the 'Heil Hitler salute' and the other guards became nervous.¹⁵

One of the ways in which the prisoners tried to make these guards – and their memory of them – less frightening was to mock them behind their backs, or to ridicule and caricature them in their memoirs. Thus, Ludwig became 'Ludwig with the buck teeth' or 'Ginger'. Otto was described as 'a perfect joke, quite a music hall or pantomime character' who 'did his best to be taken seriously but never quite succeeded'. He 'had a spinal defect and walked with a limp' and was a 'short, fat, pot-bellied man with a "Punch"-shaped nose . . . stupid and a bully, always yelling . . . to maintain his authority' and turning red while doing so. 'Big' Heinrich was a 'tall, slender man of regular features, was quiet . . . but he was dangerous and needed to be watched'. He also had wooden blocks inside his boots as he'd apparently lost his toes through frostbite when in Stalingrad. When angry, the *Chef* was described as a 'pantomime of outraged German pride' with 'skips and dances' to accompany his 'tirade'.¹⁶

It was part of the prisoners' sense of pride and self-esteem to portray these guards as stupid and to outwit them. Thus, when one of the prisoners was caught trying to escape from the prison and was accused by Heinrich and Otto of making fools of them, the memoirist commented that they had been fools long before he came on the scene.¹⁷ The guards were also mocked in song, and evening singing sessions would start with a song in which the prisoners all joined, where the words had been arranged to tease the jailers. Each jailer was given a nick-name for this purpose.¹⁸

The German guards were not, however, the buffoons they were made out to be. They could be dangerous and had the power to put prisoners on *Streng* and/or solitary confinement. Using a metal soup ladle, the *Chef* once beat up a prisoner who had tried to escape, causing cracked ribs, although he apologised for this the next day.¹⁹ The *Chef* would have been held responsible and punished for the loss of a prisoner on his watch, and so this display of fury was as understandable as it was unacceptable to the modern reader.

The German prison guards could also be kind, gentle and humane: Heinrich was said to be the most relaxed of the guards and occasionally let families visit prisoners in B-Block or allowed in suspect parcels. He also hid a copy of a magazine and chocolate in the clothes of a young prisoner in solitary confinement; the *Chef* hugged the same boy after he'd been allowed out to fetch his stolen gun which could then be used to convict him and perhaps earn him the death sentence. He also gave a woollen blanket to a female prisoner to help her survive the bitter winter cold of her cell.[20]

Otto was also extremely kind to Lucy Schwob, whose health deteriorated in prison during the harsh winter of 1944. He brought her food reserved for high-ranking officers to encourage her to eat, hot water to use in her milk bottle used as a hot-water bottle, and delivered a blanket secured from the *Chef*.

The German guards would also smuggle parcels out of the prison on occasion; after Joe Mière had been beaten up and his teeth knocked out by the *GFP*, Ludwig smuggled the bloody shirt and teeth out to Mière's mother.[21] Otto would occasionally leave several cell doors open at once on B-Block so that prisoners could stretch their legs, communicate with each other and compile autograph albums.[22] Another un-named guard allowed American POW George Haas to sit by the stove in his office, even in his absence, which gave Haas the opportunity to listen to the radio. However, Haas saw only self-interest in this kindness, suggesting that the guard knew that the tide of the war had turned and that he wanted to be treated well when he became a POW.[23] It was in the interest of the guards to be kinder to the prisoners after Red Cross parcels came to the Island from late December 1944 onwards because, although some prisoners made a great show of smoking Red Cross cigarettes and eating chocolate in front of them, some also shared their new luxuries with guards.[24]

Each of these guards claimed to be anti-Nazi, but only when out of earshot of the others. Haas managed to work this to his favour by playing them off against each other, which he claimed was possible because they respected his status as an American officer. The guards were willing to do him small favours as long as they were not caught doing so, such as bringing him food, drink and reading matter.[25]

It seems that in the last few months of the war, the German jailers were concerned about their ultimate fate given that they were losing the war. Tensions were building between them, and this encouraged them to speak more freely to the prisoners on occasion. Suzanne Malherbe once witnessed this side of the *Chef*. While reading a letter from his wife, he confessed to her, with a finger on his lips, that he hated the Nazis, and that his deputy, big Heinrich, was plotting to bring him down and make him look like a communist. He told her that he lived 'in anguish, in terror, and impatient for an Allied victory' and lamented being stuck in the prison, which Suzanne found somewhat ironic.[26]

In short, memories of the German guards were mixed: they were comic figures to be made fun of in memoirs – after all, life on the military side was unpleasant and more dangerous. Such dark memories, which haunted political prisoners until they wrote their memoirs in old age, needed to be vanquished and tempered with remembered instances of acts of kindness and humanity. The departures from the comedy caricatures in unpublished diaries and letters, on the other hand, are especially valuable in allowing us an insight into the jailers as they really were and the troubles they faced as the war came to an end and their fates were unknown.

Memoirs reveal that the local warders on the civilian side were treated with disdain and disrespect; this aspect of their treatment was emphasised in memoirs to highlight the illegitimacy of the political prisoners' detention. At the same time, the prison regime was more relaxed on the civilian side and prisoners took advantage of this.

Ernest Briard (Prison Governor) and Dina Briard (Prison Matron). **(Copyright Jersey Heritage Collections refs. D/S/A/4/A1680 & A1676)**

As already noted, Ernest Briard was the Jersey governor of the prison and his wife, Dina, was one of the two prison matrons, but his jurisdiction during the Occupation was over the civilian side alone. He was hated and was perceived to be 'always fawning to his German masters'. Anthony Faramus accused him and his deputy of having a scheme to:

> Supplement their own beggarly larders. Whereas in normal circumstances food parcels were prohibited, the wily pair winked at the rule, and friends and families of prisoners were encouraged to bring in foodstuffs; legitimate rations which had been scraped together and provisions brought on the black market were left at the gate for examination and then systematically nobbled, only a small proportion reaching the cells.[27]

Briard was someone who 'could have been more supportive' and 'a frightened man . . . who did very little' for political prisoners. He bullied his own staff[28] and was described as a 'cold, unapproachable disciplinarian . . . incapable of differentiating between political prisoners and common criminals'.[29] This was a cardinal sin among the political prisoners, who did not perceive themselves to have been legitimately imprisoned. Briard was even threatened with denunciation as a collaborator by one of the prisoners unless he rescued a young teenager from solitary confinement and allowed him into the civilian side of the prison when the Germans were not carrying out an inspection.[30] Briard was not always unapproachable; young Pauline Lamy, in prison aged 22 for listening to the radio, had Briard's signature – and that of his wife – at the very back of her political prisoner autograph book![31] Accompanied by the date of September 1944, this was not a post-war souvenir. That it was written upside down on the final page, thus making it appear as the very first entry (from a different perspective) indicates Briard's desire to exert his authority and status within the prison.

There were thought to be eight Jersey prison warders, although this number may have increased as the prison grew more overcrowded in late 1944.[32] The other warders were mostly ex-soldiers of the First World War, like their German counterparts. They resented having to salute all Wehrmacht officers, as they were ordered to do. At the beginning of the Occupation all of them took their war medals off their tunics, but later, as an act of resistance, they replaced them.[33] Despite this show of patriotism, to the political prisoners these men ranged from being 'right bastards' and 'jobsworths' to 'decent men caught in an unenviable position'[34] and men who 'treated the political prisoners with respect and kindness'.[35] While some

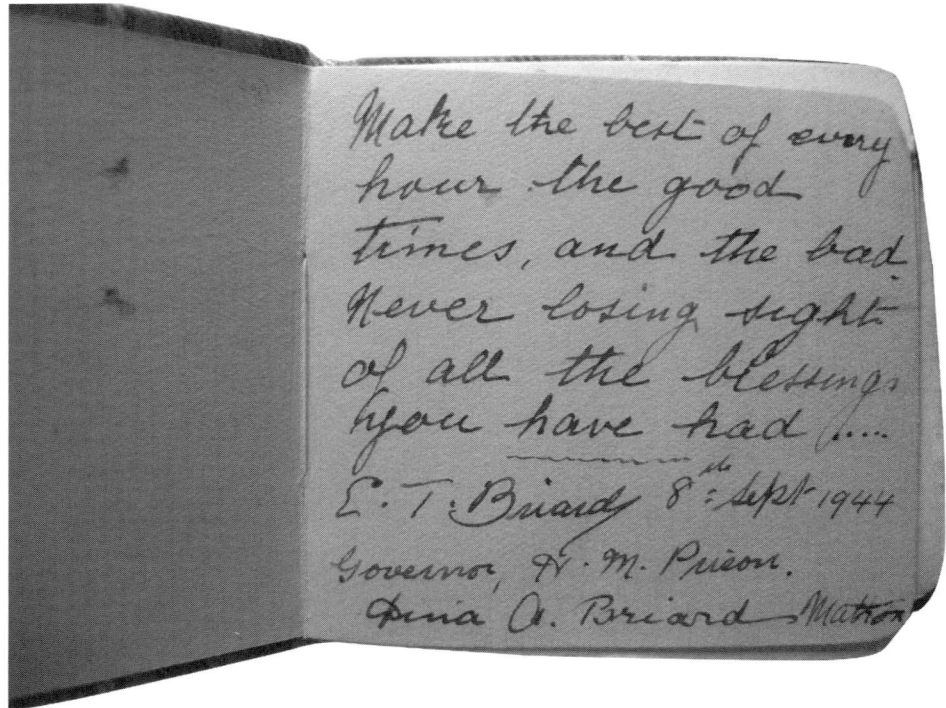

Ernest Briard's signature in Pauline Lamy's autograph book. (Courtesy Paulette de la Haye)

of them turned a blind eye to minor infringements of rules, others were not afraid to give prisoners a dressing down for such misdeeds.[36]

Prisoners showed their disdain for the Jersey guards through lack of respect and breaking the rules, especially when asked to observe them. Thus, when Briard came to Le Quesne's cell to ask the inmates to keep the volume down, one of them threw a pillow at him and knocked his hat off.[37] When a warder 'shoved and shouted at' one of the political prisoners, he was grabbed and beaten up. Even when punished for this assault, the prisoners were furious because they considered the guards to have no jurisdiction over them. The prisoners were much more responsive when treated with respect, and had better words to say about a warder who addressed them as 'gentlemen' and was helpful and courteous.[38] In a reversal of positions, the convicted political prisoners in A-Block preferred to exert their authority over the guards, noting that they 'didn't take any nonsense' from even the governor.[39]

One illustration of this is told in an anecdote by Joe Mière who, by April 1945, was imprisoned in the 'bungalow'. When he originally entered the prison, Mière had a Union Flag folded up inside his jacket pocket. Although it was confiscated by the Germans, it was returned to him, somewhat remarkably, when he entered the civilian side of the prison. The flag was hung up on a door in the bungalow and the words 'Political Prisoners Jersey 1945' were added. As an important German general was due to visit the prison, the governor and head warder were carrying out an inspection and asked the prisoners to hide all 'knives and books, etc.' before he arrived.[40] Presumably he wanted to give the impression that no contraband existed in the prison and that he was running a tight ship. Briard demanded that the flag be taken down and the prisoners refused, threatening anyone who tried to do so with violence. The governor had little choice but to walk away.[41]

We should not assume, however, that the political prisoners had carte blanche to behave how they wished. Memories of disrespect towards Jersey prison guards conveyed in memoirs were shows of bravado. The other side of the coin is represented in a book of 'offences and punishments' that had taken place inside Jersey Prison. Now in Jersey Archives, this book shows that prisoners were confined to their cells, had food or blankets removed or were even birched for offences such as bad language, insolence towards warders, passing notes to other prisoners, attempting to speak to prisoners of the opposite sex, deliberately destroying furniture in the cell or for obtaining contraband.[42] However, it is unclear whether these punishments were for civil prisoners only or for political and non-political prisoners alike.

It is likely that the warders were intimidated by the prisoners; indeed, the prisoners tried to intimidate them – something that never happened on the military side of the prison, where the Germans were firmly in control and only mocked behind their backs. Some warders were sympathetic to the prisoners, whether as individuals or because they supported their cause, and this was expressed through the facilitation of minor rule-breaking. Thus, one or two male prisoners are reported to have made short visits to the female side in A-Block, which could only have been carried out with the connivance of a warder because of the thick door that separated the two sides.[43]

Chapter 6
Solidarity, Legitimacy and Resistance

A belief in the legitimacy and pride in their acts of resistance was a cornerstone of political prisoner identity. This belief lay at the heart of the full range of protest, defiance and non-compliance with prison rules, the three overlapping forms of resistance that I outline here. A range of options was available to prisoners who wanted to exert their will and their agency; they were not powerless to act, although their opportunities and abilities were severely reduced on the military side of the prison. Even there, they exerted their right to stand up for what they believed was right and to do all they could to protest against illegitimate treatment of other prisoners.

For prisoners who wanted to protest in a legitimate way, the option existed for letters or petitions of complaint to the Prison Board or to the Bailiff directly, in his dual position as Bailiff and member of the Prison Board. This was not without risk, as one's prison record could be marked for being less than a model prisoner; there is even some evidence that prisoners did not have the right to petition in the early part of the Occupation.[1] A more immediate form of protest, often at the treatment of another prisoner, included shouting at the guards and hammering on the cell door until somebody took notice. Defiance, meanwhile, covered a range of behaviours in the civilian side of the prison, such as singing loudly in the evening or night time, after the cells had been locked – singing loud enough for one's voice to carry to other cells so that a whole corridor or floor could join in the communal singing (and so that every prisoner might know who was newly silent or had been taken away). This was a common way of vocally creating and expressing solidarity with fellow political prisoners. Defiance, then, was spontaneous, immediate, often vocal but sometimes silent, and was often carried out in a spirit of good-humour rather than anger, unlike protest. It also included non-compliance with the prison rules, which principally involved smuggling parcels, food and contraband in and out of the prison, and usually entailed the help of other prisoners, family and friends, and a sympathetic guard or warder. It involved other forms of circumvention of the system, but the most extreme form of non-compliance was escape or attempted escape, and a number of prisoners managed this from both the military and civilian side.

Protest

Protesting to or petitioning the authorities against perceived injustices within the prison system could be an effective method of change, but the authorities were not always willing or able to do what the prisoners asked. One of the earliest instances of protest during the Occupation took place when François Scornet entered the prison in 1941. Scornet led a group of young Frenchmen who had escaped from France with the hope of getting to England. They arrived instead in Guernsey and were taken to Jersey where they were placed in prison. Two prisoners, Eddie Chapman and Anthony Faramus, encountered them there. The Frenchmen became popular in prison through their disobedience and non-compliance. They danced, sang, shouted, drew graffiti on the walls and squatted instead of standing to attention in the face of visiting German officers.[2] However, at their court martial, Scornet received the death penalty and his friends were sentenced to hard labour on the continent. Other prisoners who had befriended Scornet were so disturbed and distressed by this verdict that they petitioned the Bailiff and Attorney-General, although this was not possible to do directly. Instead they had to give notice to a senior warder, who would then inform the head warder, who would then approach the governor, Briard. On this occasion, it seems that Briard considered it to be 'contemptuous and against discipline' for prisoners to 'dare put their name to paper, for whatever reason', although it seems more likely that he knew that it was impossible to go against the result of a German court martial.[3] At this stage in the Occupation, the authorities were still learning how far they could go in bargaining with the Germans and it seems that whether or not Briard forwarded the petition (and there is no surviving archival evidence to suggest that he did), the local authorities were not prepared to take risks or ask for favours for someone who was not one of their own countryman.

After 1941, there is a lack of evidence of any further examples of protest by political prisoners until October 1944. At this stage, both the archival and the published evidence tallies in showing that protest and liaison with members of the Prison Board or Bailiff became more regular, was taken seriously and was acted upon. Whether the lacuna between 1941 and 1944 is real, or whether the change in 1944 was due to the formation of political prisoner consciousness and identity due to a more static prison population after the Germans could no longer deport people, is unknown. It is possible that a lack of extant records is a hindrance in answering this question. In any event, evidence for protest carried out by prisoners and their family members increased over time. It seems that, by 1944, the Bailiff had become more muscular in his dealings with the Germans and was more ready to listen to prisoners and others. He would also have been aware that he had to be seen to be on the side of the people rather than the Germans, and so public perception was very important in his dealings. At the same time, the acts of resistance of the would-be political prisoners were making things difficult for him in his relationship with the German authorities.

Joe Mière recounted a conversation that he had with Coutanche at some point after Coutanche's 1961 retirement from office. As Coutanche died in 1973, the conversation most likely happened in the 1960s.

> It was all right for you young hot heads, you were very young and only saw your side of the German Occupation, but every time you got in trouble with the Germans it was I who had to go to College House and face the full anger for your actions. It made it very difficult for me to negotiate with the Kommandant to ease restrictions on our people.[4]

That the Bailiff minded how he was perceived locally is also suggested in the diary of Deputy Edward Le Quesne. After his spell in prison for wireless offences in October 1944, he went to see Baron von Aufsess, Head of Civil Affairs in the German Field Command, about securing an early release for all those in prison at that time for similar offences. The Baron promised to do his utmost to help. In his diary entry for 25 October 1944, Le Quesne reported that, 'The Bailiff seems hardly overjoyed at this result, possibly fearing that any success on my part may suggest that he has not done his share in looking after the interest of his people.'[5]

The Germans were also aware of the importance of public perception. In von Aufsess' diary, in an entry for 7 October 1944, he noted the 'foolish blunder' that had been made which allowed Le Quesne out of prison early:

> After he had served only two weeks of his seven months' sentence, he has been freed and the rest remitted. This does nothing to help his cause or our own. It brings our reputation for impartial justice into disrepute, and leads to the obvious accusation that we have one law for the highly-placed and another for the ordinary citizen. Although I would willingly have helped him in the first place and hushed the matter up if it had been brought to my notice in time, I cannot agree with this reversal of judgement and it took place without my agreement.[6]

Le Quesne was obviously mistaken about the source of the 'foolish blunder'; von Aufsess noted in his diary for 24 October 1944 that he had received a letter from

Le Quesne, thanking him for Aufsess' testimony on his behalf and his resulting early release from prison. Interestingly, von Aufsess did not make any reference about Le Quesne misunderstanding the reason for his early release and nor did he correct him. Perhaps von Aufsess wanted to appear benevolent to local officials in order to keep good relations between the two sides.

On 31 October 1944, Le Quesne noted in his diary that his efforts on behalf of the political prisoners had been successful and that many had been released from prison. However, it seems that self-interest rather than benevolence or altruism may have motivated the Germans to act. On 1 November 1944, von Aufsess noted in his diary that 'our press announcement of the freeing of all prisoners held for possessing wireless sets . . . should add further oil to troubled waters'.[7] As the waters had been troubled by German indications of the requisition of all remaining civilian supplies, it is clear that Le Quesne's request and the resulting German concession was merely a move in the greater chess game of the Occupation.

While Le Quesne was still in prison, and after only five days incarceration, he had sufficiently succumbed to the solidarity and group spirit of the political prisoners. Perhaps as part of wanting to be accepted by the group, he used his position and influence to ask for concessions and had been nominated as spokesperson because of this. He later reported in his diary that he had been:

> Fortunate enough to be able to secure bedsteads, an extra hour's exercise per day, the right to promenade round the governor's courtyard, a water tap upstairs and wash hand basins in the corridor instead of having to do our washing in the cells as at present. Not a bad day's work, but I want to do more for the boys before I leave here.[8]

We don't know whether or which of these concessions were honoured as no other prisoner later commented on new facilities. Presumably the prisoners felt that they were on a winning streak with Le Quesne as their spokesman. After getting in trouble for holding a 'smoking concert' a couple of nights previously, the political prisoners got together, again elected Le Quesne to speak for them, and asked the Governor to meet them to air their grievances against him for his remonstrations against their concert. Again, we do not know the outcome, but apparently Briard heard some 'straight talk' at the meeting, indicating that the prisoners were not afraid to state their case and the illegitimacy of prison rules in their eyes.[9]

By 1945, the political prisoners were regularly flexing their muscles, no longer fearing any negative consequences to making demands. They petitioned the Bailiff on 9 February to ask him to visit them at the prison because they felt that they were being treated unjustly with respect to the distribution of Red Cross parcels. Three days later the Bailiff visited them with two other members of the Prison Board and noted that he:

> Saw the Petitioners, who stated they acted on behalf of all the Political Prisoners. Subsequently saw all the other Political Prisoners. I explained the position with regard to Red Cross Parcels. The Petitioners made requests i.e. (1) Exercise (2) Suet (3) Fish. I asked the Board to consider these matters sympathetically, which I feel satisfied they will do. Before leaving I wrote an official entry in the Visitor's [*sic*] Book.[10]

It is interesting to note that the Bailiff was motivated to leave his signature in the visitors' book, to make it clear that he had visited and intervened on their behalf. He was also motivated to make a note in his official papers that he did so. It seems that Coutanche not only cared about how he was seen by prisoners and others, but he also had half an eye on how he would be judged after the Occupation. This is not the first example of Coutanche doing so. In September 1942, he also left eleven pages of hurried notes in his files about his protests to the Germans about the forced deportation of English-born Islanders to civilian internment camps in Germany.[11]

Coutanche's visit to the prison was not just to discuss Red Cross parcels. A handwritten note in his files confirms that he also visited the prison because: 'some of the parents of the young men imprisoned on the military side of the Public Prison (and, therefore, entirely outside the control of the Prison Board) have complained to me of (1) lack of sufficient food (2) ill-treatment, amounting in some cases to physical cruelty'.[12] It seems likely that at least some of the 'parents' in question were actually the mothers of Joe Mière and his friend Frank Le Pennec. Joe had smuggled out of the prison his blood-stained shirt and bits of teeth using a friendly German prison guard. The two mothers went to complain to the Kommandant but were escorted out of the building and accused of being mad. It seems likely that the women then complained to the Bailiff. In later years, Alexander Coutanche said to Joe that he remembered his mother coming to visit and informing him that the German police were treating Joe in a 'very brutal manner' with beatings and had knocked his teeth out.[13]

Thus, when Coutanche visited the prison on 12 February 1945, he spoke to the Receiver General, Major Giffard, who was the Honorary Secretary of the Prison Board.

He told Coutanche that prisoners who were transferred to the civil side of the prison after time spent on the military side would have every opportunity to complain to prison officials and that 'no such complaint appears to have been received'. However, Major Giffard promised Coutanche that he would make 'further discreet enquiries' and report back. Meanwhile, while at the prison, Coutanche saw the political prisoners and 'no one made any complaint. Maybe no one whom I saw had been exposed to any ill-treatment.'[14]

A week later he discussed prison conditions with Baron von Aufsess and also Dr Kopplemann, who was in charge of prisons. He told them that he had received formal complaints of cruelty and was told that immediate enquiries would be made. Coutanche suggested that he be allowed to visit the military side of the prison to talk to the prisoners there (as this was where the ill-treatment was taking place), and was promised that his request would 'receive consideration'.[15] Although we do not know the outcome of this, Mière reported that the ill-treatment stopped and that Coutanche suggested that his intervention on Joe's behalf must have borne fruit.[16]

On the same day that Coutanche visited the prison with President of the Prison Board, Charles Sidney Le Gros, and Major Giffard (i.e. on 12 February 1945), Le Gros met with Noel McKinstry, the Medical Officer for Health, and asked him to inspect the prison with his medical colleagues because it was badly overcrowded. Although there is no supportive evidence of this, it is possible that the meeting was requested by Coutanche. In any event, a report was requested by the Prison Board.[17] Their report highlighted issues of gross overcrowding, squalor, scabies, unpleasant odours, a risk of epidemics of meningitis and TB, dampness and totally inadequate cooking facilities.[18] Interestingly, they also referred to the 'storm of criticism that the prison has invoked', which indicates that there was pressure on local authorities from outside the prison to improve conditions.

Following correspondence with Le Gros, McKinstry was compelled to write again to point out that his indication of prison overcrowding was emphasised, 'not with a view to provide more prison accommodation but with a view to efforts being made to effect a reduction in the number of prisoners. We had hoped that our report would strengthen your hand in making representations to the Germans about the gross overcrowding that undoubtedly prevails.'[19] Meanwhile Le Gros had written to the Bailiff with a list of prisoners and their sentences to see if any could be released early.[20] The Bailiff had a meeting with the Platzkommandant Captain von Cleve and Baron von Aufsess on 11 April 1945 and handed over a list of political prisoners (probably only those who had already been sentenced) and urged them to:

> Give sympathetic consideration to a possible remission of sentence upon these prisoners. Captain von Cleve promised to give the matter his immediate consideration, but I gained the impression as I have gained on previous occasions when I have made similar requests; namely that whilst wireless offences were regarded with some sympathy, there were other classes of offences which did not call forth similar sentiments on the part of the Occupying Authorities.[21]

Rather than any remission of sentences on this occasion, the Germans instead had already decided to deal with the problem by transferring a number of prisoners across the road to the Chelsea Hotel, where 'two corridors with a total of 30 rooms' were to be made available forthwith.[22] On 3 May the Prison Board advertised for new prison staff,[23] but there is no evidence that the Chelsea Hotel was ever actually used to house prisoners before the Occupation ended. Kevin Le Cocq, for example, recalls 'expecting at any moment to be ordered into this new annex', but the order never came.[24]

In summary, we can see that protesting against the prison regime was carried out by prisoners, their family members, and by the medical authorities. By the final year of the war, the Bailiff was more willing to act and to be seen to be acting. The prisoners had also found their voice and had long since lost their fear and respect for authority and prison rules. Their disregard for the rules comes across most clearly in instances of disobedience, which occurred at both an individual and communal level, where prisoners took strength from their mass action.

Defiance and Non-Compliance

Defiance was mainly a tool of prisoner solidarity and an expression of identity, but also a way of boosting morale and even passing the time. Raising their voices together, principally through the medium of singing, was a strong bonding tool. Group singing is a recurring theme in Le Quesne's diary. During his fortnight's stay in prison, he records it taking place on at least eight different occasions. It was used to say goodbye to people who were leaving the prison at the end of their sentences. Although the usual leaving song was 'For He's a Jolly Good Fellow', a French prisoner, André Aune, received the Marseillaise when it was his turn to leave.

Prisoners also sang patriotic songs which were likely to have aggravated the nearby Germans and thus worried the local warders; Le Quesne records the singing of the National Anthem at the end of one evening.[25] The most popular time for singing was in the evening. This was perceived to be disruptive by the warders, who knew defiant behaviour when they saw it and whose only sanction was to lock the prisoners in their cells or to take away their musical instruments.[26] Le Quesne recorded that:

> We had a smoking concert in the evening. First of all Briard called in and told us we were not to 'kick up a row' . . . Then the fun began. We all started singing 'Pack up your troubles' at the top of our voices and the ordinary prisoners locked up in their cells began joining in; you never heard such a din. Briard then sent two warders to warn us that we would all be locked up if we didn't stop . . . Then [we] started singing again. Briard then reappeared and started laying down the law so we started 'Auld Lang Syne' for his benefit, but that finished it, so off we had to go to bed, all satisfied that we had had a ripping time, contrary to rules and regulations.[27]

The singing in one block could be heard in other blocks, which was a way of creating solidarity between prisoners on different sides of the prison. Singing on the women's side of the civilian wing was also joined in by the men on the other side. When it came to singing by individuals or between separated couples, it was a way of seeing who was still alive or in the prison. Prisoners who came in as a group but were separated could use this to communicate with each other to see who was still present. Singing also took place on the German side of the prison and was used to unite prisoners locked up in their cells, to raise morale, and could be an act of resistance. On one occasion, a group of prisoners having a 'jazz session' imitated the sound of English planes flying overhead and dropping bombs, finishing the session with a rendition of 'There'll always be an England'. Although a passing *GFP* officer overheard them and complained, leading to the German guards bursting into B-Block, they started singing again after a decent interval.[28] There was little that the guards could do to prevent such spontaneous singing, but it also had other uses: it conveniently covered other noises, such as those made by others while trying to escape.[29]

On the military side of the prison, where prisoners were locked in their cells, communication was clearly prohibited. Therefore prisoners had to be ingenious when it came to talking or passing on messages, which was done between neighbouring cells, between cells further apart on the same corridor, between different floors of the prison block and between the military and civilian side of the prison.

Although prisoners in solitary confinement were not allowed to speak to each other in B-Block, there were three methods for communicating with the person in the next cell. If both prisoners lay on their backs with their heads close to the gap under the door, they could speak or whisper and hear each other speak.[30] This could only be done if the guard was not present, and it was a similar story for prisoners who opened their small barred windows and tried to speak window-to-window. In B-Block, heating pipes (seemingly always cold) ran along the back of each cell, and the lime and cement plaster which held the pipes in place could be scraped away with spoon handles (knives and forks were forbidden on both sides of the prison) to create a small hole between cells. Prisoners could speak or pass messages through this hole (written on smuggled paper with smuggled pencils), putting the scrapings in their chamber pots and emptying them down the toilets in the morning.[31] As a protest against the enforced silence and the lack of communication, after emptying their pots in the morning the prisoners would bang them against the wall on the way back as a form of communal protest and solidarity.[32]

In order to pass messages between different cells on the same corridor, prisoners would slide notes under each other's doors. This method was even used by incarcerated German soldiers to make contact with Jersey political prisoners, prompted by their fear following the execution of one of their number, Georg Keil,[33] on 7 April 1944, for speaking about desertion.[34] Communication between floors was possible via two methods. A prisoner could elude the guard and go downstairs with a note. Alternatively, a prisoner in a lower cell could stand on a chair or the bed, or build a scaffold with stools, and communicate with the prisoner in the cell above by whispering or sending a note, food or contraband through a hole in the floorboards.[35] Prisoners could also 'speak along the pipes'. This was a process which began by tapping the pipe to alert the attention of another prisoner, which they replied to by tapping back to show that they were ready to receive a message. By putting the ear to the pipe, one could hear the voice of other prisoner which was 'transmitted along the metal', like a 'crude telephone'. Clearly, this method of communication was not private, but could be heard only by those who placed their ears next to the pipe.[36]

Although exercise in the yard was supposed to be conducted in silence, a number of prisoners commented on being able to use the opportunity to whisper brief messages, to pass on the news to each other, to plot escape attempts or to pass on contraband or food.[37] This suggests that the silence was not always strictly policed, or that prisoners were prepared to risk being caught.

Female political prisoners who had already been sentenced and were in the civilian side of the prison took their exercise in a yard overlooked by B-Block. This offered prisoners on the military side the opportunity of passing messages between blocks. The method for doing so was outlined by Frank Keiller as follows:

> If we propped the wooden bed against the outer wall when the guards weren't about, we could climb up it – with some difficulty – and peer out of the window and talk to female prisoners at exercise in the yard below. They . . . were supervised by a civilian wardress who was sympathetic. It was easy to whisper down to them and to pass on messages, provided we kept an eye on the Judas hole and listened for noises in the corridor. At times, we even lowered small articles or notes on a piece of string, and sometimes got something back.[38]

Wendy Janvrin-Tipping, daughter of political prisoner Muriel Costard, and niece of Muriel's sister, Evelyn Janvrin, wrote that when Evelyn and Alice Thaureux (who shared a cell) exercised in the yard, Alice would call out to her boyfriend, German soldier Nikolaus Schmitz. Alice and her family had sheltered Nikolaus after he had deserted. When caught (or rather, informed upon[39]), both Nikolaus and Alice were given a death sentence, although Alice's was commuted to ten years imprisonment after intervention by the Bailiff. Nikolaus was executed on the parade ground at Fort Regent on 27 April 1945, despite trying to commit suicide the night before by swallowing rusty nails, as mentioned earlier.[40]

An almost identical testimony of this method of communication was provided by Lucy Schwob, thus confirming the helpfulness of the female warder in allowing this kind of interaction between political prisoners.[41] It was also possible for prisoners on the civilian side to throw messages over the wall which separated the blocks into the yard used by the prisoners on the military side.[42] Messages were also passed between prisoners as they stood in the queue for washing and shaving in the morning.[43]

Again, the only way for prisoners on the military side of the prison to have access to paper was to receive it from other prisoners, often via the methods described above. On the civilian side of the prison, paper could be ripped out of books; the prayer books in the prison chapel were a good source of supply.[44] Library books were also used. When François Scornet was imprisoned in Jersey Prison before his execution in 1941, using a pin he pricked his name, the date of his execution and '*Vive La France*' into the edges of the page of a prison library book.[45] On the military side of the prison, pages of library books were also used, as was the

Solidarity, Legitimacy and Resistance 73

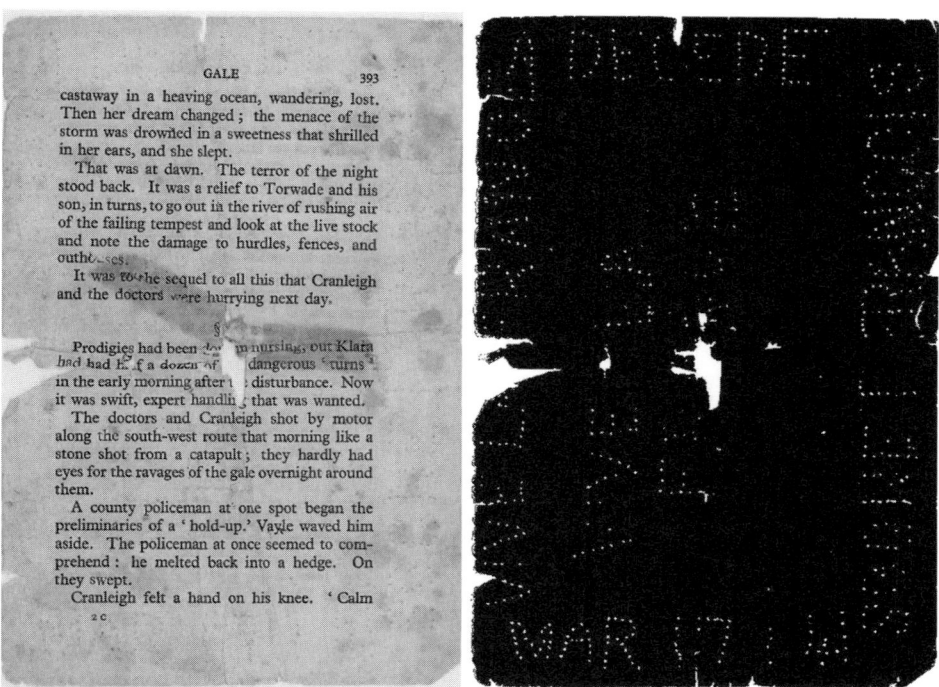

Page of a library book pricked with a pin by François Scornet to create words of defiance. (Copyright Société Jersiaise, reference GO3/1)

jailers' toilet paper, which was often stolen and used as writing paper much to the amusement of the prisoners.[46]

Paper also entered the prison in the form of notes smuggled in by friends and relatives of those in A-Block who were allowed to visit every fortnight, although this became more frequent at the end of the war.[47] Writing paper was sometimes brought in by Jersey warders, or, with the help of friendly guards, to those on the military side. Letters were also carried out of the prison by departing prisoners who had finished their sentence.[48]

It seems that although prisoners on B-Block were not officially allowed family visits or parcels, it was not unusual for guards to turn a blind eye for certain prisoners. Peter Gray's mother smuggled a note in the spine of a book for her son, but Otto, the 'little guard', discovered it.[49] That it was Otto who had been ready to relax the rules and sneak in a book (until the note was discovered), correlates with unverified reports that he could be bribed with eggs or tobacco to smuggle letters in and out of the prison.[50] Families could collect or deliver laundry twice a week.[51] Such a service was also used as a method of passing messages.[52]

Prisoners without friends on the outside either had to wear the same clothes for long periods of time or else were given clothes charitably donated.[53]

Although one needed a friendly guard who was not inclined to search parcels thoroughly, it seems that many small items of contraband were smuggled into the prison via food parcels from families or through the fence which prisoners on the civilian side could access during their walks. Indeed, many of the extant letters from prisoners to their families seem to comprise requests for food and contraband, with advice on how to sneak it in.[54] One of the letters written by a prisoner and sent home in March 1945 stated quite clearly that 'parcels in or out and not searched in any way whatsoever . . . there is no risk whatsoever'.[55] This matches an entry in George Le Marquand's diary for February 1945, which says that after complaints to the governor, political prisoners' parcels coming into A-Block would no longer be searched.[56] This suggests that towards the end of the war, rules were relaxed for political prisoners as they began to find their voice and demand special treatment befitting their status.

On the military side of the prison, food parcels were sometimes allowed, and a smuggled letter to his parents during his imprisonment reveals that Francis Harris begged his parents to wrap his knife, sharpening stone, matches, writing paper, needle and thread, in waterproof paper, inside a pie dish, assuring them that the Germans 'don't break open food'. We do not know whether they were wholly successful, but Harris still has today the needle and thread that he had with him in prison.[57]

Even some of the components needed to manufacture a crystal radio set were smuggled in. André Aune, imprisoned for six months for making crystal radio sets in April 1944, even managed to make one while inside. The earpiece was thrown over the wall by a friend of one of the other prisoners.[58] Peter Noel, imprisoned in November 1944 for attempting to escape from the Island, was also said to have a hidden crystal set in his cell.[59] Prisoners could also keep up with the news by other means: American officer and POW, Lieutenant George Haas, managed to listen to the radio in the office of a German guard in his absence, as we saw earlier. One of the German guards' servants, 'Karlschen', who carried out administrative tasks, used to write down the news from the guards' radio and pass it on to Lucy Schwob.[60] As the war drew to a close, Islanders became more daring to the extent that Lucy Schwob noted that the friends and family of prisoners brought war news with them on visits, and that prisoners received 'long, clearly written BBC bulletins which they circulated under the warder's nose'. This was presumably on the civilian side of the prison, given that those on the military side were not allowed visitors.⁶¹ Even so, the obviously imminent end to the war made Islanders less concerned about the repercussions of their actions.

Just as prison guards were often instrumental in allowing contraband into the prison and smuggling letters and objects out of the prison, circumvention of the prison system also took place without their connivance. Prisoners took delight in finding ways to prevent cell doors locking or in re-arranging the wiring and turning prison lights back on after the warders had turned them off and retired for the evening.⁶² Often this involved the use of objects to which prisoners should not have had access. For example, Eddie Chapman related his discovery of a gimlet and hacksaw, left behind in the prisoners' toilet by a visiting carpenter, which enabled him to cut out the lock.⁶³ Other prisoners placed a thin strip of plastic or cardboard between the lock and a frame to prevent the door from locking properly, although this was done purely to annoy the guards, as it seems that nobody used this method to escape.⁶⁴ Another prisoner, who was skilled at picking locks, used a piece of curved metal to let himself and others out of their cells in B-Block. Again, this was not done with the intention of escaping, but only so that the prisoners could chat to each other.⁶⁵ It is possibly through this method that George Le Marquand was able to report in his diary that he 'got on the wrong wing' and 'had warders in hell of a panic'.⁶⁶

The most extreme way in which prisoners defied incarceration was through escape – not just from their cells or their block, but from the prison altogether. This was achieved through the creative use of the mundane objects already available to the prisoners in their cells and their corridor. On getting help in picking the lock of his cell door and that of a store room and an exit door beyond, Richard Weithley used a bench, a table and a steel box in the store room to climb over a 10ft prison wall. He was caught. On his second attempt he used a section of angle iron, already welded into an L-shape, from the supports of cables and pipes running along the prison corridor. This he planned to use as a grapnel. Lengths of blankets were turned into ropes and, when the moment to escape arrived, the electricity cables in the corridor were torn down to stop the use of the emergency bell. However, once again he was caught as the makeshift escape equipment proved inadequate to the task.⁶⁷

In February 1945, Frank Keiller decided to make the most of the long hosepipe in his corridor in A-Block which, together with a fire bucket and stirrup pump, was kept there to deal with potential incendiary bombs. It was to serve as a rope substitute. He also stole a chisel and screwdriver from the prison workshop when the warder's attention was diverted, and used these to remove the wooden bars of the prison 'bungalow', in which he was incarcerated. Prison blankets were placed on top of the broken glass which was cemented on top of the outer wall of the prison. Keiller's escape was successful, but at great personal injury. After these escapes, in March 1945 the Germans set about making the prison more secure, adding more barbed wire and putting 'detonators around the prison walls' and notices saying *Achtung Minen*.[68]

Help From Medical Staff at the Hospital

In addition to protest and defiant behaviour by the prisoners, there were others who were prepared to break the rules. Although the medical staff of the next door hospital could not directly help prisoners escape, doctors and nurses did what they could to help them and we can only assume that the lines of communication between the hospital and the prison were kept open by prisoners who needed treatment from time to time and who were able to talk about their friends who also needed help. Communication between the hospital and prison was carried out by semaphore; Nurse Renée Griffin would signal the news from her window to prisoners, and they thanked her by presenting her with one of their signed autograph books.[69]

Medical staff were able to offer help in the form of taking food across for ill and starving patients and were also able to give more practical assistance. Frank Keiller, who was suffering from either what he described as 'famine diarrhoea' or food poisoning and was lying semi-conscious in his cell, was brought hospital food by one of the nurses who delivered it to the guard room.[70] Nurses from the hospital would also pickle cockles and mussels from the beach and send them over to the prison.[71] Later on, when he needed a stitch in his gum after a tooth extraction, Dr Hanna encouraged Keiller to add some red ink to the kidney dish he was spitting into, sufficient for him to be admitted to hospital for a few days of 'comfort, beautiful warmth, hot baths, and more food than I had seen for a long time'[72] After his escape from prison, the heavily bleeding Keiller was let into the medical officers' quarters where they bandaged him up before letting him go. While he was on the run and moving between safe houses, Dr McKinstry, the Island's Medical Officer of Health, got him a false identity card and ration book.[73]

Richard Weithley, who, like Keiller, was a teenager, also had need of medical attention after a self-inflicted wound. He had hoped to escape while in hospital, but as he was accompanied there by the German guard Heinrich, he had no opportunity.

Nurse Renée Griffin's autograph book. (Copyright Société Jersiaise, ref. GO3/12)

All the same, the nurses were very kind to him and gave him a cup of tea and some magazines and a book, which would have been much appreciated on the military side of the prison.[74]

Francis Harris, also a teenager, needed regular hospital treatment while in prison after injuring his eye before his arrest. Although he was taken to the hospital under armed guard, Sister Morgan, the casualty sister, made Heinrich and Otto wait outside in the waiting room. Meanwhile Francis was given hospital food and allowed illicit meetings with his family, organised by a Sister Morgan, long after he needed any further treatment on his eye.[75]

Unlike the Jersey Prison warders, the hospital staff were free to show their support of the prisoners in practical ways; they were not bound by prison rules and did what they could to help prisoners. They were even keen to use their own power and influence, such as it was, to help political prisoners.

In March 1944, Dr McKinstry wrote to the Bailiff to complain about the food rations given to the political prisoners on the civilian side of the prison. Not only had the governor reduced the weight and regularity of food parcels from outside but,

McKinstry implied, he had also placed 'unnecessary difficulties' in the way of giving TB prisoners the extra rations they required. In no uncertain terms, McKinstry wrote that, 'These men have committed no offence against our laws, yet it would seem that they are forced to subsist on a diet which greatly adds to the severity of their punishment'. In a clear criticism of the governor's actions, he complained that the governor had not been willing to act without asking the permission from the German authorities, who then communicated with the Attorney-General, who then wrote to McKinstry. He complained that 'I consider all this delay unnecessary and even the permission of the German Authorities need not have been sought. Action could have been taken until such time as the German Authorities saw fit to interfere.'[76]

Although we do not know how the Bailiff responded, such plain speech indicating McKinstry's political position and preferred approach when dealing with the Germans was daring but would no doubt have been welcomed by the prisoners. They were not the only ones who believed that Briard was overly compliant in his actions with the Germans; that such a perception was shared by a man of McKinstry's standing and authority is telling.

Chapter 7
'The 'Calendars . . . of Previous Prisoners': Graffiti and Interior Decoration

Defiant behaviour by the prisoners was not limited to confrontational acts. Graffiti, which was strictly forbidden, would have been equally satisfying for some. However, when Jersey Prison was demolished in the mid-1970s, all record of graffiti on the walls dating to the Occupation was lost. A 1936 account of the prison refers to some 'interesting carvings' on the first floor of A-Block in the wooden cell 'where violent prisoners were put'. The carvings were said to 'date back about 100 years and represent transportation of prisoners to Australia'.[1] When Frank Keiller arrived in his prison cell, he noted that 'the scrofulous walls wore peeling whitewash on stone and were decorated with old and new graffiti: the calendars and sadness of previous prisoners'.[2]

We can be sure that graffiti, or at least some kind of 'interior decoration' of the cells, took place at the hands of the inmates during the Occupation, because political prisoners referred to it in their memoirs. Although we have fewer than half a dozen references to Occupation period decoration of the walls, we can use these descriptions to begin to comment on the reasons for the graffiti and the messages which they communicated to others.

Throughout the Occupation, and certainly during the last year, political prisoners were moved around from cell to cell; this much is confirmed by all memoirs. Not only were prisoners moved from the military to the civilian side of the prison, but as the prison filled up and certain groups of prisoners had to be separated, it was necessary to move people about and the prisoners would have been soon aware of this. This meant that any graffiti was read by others and was perhaps meant to receive an audience of more than one person. In fact, Francis Le Sueur was quite explicit in his memoir about writing a message for two separate audiences: both for the benefit of the Ukrainian or Russian forced or slave labourers who were employed to keep the German section of the prison clean, and something that 'might not be entirely to the taste of the prison personnel'. Using his prison-issue spoon, he used the 'pointed end' to write something 'with a demoralising flavour . . .

"In Russland, der Wehrmact ist kaput" [*sic*]'. He also added a large hammer and sickle, and Le Sueur noted that the Ukrainians saw it and gave him a 'thumbs up'.[3] In fact, this graffiti was triggered by the refusal of a German guard to let him have pencil and paper – something that was forbidden in the military wing. So by refusing him contraband, the Germans inspired a prisoner to indulge in a form of communication even more *verboten* – and more permanent. We can also be sure that the Germans and other prisoners saw this graffiti because Le Sueur tells us that another political prisoner incarcerated for a wireless offence was told by the German guards to scrub the graffiti off the wall, although this proved impossible as it had been too deeply engraved.

Similar anti-German comments were scratched on the wall by François Scornet. Eddie Chapman, who was imprisoned with him in 1941, noted that Scornet and his friends 'drew caricatures of Hitler and Goering on the walls'.[4] Again, the fact that Chapman was able to comment on this indicates that the graffiti (a form of common language overcoming any language barrier) was intended for an audience of other, sympathetic, political prisoners, as well as for the German guards, who they knew would be annoyed by such artwork.

There is also a reference to a slightly more subtle, semi-encoded graffito: Lucy Schwob noted in a number of sources that she, and perhaps others, used 'an old nail or such loot' to scratch 'on the paint of the cell doors' and 'on the wall of our cell' the political prisoners' slogan, '*ANY MINUTE NOW*'. This was a statement with many meanings: any minute now they would be liberated. Any minute now the Allies would come. Any minute now the war would be over, the Germans would be defeated, and they would get their just deserts. Schwob wrote that she liked the ambiguity of the slogan; it was a way of asserting the political prisoner voice – a cheerful, impudent voice.[5] Schwob also noted that the slogan was scratched on the tins which replaced worn out pots for meals, indicating the transferable and portable nature of graffiti. As the meal tins were collected in and reused every day, this rebellious, resistant sentiment would have been seen by many prisoners and even passed around the prison block in an entirely official capacity at mealtimes. In this way, the message would spread and others would be encouraged to replicate it. In fact, Schwob refers to it being traced on 'tins' and 'doors' (plural), thereby implying that this was a common practice.[6] It is interesting at this juncture to note that this political prisoner slogan was not just a motto that emerged at the same time as political prisoner consciousness in the second half of 1944. In a prison letter written by Joseph Tierney, imprisoned between April and September 1943, he wrote to his wife 'it might not be so very long before we are together again.

You know our motto here, don't you. "Any time now"!' He also ended that letter with the words 'Don't forget I might be home ANY TIME NOW!'[7] Such was the importance of this motto, and its multiple meanings, that Tierney composed a poem of the same time, which is reproduced at the start of this book. It seems likely, then, that this motto and the sentiment behind it circulated even before 1943 as a prisoner voice of defiance against the occupier.

There is an overlap between graffiti as a statement of defiance, and graffiti as decoration to cheer up a depressing and chilling prison cell. As artists, it was perhaps natural for Lucy Schwob and Suzanne Malherbe to choose to decorate their cell in this way, even though it was forbidden to do so. In her post-war notes of her time in prison, Schwob wrote that '*c'était la mode parmi nous*' [it was the fashion among us] to use beetroot syrup as a form of glue to stick pictures on the door of their cell. She explained that after their release, they were permitted by the jailers to show their friend their cell, which had been decorated since Christmas with flowers, butterflies, holly and eucalyptus, with inscriptions and photomontages. Since April, the door had also been decorated with little Allied flags.[8]

It is interesting to compare what was written or pasted on walls with what was put on the inside of doors; for while the guards could look through the peep-hole or walk into the cell and see the graffiti on walls, as soon as they opened the door they would be unable to see what was on the other side of it without closing the door. Therefore, we might infer that, as far as the military wing of the prison was concerned, graffiti on the inside of doors was more for the benefit of the prisoner or the inmate of that room. That which was on walls might have been more intended to provoke the guards or for other passing people to see, such as other prisoners on the corridor who might steal the chance to look furtively through the peep-hole when passing. Thus, the photomontages of Lucy Schwob were on the door, yet the political prisoners' slogan was written on the wall.

One might also expect the most subversive messages to be placed on the door – something that the prisoner alone might gain satisfaction from without getting into trouble with the guards. In a letter written in 1950, Schwob recalled that, against the rules, she stuck on her cell door an image of (presumably Allied) tanks moving towards Berlin, taken from a propaganda newsletter for the German troops that had been printed in England and dropped on the Island by the RAF. The publication had found its way into the prison through the clandestine 'prison post.' In April, they were given a German magazine under their door. In this publication, a rather inept artist had attempted a picture that, to the eyes of Schwob and Malherbe, looked like a decapitated and mutilated head of Hitler – although this is clearly not what the artist intended.

They also stuck this on the door of their cell with beetroot-syrup glue.[9] This illustration had the effect of cheering up the grey paint of their cell door with an ambiguous yet dangerously subversive image, and when the death of Hitler followed soon afterwards, it seemed to them that their picture had presaged the event.

Schwob and Malherbe were not the only prisoners who took comfort from images of the Allied machinery of war, and who perhaps looked upon them as a form of wish fulfilment or 'sympathetic magic'. Francis Harris had been given old copies of *Signal* and *Adler* magazines by a guard, and he used them to copy images of British and American aircraft planes on his cell wall, using charcoal from discarded fires.[10]

In summary, therefore, graffiti and decoration of the cell and prison-issue objects such as food tins had many purposes. It was certainly a form of protest or disobedience as it was forbidden. It is interesting to note that all the recorded examples stem from the military side of the prison, although we have no way of knowing how representative this was. As we have seen, prisoners under German guard were on the whole more compliant than those on the civilian side. They were more cautious, even scared, of the guards and so had to be non-confrontational in their mode of resistance. In this context, we should not be surprised to discover that graffiti might have predominated on this side of the prison, and that the most subversive images were hidden on the back of the cell doors. Although we can describe graffiti as non-confrontational, this does not mean that the guards did not see it; sometimes they were even the intended audience. However, graffiti was also aimed at others, including other prisoners and people under the control of the Germans, such as their Russian and Ukrainian servants. It was, above all, a mode of silent communication – a useful tool in a building where talking was not allowed – a material expression of unspoken sentiments?

Graffiti and decoration were also a way of cheering up the cell inmate and of giving the prisoner a way of passing the time, of doing something creative to take their minds off the cold, their hunger and their circumstances. It added colour to the room and gave them a different scene to gaze upon, to wish for and to use to boost their morale. We should not be surprised that in the depths of an icy winter, Lucy Schob decorated her cell with butterflies and flowers, symbols of summer, warmth and life. Similarly, Francis Harris, in prison for firearms offences, was able to feel psychologically that he was doing something for the Allied cause by drawing Allied planes, adding them to the number that was at that moment fighting the Germans. Schwob, too, in her selection of a decapitated Hitler, was able to focus her mental energies on this image, no doubt wishing ardently for it to be real, and feeling unsettled when she learned that Hitler had actually died, as if her artwork had somehow contributed to his death.

Chapter 8
'Yielding to so Rare a Pleasure': Autograph Books and Artwork

A different form of artistic output also exists from the prison: the small number of autograph books in public archives and in private ownership. These were originally smuggled into the prison by family and friends of prisoners.[1] They were circulated by political prisoners from the autumn of 1944 onwards and record a number of themes. While a slightly larger corpus of political prisoner artwork also survives in the form of certificates and illustrated lists of autographs, these are considered alongside the autograph books here as the images are often the same and painted or sketched by the same people at the same time. Close reading of these sources can reveal a multitude of themes and meanings and reasons for their production. While they primarily built bonds of friendship and community between the prisoners, helping them to get to know each other through their offences, they were also used to develop political prisoner consciousness, and thus a particularly powerful kind of material culture. Autograph books and certificates were also an alternative method of record keeping and of recording the experience of imprisonment. Francis Harris believed that 'they formed some sort of "guarantee" that should any inmate disappear, there would be a record of some sort'.[2]

It would have been natural for the young people on the political prisoner block to bond and make friendships with each other and to reach out to each other to combat their fear and isolation. Most of the people who wrote entries in Peter Gray's or Nurse Renée Griffin's autograph books, for example, wrote their age as a way of finding out who were natural members of the gang of young offenders. There is a sense that the teenagers gave their ages alongside a sketch of their offence both to prove that they were old enough to be taken seriously while at the same time using their youth to emphasise the injustice of their imprisonment. However, older prisoners followed the younger ones in declaring their age alongside their crime, perhaps as a way of asking to be part of the group because of their offences, despite their age; 61-year-old Harry Durtnall wrote his age alongside a drawing of a radio broadcasting the BBC Home Service.[3]

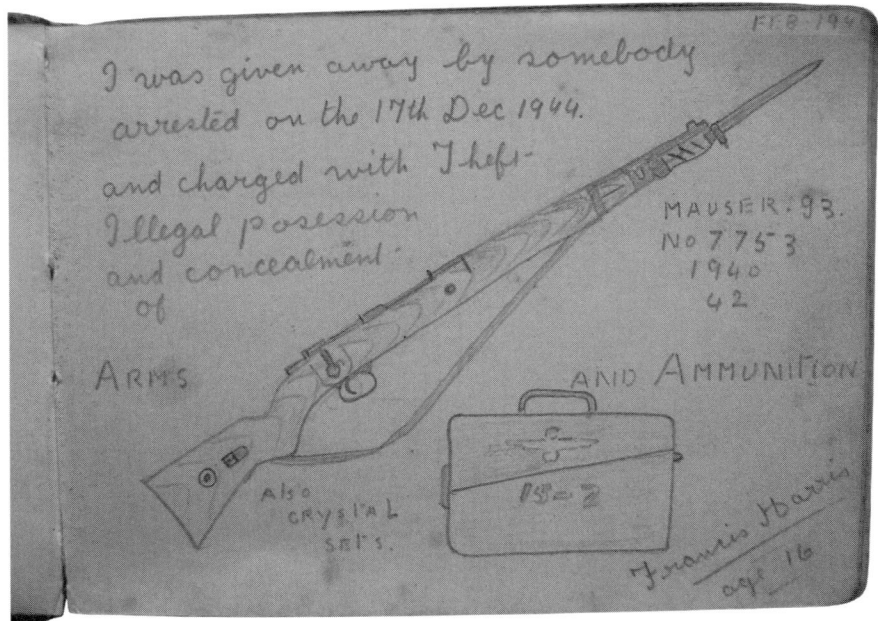

Page from Nurse Renée Griffin's autograph book signed by Peter Gray. (Copyright Société Jersiaise, ref. GO3/12)

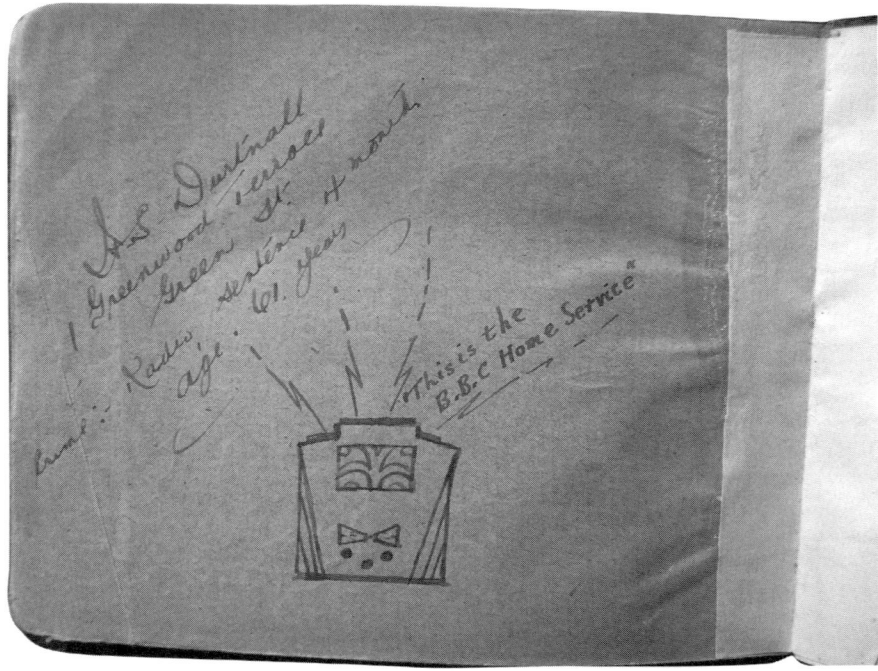

Page from Peter Gray's autograph book signed by Harry Durtnall. (Copyright Peter Gray)

It is likely that the autograph books and political prisoner certificates were circulated as a way of getting to know the inhabitants of the other cells and to find out what sort of company they were keeping. It was also a way of expressing their credentials to each other and proving their patriotism and commitment to the cause. Examples of two typical autograph books, complete with beautiful artwork, belonging to political prisoners and sisters Murial Costard and Evelyn Janvrin, have been published elsewhere by Wendy Janvrin-Tipping.[4]

The certificate, the most ubiquitous of political prisoner artwork in the possession of most political prisoners interviewed, can be viewed as a seal of approval. It was evidence that they, among the general population, had acted properly and patriotically against the occupiers by their act of resistance and subsequent arrest and imprisonment. It was their badge of honour. Certificates, more than autograph books, are thus vehicles of patriotic insignia and symbols, and are usually replete with V-signs, victory laurels, flags, coats of arms, symbols of monarchy and the armed forces, and patriotic colours.[5]

Political prisoners also defined themselves by their offences, and this is why their artwork and entries in autograph books are dominated by these kinds of images

Example of patriotic artwork in autograph book belonging to Evelyn Janvrin. (Copyright Wendy Janvrin-Tipping)

and statements. Thus, the most typical entry in autograph books lists only the name of the prisoner, their offence and their date of arrest or imprisonment. Even this kind of simple statement would serve to introduce new members to the older members of the political prisoner gang.

Above: *Belza Turner's political prisoner certificate.* (Copyright and courtesy Barbara Greene, daughter of Belza Turner)

Left: *Belza Turner.* (Courtesy Barbara Greene)

Image of Britannia in Muriel Costard's autograph book. (Copyright and courtesy of Wendy Janvrin-Tipping)

To emphasise the importance of the patriotic nature of their offences, some of the artists exaggerated or employed artistic licence to make clear their agenda. In Muriel Costard's autograph book, for example, Denis McLinton, sentenced to two years for attempting to escape from the Island, painted an image of Britannia standing up in a boat, trident and shield held in readiness, and flanked by three war ships.[6] The caption underneath reads 'Britannia Rules', and whether she is sailing to the rescue of Jersey or escaping from the Island as McLinton did, the patriotic message is clear. Patriotism is also emphasised in statements such as '*God Save the King*', added at the bottom of details of their convictions by Hugh Le Cloche and Frederick Emmett.[7] Muriel Costard added '*England for Ever. The Land of the Free*', to hers. Peter Noel's entry, showing a painted image of Britannia seated, the Union Jack, the Royal Standard and the caption '*Britons Awake*', makes clear his loyalties.[8]

Such statements are relatively common throughout all autograph books, especially among those arrested for attempting to escape from the Island.

Others portrayed their resistance in more idealistic forms, using cartoon sketches of themselves carrying out the act of resistance which they were thwarted from fulfilling because they were caught. There is a series of four sketches which illustrates this theme, drawn by members of the 'Underground Retaliation Movement' (URM). The group comprised 19-year-olds Arnold Bennett and Bernard Hassall Carratu, 16-year-old Peter Gray and 22-year-old Claude Saunders.

We know that the four were members of one of the several small teenage gangs in St Helier, identified by Willmot,[9] whose objective was to steal German weapons and equipment that might one day be used to help liberate the Island alongside Allied soldiers. These four young men of the URM also wanted to 'do something about informers' by bombing a hairdressing salon in St Helier owned by a man who was notoriously pro-German. Although the young men were informed upon before the attack could take place, they had apparently

Image of Peter Gray in Nurse Renée Griffin's autograph book. (Copyright Société Jersiaise, ref. GO3/12)

stockpiled the explosives needed. Despite this, their autograph book cartoons depict themselves in the act of carrying out the attack.

Thus, Arnold Bennett drew himself as 'Commander in Chief' of the URM, sitting at a table speaking into a radio transmitter. Boxes of TNT and a bomb sit waiting behind him on the floor, and a gun in a holster hangs off a coat peg. The caption reads 'Sentenced to 6 years for attempted murder etc etc'. 'Lieutenant' Bernard Hassall, wearing the same 'URM' arm band as Bennett, is featured on the next page of the book. He drew himself heading towards the hairdressing salon in St Helier, stick of TNT in one hand and pocket and revolver in the other, wearing a hat low over his eyes and a handkerchief over his face. The caption reads 'B.E. Hassall (Lieutenant). Sentenced to 6 years Penal Servitude for Attempted Murder etc. etc. Also for being in possession of arms and photographs of military importance.' In Peter Gray's sketch, he stands outside the same hairdresser, URM armband on display, rifle under his arm and dynamite in his back pocket. The caption states that he has been 'sentenced to 14 months for arms and ammunition, and wireless sets, also attempted murder'. Gray was given a lesser sentence, presumably because he was younger than the others. The last image of the four shows Saunders wearing boxing gloves, standing next to a table upon which burns a stick of dynamite. The speech bubble reads 'Will I or won't I. Shucks', and the caption says that he was sentenced to four months for not reporting arms and ammunition. Not part of their gang, but drawn in the same style, 18-year-old Victor Webb has copied Arnold Bennett's image almost exactly, but this time it is crates of cameras, crystal sets and leaflets on the floor around him rather than dynamite. The caption states that he was arrested for 'being in possession of crystal sets, revolvers, cameras and photographs of military importance'.[10]

While these young men had not yet carried out their intended offence, their cartoons allowed them to carry it out vicariously, but their positions as members of a team are clear. In Peter Grey's own autograph book, by contrast, the group of four did not repeat their cartoons. Instead they simply stated their sentences, but this time with a different spin. While Gray listed his stockpile of weapons ('1 rifle, 1 pistol, 26 sticks of dynamite, 2 bayonets, 1 German helmet and belt, 2 radios and 14 leaflets and 158 rifle cartridges'), Bennett proudly stated his 'leadership of Underground Retaliation Movement' and Hassall drew a dagger dripping with blood underneath the statement 'attempted extermination of a Quisling'. This time they are almost showing off to each other, trying to outdo each other with their bravado. As this autograph book appears to have been filled in towards the end of April 1945, whereas the earlier one was compiled mid-March, their team spirit

Victor Webb's entry in Nurse Renée Griffin's autograph book. (Copyright Société Jersiaise, ref. GO3/12)

appears to have dissipated and to have been replaced by anger and a readiness to fight as soon as they were let out. To confirm this, Peter Gray used his autograph book to write down the names of the prison warders, perhaps to remind himself to take revenge after the war, especially given the remit of the URM.

As well as being a vehicle for wish fulfilment or showing off to each other, autograph books were also a way of building camaraderie and friendship between those imprisoned and were presumably slid under each other's doors for completion and passing on. They also provided a guarantee that if anything happened to any one of them, then even if the official records were faked, adjusted or destroyed, the political prisoners would have their own records.

Autograph books could also be solemn. They could act as memorials for friends who had died in the struggle against the Germans. George Le Marquand and Kenneth Collins, sentenced in October 1944 for attempted escape from the Island, used their pages in nurse Renee Griffin's and Peter Gray's autograph books to remember their friend, Douglas Le Marchand, 'who was shot during the attempt'.

The autograph book could also be used to express political prisoner morality, where contempt about informers on the outside could be expressed and the

'Yielding to so Rare a Pleasure': Autograph Books and Artwork 91

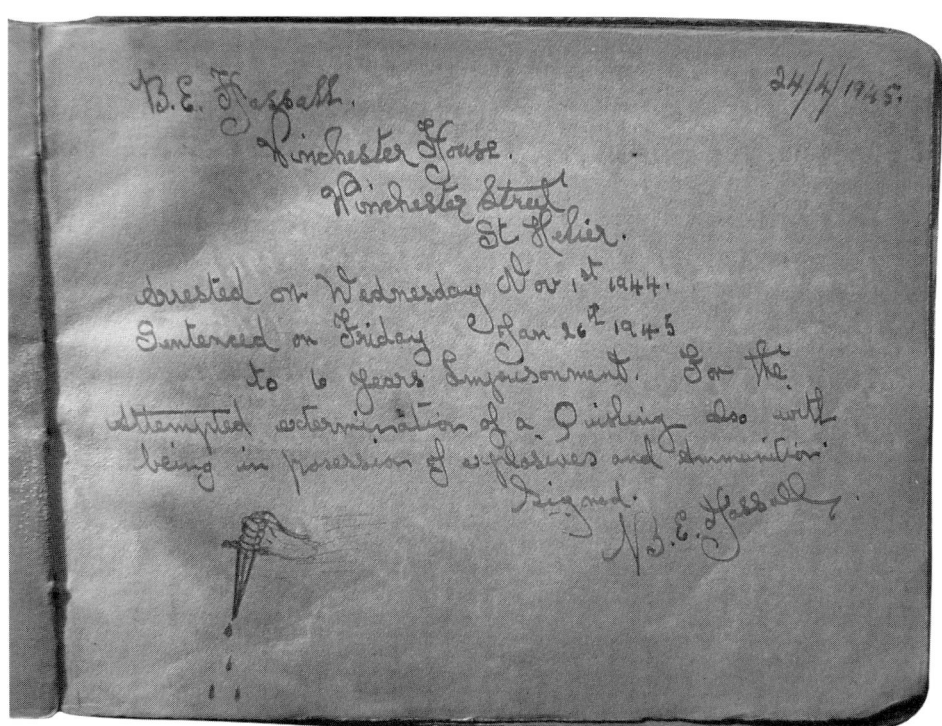

Above: *Bernard Hassall's entry in Peter Gray's autograph book.* (Copyright Peter Gray)

Right: *George Le Marquand's entry in Nurse Renée Griffin's autograph book.* (Copyright Société Jersiaise, ref. GO3/12)

behaviour of the political prisoner held up as an ideal. Ernest Canivet wrote that he was sentenced to six months for 'possessing a crystal receiver, taking it to a so-called friend's house, and allowing the occupant to listen "to foreign stations and enemy propaganda". Here in this prison I am happy to say I met a grand lot of fellows and feel "quite at home".' Edward Rutherford, convicted for making a wireless, sketched three monkeys. The first speaks no evil. The second sees no evil. The third listens to the radio.[11] Among the political prisoners, legitimate action in the face of enemy occupation was defined and endorsed. The 16-year-old Francis Harris was soon to realise that he was among like-minded friends in prison, and so his pencil sketch of a Mauser rifle extends diagonally across the page, flanked on one side by a box of German ammunition. His entry proclaims that he was 'given away by somebody' and 'charged with theft, illegal possession and concealment of arms'.

A number of additions to autograph books show bravado, and attempt to cheer and boost morale. Philip Buesnel's entry shows a smiling character in prison garb sitting in a cell with the caption 'all's well that ends well', and Dutchman Siebe Koster's poem declares that his 'spirits are at the brim of the pail'.[12] Denis Webb

Edward Rutherford's entry in Nurse Renée Griffin's autograph book. (**Copyright Société Jersiaise, ref. GO3/12**)

encourages the others with the words 'any day now'[13] (a variation on the political prisoner's catch phrase to declare imminent release). Three pages after Buesnel's entry, Frank Keiller reproduces his sketch of a prisoner sitting in his cell.[14] By using the same images as each other and copying the form of other's artwork, they are communicating directly to each other and creating fellow feeling, emphasising the similarity of their predicaments.

The two images of prisoners in their cells remind us that political prisoner artwork allows us access into the conditions of confinement through images of cell interiors and views through the doorway, both outside looking in and inside looking out. While Roy Sanderson drew a simple sketch of an open door, looking into cell number 10, four pages later Suzanne Malherbe drew the view through a keyhole of the back garden of the prison.[15] The same image is repeated in Evelyn Janvrin's diary, but with a visitor poking their head around the wall.[16] In the artwork depicted on the political prisoner autograph sheet of Allan Costard, his offences are depicted by Bernard Hassall. The final image shows him and his friends sitting in despair in their cells, heads in their hands, after having been sentenced by the German court.[17] Despite the good cheer circulating in the

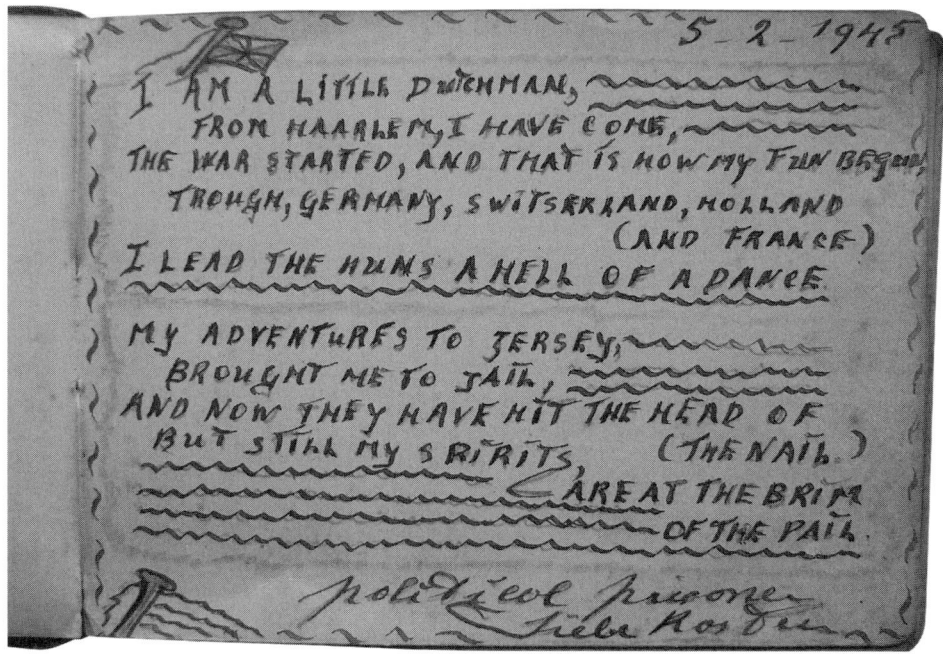

Siebe Koster's entry in Nurse Renée Griffin's autograph book. (**Copyright Société Jersiaise, ref. GO3/12**)

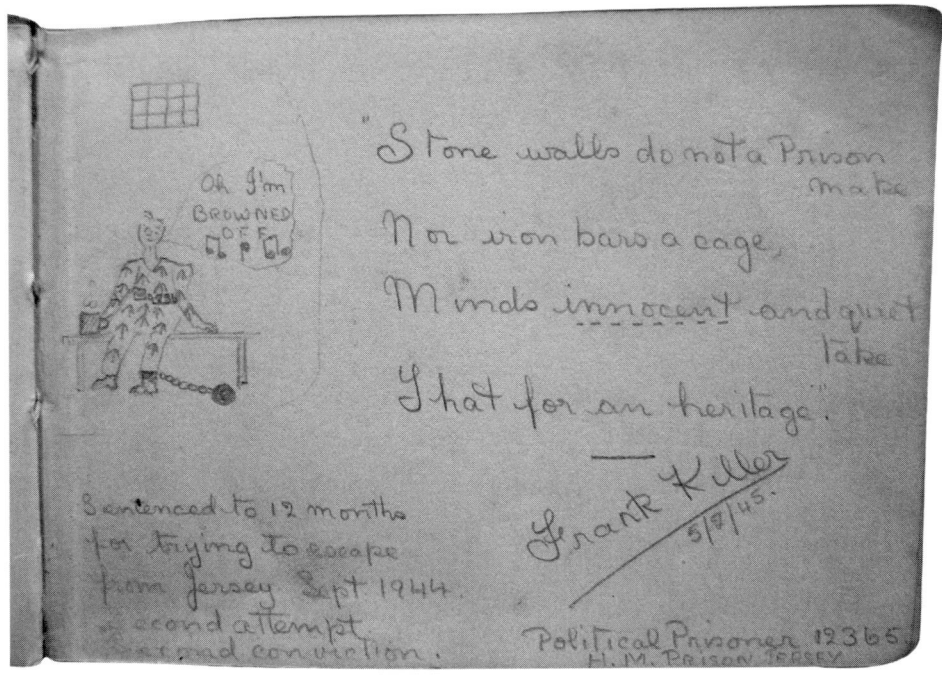

Frank Keiller's entry in Nurse Renée Griffin's autograph book. (Copyright Société Jersiaise, ref. GO3/12)

autograph books, this piece of artwork is likely to give us a truer understanding of the emotions experienced by the occupants of Jersey Prison.

Some political prisoners wrote poems in their autograph books, and while many of these are about their offences and their patriotism, some give us an eloquent insight into the experience of being in Jersey Prison:

> Grey granite buildings and unpleasant smells
> The strident notes of cracked prison bells
> Dark gravelled paths, so sad and so neat
> The clacking noise of clogged convicts' feet.
> Whitewashed cells, like animals' stalls,
> And lines of high forbidding walls.
> Views of housetops and chimney peaks
> These are my impressions of 4 Gloucester Street.[18]

There are also entries by those whose acts were perhaps not necessarily or clearly resistant or patriotic in motive, and it appears that these individuals went to some

'Yielding to so Rare a Pleasure': Autograph Books and Artwork 95

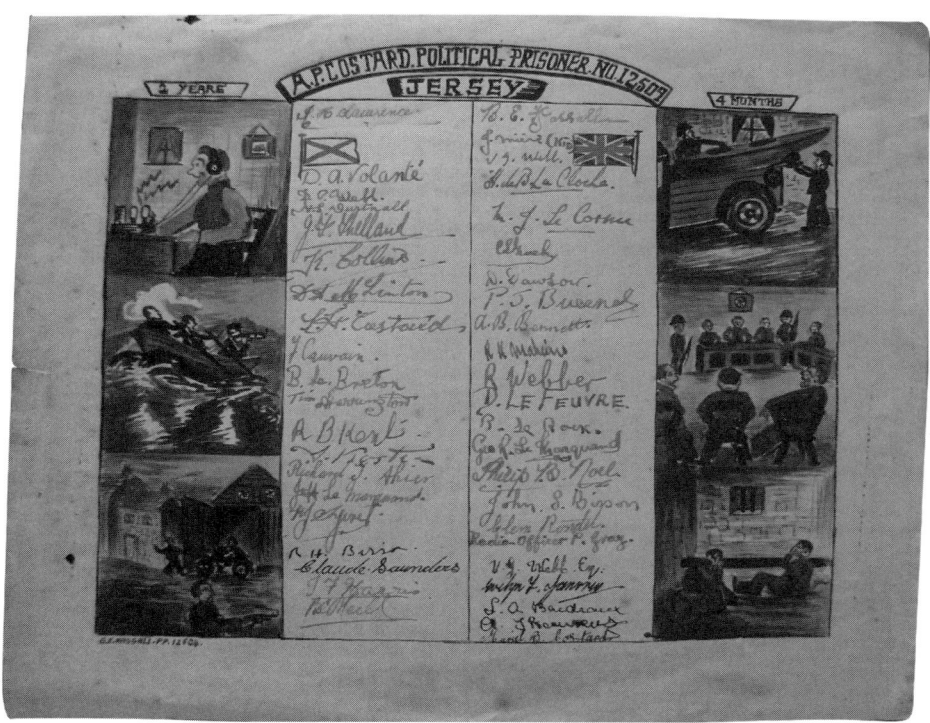

Prison artwork by Allan Costard. (Copyright and courtesy of Wendy Janvrin-Tipping)

effort to enhance their standing in the eyes of their new friends. A farmer who had sold wheat to a black marketeer rather than the Germans composed a poem making clear his loyalties. A man convicted for 'disturbing the working peace' wrote that it was 'only the third time' that he had been imprisoned, but that he continued to 'annoy the Germans all the same'.[19]

Although autograph books were passed around among all political prisoners, they could also be used for writing personal messages to the owner. Thus Muriel Costard's book revealed a message from Lucy Schwob, who wrote 'friendship at first sight – the only opportunity we had, and a snatched one – but through Evelyn, Denis and other friends it was confirmed and will soon be again and again through freedom'. Underneath this, Schwob drew an image of a big red, white and blue French flag that she had been making before her arrest, embroidered with a Free French cross flanked by the words '*La Liberté ou la Mort*' and '*Vivre pour Vaincre*'. On the following page she wrote in French an 'extract from a plan for a short story' to entertain Muriel. As if echoing the newly established form of writing longer entries, 27-year-old Ukrainian prisoner Michael Jourablo took the opportunity to tell his story of fighting, capture, imprisonment and forced labour across Europe, followed by sixteen months spent on a Jersey farm in hiding.[20] James Thelland, too, composed a 'Prisoners alphabet' over the page, which encompassed themes of patriotism, victory, complaints about food, dislike of the occupiers, methods of confession extraction and moods of the prisoners, from anguish to zeal.[21] These entries help Costard's autograph book to increase in value as an object that acts as a testimony to the conditions of the past.

In Evelyn Janvrin's autograph book, Lucy Schwab wrote a potted autobiography followed by an extract from a short story. By the end of the third page, she writes 'dear Evelyn – forgive my taking so much space in your album. The temptation of yielding to so rare a pleasure was too great for me. And still remains unsaid the most important thing: my love for the plucky cheerfulness you have brought us here at the grimmest of the black bleak wintertime. Lucy.'[22] This reveals another value of the autograph book – the sheer pleasure of writing and communicating with others during a dark experience. Schwob continued her entry on a fifth consecutive page with a political prisoner manifesto.

> In the name of the Nameless who stood against Evil, each to the utmost of his power and conscience, of those who in spite of all odds have found Truth and acted accordingly, of those who do so outside the prison and even perhaps inside, of those who fell in the fight and died – but not in vain, in the name of those who cannot yet or nevermore speak for themselves, I say: let us keep united in the making of a better life for the <u>individual common man or woman</u>, a life with more comfort, leisure and freedom of choice. Let us keep sincere and united in this purpose for it is the only way to prevent the perpetual recurrence of tyranny and war . . . Lucy Schwob, 9 April 1945 [original emphasis preserved].[23]

Thus, the autograph book also becomes a vision for the future and an instrument of education and political instruction that would speak to all incarcerated in Jersey Prison.

Unable to follow in quite the same vein or with the same skill, the next entry by James Thelland is at least able to respond to Schwob's autobiography. He attempts his own in verse, following his journey from theft of bicycles and possession of radios to tangling with the Gestapo and imprisonment. The poem ends firmly looking to the future and the arrival of the 'Tommies'. 'And we'll all have lots of fun, laughing at the beaten Hun.'[24] Thelland's entry shows us how prisoners responded to each other's entries, each in their own way. The entries in the autograph book thus do not always stand alone; they can be read as a conversation, a call and response, often spilling into other volumes.

'Yielding to so Rare a Pleasure': Autograph Books and Artwork   97

As Guernsey and Jersey prisons no longer exist and have been demolished, no traces of wartime graffiti remain except in the diaries, letters and memoirs of political prisoners. We might perhaps suggest that graffiti on the military side of the prison formed the equivalent of the autograph books on the civilian side. The two outputs might be considered together as complementary forms and one can teach us about the interpretation of the other. Thus we might consider the extent to which graffiti formed a record of the presence of the prisoner; a trace that would still exist if the prisoner was taken away to an unknown fate. While autograph books circulated on the civilian side of the prison, so prisoners circulated between cells and were able to read what had been left behind by nameless predecessors. Autograph books could also be used for subversive and non-confrontational messages and statements of resistance between prisoners. We have already observed the role of autograph books as wish fulfilment; how some of the prisoners were able to draw themselves carrying out an offence which they had been caught before committing. Graffiti and autograph books also had fundamental differences: one was anonymous, although the identity of the artist of fresh graffiti could be hardly denied, given their presence in the cell. The other artistic output, by definition, involved identification. Graffiti was, to all intents and purposes, permanent and on display. Autograph books were transient; the images could be covered; the books could be hidden or spirited away. For these reasons they are interesting to compare as two inter-related phenomena.

Image of the demolition of Jersey Prison. (Copyright Jersey Archives ref. L/A/75/A3/1/39D)

The remains of the stones of the 1812 block of Jersey Prison today. (Copyright Gilly Carr)

Chapter 9
'Any Time Now!' The End is Nigh?

Our knowledge of the prison in May 1945 is detailed, commented upon by diarists, memoirists, letter writers and archival sources. At the end of the Occupation, but before the British troops arrived, Bailiff Alexander Coutanche relates in his memoirs for 8 May 1945, written in 1975: 'I had a number of things to do. My first thought was for the prisons and I made my way, partly on foot and partly by car, to the Public gaol in order first of all to release some political prisoners who were still there . . .'.[1] We cannot know whether Coutanche did this because his own prison visits and personal convictions had made him sympathetic to the cause of political prisoners, or whether he wished to avoid the 'storm of criticism' and wrath of parental anger. It was probably a mixture of both. Either way, tellingly, Coutanche did not release all the prisoners but only a sub-section – he was perhaps not as sympathetic as he wished to appear.

Although Coutanche records (thirty years after the event) that he went to the prison on 8 May, Le Quesne noted in his diary for 7 May that he was informed that 'as an indication of the German attitude . . . all political prisoners would be released at noon. At 5pm they were not yet free but many were at 6pm.'[2] Leslie Sinel also recorded in his diary for 7 May that 'At 6pm, about 30 political prisoners were released' and, for the following day, that 'the Bailiff said that some political prisoners had been released'.[3] He also noted on 8 May that, 'it was funny to see young men coming out of prison carrying their beds', although at least one of these was Joe Mière leaving the prison for a second time after being sent back by his mother to collect his mattress.[4] Although a number of diarists note that 'about 30' people were released on 7 May, a German document exists which lists only twenty-three people who were to be released that day, 'granted remission of sentence as a test of good conduct'. Two of those released were on the military side of the prison at that time.[5]

Lucy Schwob and Suzanne Malherbe were not among those released on 7 May. Schwob wrote of that day five years later, saying that:

> Some Jersey prisoners, amongst them political prisoners incarcerated in the civil prison, who had not yet finished their time, were released, one by one. Climbing up

on a stool, balanced on a bed, leaning against a wall and heaving ourselves up to the bars, we could see through the window he or she to whom we shouted something along the lines of 'see you soon, see you very soon!' and we sung in chorus the departure song 'for he (or she) is a jolly good fellow' . . .[6]

Mière also recorded that political prisoners were freed by Coutanche from the civilian side of the prison on 7 May. The Bailiff took them across the road to the dining hall of the Chelsea Hotel and told them 'not to kick a dog when it's down, in other words, not to make trouble and leave the Germans alone'.[7] Mière also testified that 'outside the main gate in Gloucester Street there was a crowd of people, family and friends, waiting to welcome us as we regained our freedom. The crowd cheered us as we came through the prison side gate.'[8] Presumably word had got out about their impending release and more people than just Le Quesne knew that it was imminent.

Examining the list of twenty-three people released that day, we can see that they do not include any of those imprisoned for firearms offences. We know that Peter Gray, convicted for being in possession for arms and ammunition, was kept behind; Francis Harris, not yet sentenced but in prison for firearms offences, stayed behind, as did Mickey Neal, also accused of theft of arms.[9] In his memoirs, Gray wrote that the political prisoners lined up in the prison yard on 7 May and a local government official read out a list of names of those who were to be released. He stated that 'around ten people' were not on the list. They were ordered by the same official to await prosecution by the Jersey authorities. The remaining prisoners were so angry that they created an uproar that night, the next morning and into the next day, until they were released to the 'great crowds' that were waiting outside the prison gates.[10] Joe Mière subsequently testified that Peter Gray later told him that the prisoners being held by the Germans in blocks B and C were those not released, on the Bailiff and Attorney-General's orders until the Attorney-General was sure that the political prisoners still held had not broken any Jersey law, or had not damaged any civilian property or stolen any civilian goods. There was, he said:

> A hell of a fuss made by the families to the Bailiff . . . the Bailiff could see big trouble in view . . . [and] he over-ruled the Attorney-General's order, and after consulting the German and British authorities, the rest of the political prisoners in B and C blocks were released on the morning of the 9th of May 1945.[11]

Some prisoners were also released on 8 May, as mentioned by Leslie Sinel in his diary.[12] Lucy Schwob, not released until the following day, also recorded a continuous departure on 8 May as people left one by one from the military side as well, noting that, as soon as they were free, some prisoners found a way of climbing onto the roof of the hospital. For several hours the joyous cries and the departure song were incessant.[13]

Left alone at the end, Schwob wrote that the prison contained only her, Malherbe and the Germans. It is possible that the women had been accidentally overlooked, or that nobody dared to free them without German permission. 'You can imagine our impatience . . . the atmosphere at the KWHA seemed gloomy to me. The rare and stifled noises gave a feeling of oppression.'[14]

Although Mière credits the Bailiff with securing the release of all remaining prisoners, some were liberated from the prison by other means. The father of Francis Harris went to the prison in the early morning of 9 May and took his revolver with him. Although he was told by a German prison guard that it was not yet time for the release of the prisoners, Mr Harris pointed his gun and demanded Francis' release, which was granted immediately.[15] Richard Weithley (who had also stolen firearms), on the other hand, wrote in his memoirs that his cell doors were 'flung open' by British soldiers soon after midday.[16]

While some liberating soldiers may have helped the last few prisoners leave the building, they also had another job to do in rounding up members of the *GFP* and imprisoning them. Joe Mière said that they were locked up in prison cells which were occupied by political prisoners three days earlier.[17] He also recorded that British officers took his statement and that of other political prisoners about their treatment at the hands of the *Feldpolizei*, but that that the men were kept in prison for only a week before being sent to POW camps in England.[18] Richard Weithley also recorded being interviewed by 'British Intelligence' in his memoir, noting that he was taken back to the prison on two different occasions where he found members of the 'Gestapo' imprisoned in the same cell block where he had spent the latter part of his imprisonment.[19] They were not the only new inhabitants of Gloucester Street after the Occupation; Joe Mière also recorded that Mrs Baudains and her son, George, who were 'collaborators and informers', were put in a cell in the prison for eleven months as they sought refuge from a vengeful local population. In March 1946 they were transported to England as the Jersey authorities did not know what to do with them.[20]

The overriding sense, then, is of chaos intruding into plans made hastily by the local authorities, and of the excitement, anger and joy of the crowds (or families of the incarcerated) outside the prison clashing with the ordered release of prisoners desired by the authorities. And yet there is evidence that the Jersey authorities were unsure about what to do with the last few remaining prisoners. It seems that not every single one was released.

Correspondence between the Home Office and the Bailiff of Jersey in the summer of 1945 makes the situation very clear. In the context of discussing an amnesty of prisoners, Coutanche admitted that 'many "occupation" crimes were highly detrimental to the common welfare'.[21] In the Home Office's subsequent assessment of the situation, their view was:

> Strongly against any amnesty in the Channel Islands . . . the question remains, however, whether there be cases of offenders sentenced during the German occupation which may deserve review on account of the exceptional circumstances in the Islands at that time, and the changed conditions now. Any such cases should be reviewed and submitted to us on their merits . . . It would be very undesirable that crimes which were in fact highly detrimental to the common welfare should be condoned in any way.[22]

The crimes deemed 'highly detrimental' were, in the event, larceny and burglary, and some of the young men still in prison were recommended for a remand home or approved school in England. Those who had behaved badly in prison were not released.[23] It isn't entirely clear whether others not released were political prisoners or so-called 'civilian' prisoners; larceny from German stores was among offences which led to the imprisonment of political prisoners.

Some of the political prisoners dreamed of starting an association after the war. Lucy Schwob probably was not the first to have suggested it, but she provides us with an insight into her actions in prison in October 1944 in which she tried to start one. She did not imagine that she would be a member of the association herself, because she and Suzanne were women, foreigners, and too non-conformist, however:

> Our comrades around were of a different social condition and only belonging unknowingly and from a tangential tendency, all of them different from us in all cases in their habits and intellectual interests. My project would have been the height of ridiculousness except that it was conceivable that if done by proxy but certainly in this month of October one of our comrades seemed to be qualified to form this association which I believed objectively to be very desirable. I knew that things would be facilitated from outside: the position of his family rendered him un-attackable in the most nervous milieu, the most conservative places. He personally had an excellent reputation in democratic circles as well as in others.

I noticed that he showed an impulsive gentleness towards everyone, including the Russians . . . we were in 1944. Most of the Anglo-Jersey prisoners in the KWHA were there for having hidden their radio. The songs of the BBC which flowed through our long evenings without any light, bore witness to the fact that they hadn't only hidden their radios . . . I was strictly isolated. My desire surmounted the obstacles. I managed to escape the surveillance of the gaolers enough to write up my proposal, and go down a forbidden staircase and slide my scrap of paper under the door of number 14. My proposal did not specify my choice. It addressed itself to three friends in number 14. F was one of the three. Each of these little groups of friends from school or college had a feeling of class or clan. None of these groups was inclined to fraternise with the others beyond their present conditions. I ignored that then.[24]

Lucy had chosen 'F' to start the organisation for her as a more acceptable candidate, but we don't know who 'F' was and whether F was the initial of their first name or surname. It is possible that it was Frank Keiller (or Killer as he was then), a Victoria College schoolboy whose father was the vicar of St Mark's Church, but he was likely to have still been suffering in solitary confinement at this time. In any case, although Frank would one day be known through his political prisoner memoir, he was not the initiator of any political prisoner association.

Despite Leslie Sinel's reference to those coming out of prison being inducted into an 'Order of Old Glostonians' in March 1945,[25] no such lasting official organisation emerged after the Occupation. According to the *Jersey Evening Post*, however, on 8 December 1945, the Lyric Hall was filled with 'Ex-Convicts' (i.e. former political prisoners). The meeting was called because they had heard that twenty[26] of their 'former comrades in Gloucester Street were carried off to prisons in France and Germany' and had not returned. Their dependents were facing financial hardship. The Revd Mylne, a former prisoner, chaired the meeting; Deputy Edward Le Quesne, as a former prisoner, spoke as well. A committee was elected and instructed to make an appeal to the local government for immediate relief for these families, and a private fund was also started 'in order to help the dependants of comrades', the details of which were to be made public through the *Jersey Evening Post*.[27]

The Ex-Convicts wanted to discuss a further issue: raising a memorial at a suitable spot in the Island to those who died. While funds were also collected at the meeting to help those in need, in January 1947 the States of Jersey passed an act to give an extra-statutory award in respect of the death or disablement of those who were deported during the Occupation.[28] Nineteen awards were eventually made.[29]

A memorial would not be erected to the Jersey 21[30] for another fifty years, so we might assume that this bid did not meet with success. It is possible, however, that when the States erected a memorial at Noirmont Point on the south coast of Jersey in 1947, in memory of 'those men and women of Jersey who perished in the Second World War, 1939–1945', that the Ex-Convicts were told that this included their people. We can only assume that they were – or had to be – content with this, given the lack of any other memorial bearing names until 1996. As the Ex-Convicts do not recur as a fighting force after this period, we can only assume that their political and charitable needs were met and so they disbanded, even if their bonds of friendship remained for a longer period.

The vocation of becoming a 'guardian of memory' for Jersey's political prisoners was taken up by Joe Mière. In 1948 he was demobbed from the army and started building a collection of photos and testimonies of political prisoners. In 1976 he became the deputy curator and, in 1983, curator of the German Underground Hospital in Jersey (today, the Jersey War Tunnels), where he displayed his collection. He retired in 1991. His work was done alone, as a labour of love. Although he received support and encouragement from his political prisoner friends (but not from others), he financed his own research.

Mière campaigned for a memorial to political prisoners to be placed outside the site of the demolished prison; this was achieved only in 1995 after political opposition.[31] The date chosen for the unveiling, after he was informed that Liberation Day was not an option, was 27 April. This was the fiftieth anniversary of the execution of German soldier Nikolaus Schmitz, a fellow prisoner of Mière's in B-Block, who he tried to comfort the night before Schmitz's execution.

Bailiff Philip Bailhache unveiled the political prisoner memorial with the words:

> The prison itself has gone and the people incarcerated behind its walls are a diminishing band. The site beyond these forgotten walls holds hundreds if not thousands of stories of courage and resilience, most of which never now will be told. But enough stories have been told to make it right and timely that the Island should now honour those who protested against the rule of the invader and who defied, often at enormous personal risks, the occupying force.[32]

Although those who stood up to the occupiers through committing acts of protest, defiance and resistance made things difficult for the local authorities, looking back there can be no doubt that they made the right moral choices in opposing the Nazi regime which the German occupiers were serving.

Philip Bailhache unveiling the Political Prisoner Memorial, April 1995. (Copyright *Jersey Evening Post*)

Part II
Guernsey Prison

Chapter 10
Introduction and Sources

Guernsey Prison, unlike its counterpart in Jersey, appears not to have played a special role in local memory, and nor – surprisingly – has it become a site of memory for resistors or resistance as part of the Occupation-period landscape. No memorial marks the spot of the former prison, demolished in 2003. Part of the facade was retained and reused because of its architectural merit and good quality granite. It was moved to within the modern foyer of the new Magistrate's Court in St Peter Port. Some of the land on which the old prison stood is today merely a scruffy parking lot in poor condition. There is little sense of ownership or local affection for the old prison as it is not seen as a site of martyrdom, suffering or the formation of political prisoner consciousness, unlike in Jersey.

Location of Guernsey Prison, St Peter Port, 1939 Ordnance Survey Map. (Copyright and courtesy Island Archives, Guernsey, ref. BA 96-15)

This is chiefly because those in Guernsey who were imprisoned for acts of resistance place the focus of their experience on later imprisonment in continental Nazi prisons and camps.

The extant archival records of officialdom for Guernsey Prison are very fragmented and scattered – more so than for Jersey Prison. We are thus in the position of trying to make sense of random jigsaw pieces, scattered between various files, relying on a small number of memoirs to provide the bigger picture for a building and a system that changed over time. Sometimes the pieces fit beautifully and illuminate a previously dark corner. At other times, the snippet of information floats and tells us little. For example, one undated document in a prison file provides information about the 'food supplies for civilian prisoners under German arrest'. We learn that they were allowed, among other things, 2oz (57g) a week of meat, 4oz (113g) a week of butter, 3oz (85g) of sugar and 72oz (just over 2 kg) of bread. But what date was this? How did it compare with that given to civilian prisoners not under German arrest? Without this information, this becomes a somewhat unhelpful document.[1] In a different archival file, a letter written by Major Kratzer of *Feldkommandantur* 515[2] to the President of the Controlling Committee[3] in December 1943 asks what levels of rations were issued to civilian prisoners.[4]

It seems very likely that these two documents are related, and by putting them together we might surmise that the Germans were attempting to find out what might constitute reasonable rations for prisoners under their control, or perhaps to have some baseline from which to recalculate rations for political prisoners. It might even mark the date at which the Germans started to pay for the food of the prisoners under their control. This kind of guesswork is further borne out by documents held in a third file, which – among other things – consists of a series of sheets listing prisoners of the Germans who were being fed by the Wehrmacht. These are dated from 16 April 1944 onwards and continue to be issued regularly until April 1945, as new prisoners entered the prison.[5] Each document on its own holds little value, but by studying a number of different scattered files, we can begin to work out more than the sum of their parts.

In terms of the regulations operating in Guernsey Prison, our knowledge of their similarity to those in operation in Jersey comes from a letter dated February 1942 from Mr Blampied, Sheriff and prison governor, to Fuerst von Oettingen at *Feldkommandantur* 515. In this letter, Blampied wrote that he had been informed by the Solicitor General that a letter had been received from St Helier on 22 October 1941 containing German prison regulations to be administered in Guernsey Prison. He stated that he had studied them and found in many respects that they were 'similar to our own regulations'.[6] This file does not come with any attached regulations, although another file contains German regulations for prisons in occupied France. We do not know to what extent these were followed in practice in Guernsey.[7] One prisoner of the Germans even remarked that there were no regulations about which he was informed.[8]

Because the surviving archival material relating to the prisons in Guernsey and Jersey differs, we cannot assume that together they show what existed originally. The different kinds of materials may or may not reflect different practices in each of the prison systems. There is simply no way today to find out. However, we can assume the one-time existence of particular documents, such as logbooks of prisoners kept in the German-controlled part of the prison, although no such books have yet been located. Although there is a chance that they are in the hands of one of the many private collectors of Occupation memorabilia in the Channel Islands, it seems more likely that they were destroyed at the end of the war, or at some time since.

Guernsey, unlike Jersey, does not have a genre of published literature emanating from its wartime prison. This is partly because of the lack of a wartime group identity of 'political prisoner' for those who were in Guernsey Prison, and partly because the reputations of these prisoners only began to be rehabilitated in this Island in 2015, which was after the death of almost all former inmates.[9] Only by this date was the first Resistance Memorial erected in Guernsey, signalling to other islanders that to have resisted was – perhaps – a legitimate course of action. We observed earlier that it was the memorial to Jersey's former political prisoners in 1995 that inspired a spate of published memoirs; yet by 2015, Guernsey's prisoners had passed away. The paucity of published sources in Guernsey compared with Jersey perhaps also reflects a combination of a lack of impetus to seek publication or a lack of interest from publishers – both in themselves indicative of the lack of importance attached to wartime narratives relating to Guernsey Prison. This may also explain the brevity of many sources that do exist; the prison, nor those in it, was not the star of the show.

This does not mean that we are without any memoirs relating to Guernsey Prison; simply that they are fewer in number and almost entirely unpublished and brief. The main casualty of the brevity and paucity of eyewitness testimonies is the lack of the kind of rich detail that emanates from Jersey's testimonies. This means that we have no information about graffiti on cell walls and no autograph books, for example, two sources which together were able to give us such a rich insight into Jersey Prison and the identities and relationships between prisoners. We also are unable to comment in detail about the kinds of protest, defiance and resistance within Guernsey Prison about which we know so much for Jersey.

Our knowledge of escapes, for example, comes not from those who found the ultimate way to defy their warders, but instead from notes within the prison logbook, which comprised an almost daily commentary on prison movements kept by the chief warder. This tells us, for example, that, on 16 October 1942, a Frenchman was found to have escaped from the prison by scaling the wall using his blanket, which he had cut into strips. Nine months later, on 26 June 1943, three prisoners of the Germans escaped during the night by climbing down a rope. Fifteen months later, a prisoner sentenced for a violent robbery was given a sentence of five years penal servitude and twelve strokes with the cat-o'-nine-tails. Not wishing to face the consequences of his actions, two days after his trial he escaped from the prison by 'cutting away woodwork, removing iron plate from slot in door, forcing a trap door in ceiling upstairs and breaking a pane of glass in skylight and gaining access to roof'. He was recaptured the same day and two months' hard labour were added to his sentence.[10]

Such accounts are not as thrilling as those from memoirs of Jersey Prison in their detail, but they show that escape was indeed possible. They also give us an insight into the corporal punishment employed on civil prisoners in the 1940s, and reveal one example among many of sentences of hard labour used as part of the punishment of civil prisoners at this time, about which more will be discussed later.

The most well-known memoir of incarceration in Guernsey is, without doubt, *The Silent War* by Frank Falla, published in 1967. The bid for legitimation was, as with the Jersey memoirs, the provocation for the completion of this work. Frank Falla, who had been part of the Guernsey Underground News Service (GUNS) during the Occupation, was the Channel Islander who liaised with the Foreign Office with the aim of getting compensation for victims of Nazism. The 1964 Anglo-German Agreement had allowed for the possibility that those who spent time in Nazi prisons and camps could be compensated for their experiences and permanent disabilities. These testimonies by islanders provide another source of information about the prison, as they were for former prisoners from Jersey, although very few, except those of the Guernsey policemen who we will meet later, mentioned Guernsey Prison.

When we consider the unpublished sources, our key informants of life in Guernsey Prison during the Occupation are – once again – Frank Falla (whose wartime diaries survive) and John Crossley Hayes, who was imprisoned for listening to the radio. Falla's daily diary of the Occupation years astonishingly

Frank Falla's book, The Silent War. (Copyright and courtesy Blue Ormer Books)

includes what can only have been a secret diary of his time in Guernsey Prison, which is extremely insightful. Its good condition today indicates that he managed to give it to a trusted friend to return to his mother just before he was deported to Germany.

To these memoirists we can add the words of two men who wrote much shorter accounts of their imprisonment, running to just a few pages. These include Hubert Lanyon and Cecil Duquemin, both friends of Falla's from GUNS. Gerald Domaille, in prison at around the same time, wrote a longer memoir. His recollections, like Falla's, focused more on his experiences in Nazi prisons rather than of those in Guernsey. All of these writers were in prison in 1944, and so our greatest insight into the Occupation years behind bars must inevitably be coloured by this late stage in the war. We can temper it only with the addition of the published memoirs of Frank Stroobant, deported to Laufen civilian internment camp in 1942, who spent a brief period in Guernsey Prison in the early summer of that same year. Stroobant shared a cell with one of the imprisoned Guernsey policemen, whose case is still better known inside the island than outside it.

In April 1942, eighteen of Guernsey's policemen were tried by the Germans for stealing food from German food stores. This they were doing, encouraged by the BBC, as an act of resistance, both to deprive the occupiers of food (which in any

Occupation registration card photographs of Frank Falla and John Hayes. (Copyright and courtesy Island Archives, Guernsey)

case had been requisitioned from islanders) and to distribute to starving Islanders. The BBC regularly broadcast to the occupied peoples of Europe, giving them advice on how to resist the occupiers, and although these transmissions were not aimed at Channel Islanders, nonetheless they heard them on their radios before these were banned and confiscated in June 1942.

Here we might pause to consider the expected differences between published memoirs, diaries and testimonies for compensation. It is rare to have all three sources from one person; Frank Falla is the only islander who penned all three. His prison diary is of interest for the immediacy of the feelings associated with incarceration that he portrays: of his first night in prison, 3 April 1944, he wrote that he was 'Worried to death and had little sleep all night, lying on straw-stuffed mattress on the floor'.[11] A few days later he was 'Really feeling blue about everything and homesick. Nobody brought anything for me today.'[12] While his diaries are likely to record private and entirely truthful occurrences, his memoirs were edited for a public audience and his private feelings were often hidden; his first day in prison went unrecorded. Events were also interpreted, expanded upon or summarised in his memoirs, and written with the insight gained from his later imprisonment in Germany.

Falla's later compensation testimony makes only a passing mention of Guernsey Prison but focuses primarily on his trial (in order to emphasise the illegitimacy

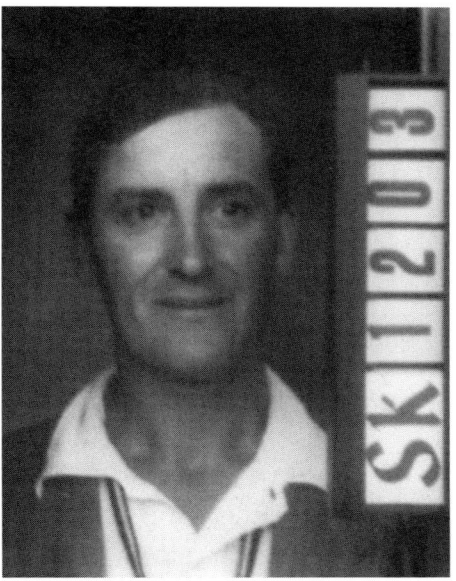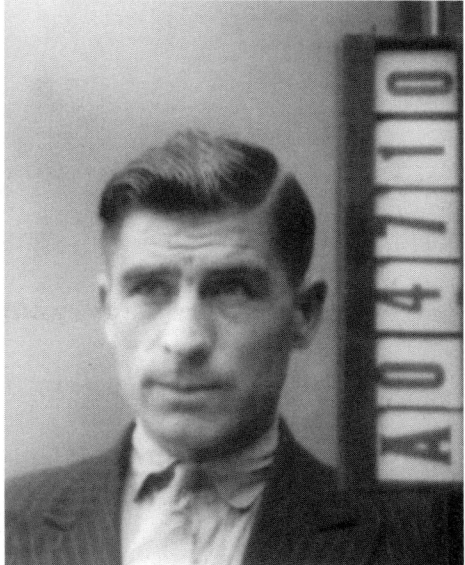

Occupation registration card photographs of Hubert Lanyon and Cecil Duquemin. (Copyright and courtesy Island Archives, Guernsey)

of proceedings) and later incarceration in Germany. After all, imprisonment within the Channel Islands was not compensated, and neither was incarceration within other so-called 'ordinary civil prisons' in France or Germany as part of the Anglo-German Agreement for compensation of 1964. We must, therefore, be aware of audience and reason for writing when we assess different source materials, not to mention the time gap between the original events and the time of writing. Falla's diary was written daily while in prison; his compensation testimony was written in 1964 and his memoirs in 1967, although both later sources had his diary to draw upon.

To the prison insights of 1942 and 1944 written by men, we can add two female experiences, both from 1942. Marie Ozanne, a major in the Salvation Army, was, effectively, imprisoned for her faith. She continued to wear her uniform and preach in public, despite being arrested for this after the Salvation Army was banned. She also wrote to the German *Feldkommandant* to tell him that God would judge him for the way the Nazis treated the Jews and forced labourers. Ozanne kept a diary, albeit with brief entries, and continued writing it during her period of imprisonment and right up to her death from peritonitis following a burst stomach ulcer in 1943.

Olive Frampton (née Allo), on the other hand, wrote her memoirs for her family in her later years and was very briefly imprisoned overnight for attending

Marie Ozanne and Olive Frampton. (Copyright and courtesy Bill Ozanne and Island Archives, Guernsey, respectively)

a party and being out after curfew without an ID card. Despite the brevity of her incarceration, Frampton's account is valuable for the insight it gives into the way that women were treated after arrest. Alongside Ozanne and Frampton, the only female voices from Guernsey prison that we have are those narrated by men, or brief references by women who were later deported to Nazi prisons and camps on the continent and whose compensation testimonies focused on places of incarceration other than Guernsey Prison. That the prison testimonies available to us were written mostly by men is, of course, also a reflection of the wider gender disparity in prison.

Chapter 11
The Changing Geography of Guernsey Prison

In terms of the layout of Guernsey Prison, all original buildings were still standing during the Occupation. The oldest part of the prison, the main block, was built between 1810 and 1812 in St Peter Port. It was intended to replace Castle Cornet as accommodation for debtors, convicted felons, petty criminals and prisoners on remand.[1] It was bordered by St James Street to the north and New Street to the east, and the perimeter wall featured a carved panel containing a crowned monogram of King George III, the reigning monarch at the time of construction.

In the partial basement or lower ground floor of the main building were originally three 'constables' cells', later sub-divided in the early twentieth century to become five, approached separately from the rest of the building and used by the constables of the parishes to lock up minor offenders for the night. The upper

Main building of Guernsey Prison. (Copyright MOLA)

Reconstructed facade inside Magistrate's Court, Guernsey. (Copyright and courtesy Jon Torode)

ground floor and the first floor contained cells with staircases at each end. Each of these floors contained an arcaded gallery, originally of seven bays, and each giving access to cells behind. The five ground-floor cells originally contained fireplaces and were used for debtors. The first floor of the building, originally intended for felons, contained nine cells. Within the prison grounds was also a house for the prison Gaoler[2] or chief warder, comprising a basement, ground floor and two upper floors.[3]

By the 1860s, demand had grown for the prison to be enlarged and improved. Between 1872 and 1875, additional buildings were constructed. These comprised a two-storey men's cell block, with seven cells on each floor, which joined the original main building; a two-storey women's cell block, with three cells on the ground floor and three on the first floor,[4] and a chapel. The main room of the chapel contained pews for men; there was a separate, smaller room containing pews for women.[5] An underground tunnel, only part of which still survives, linked the prison to the Royal Court on the other side of the street, and is thought to have been constructed near the start of the twentieth century.[6]

During the Occupation, Guernsey Prison was governed by Harold Blampied, the Sheriff, who was responsible to the Lieutenant-Governor. The Gaoler or chief warder was Albert Pike, whose wife, Lizzie Pike, was the matron and chief wardress. The Pikes were expected to live at the prison, in the Gaoler's house, and took up their position in 1937. After the death of Albert Pike on 23 January 1943, William Ferbrache became Gaoler on 13 February 1943 and his wife became the matron.

The Changing Geography of Guernsey Prison 121

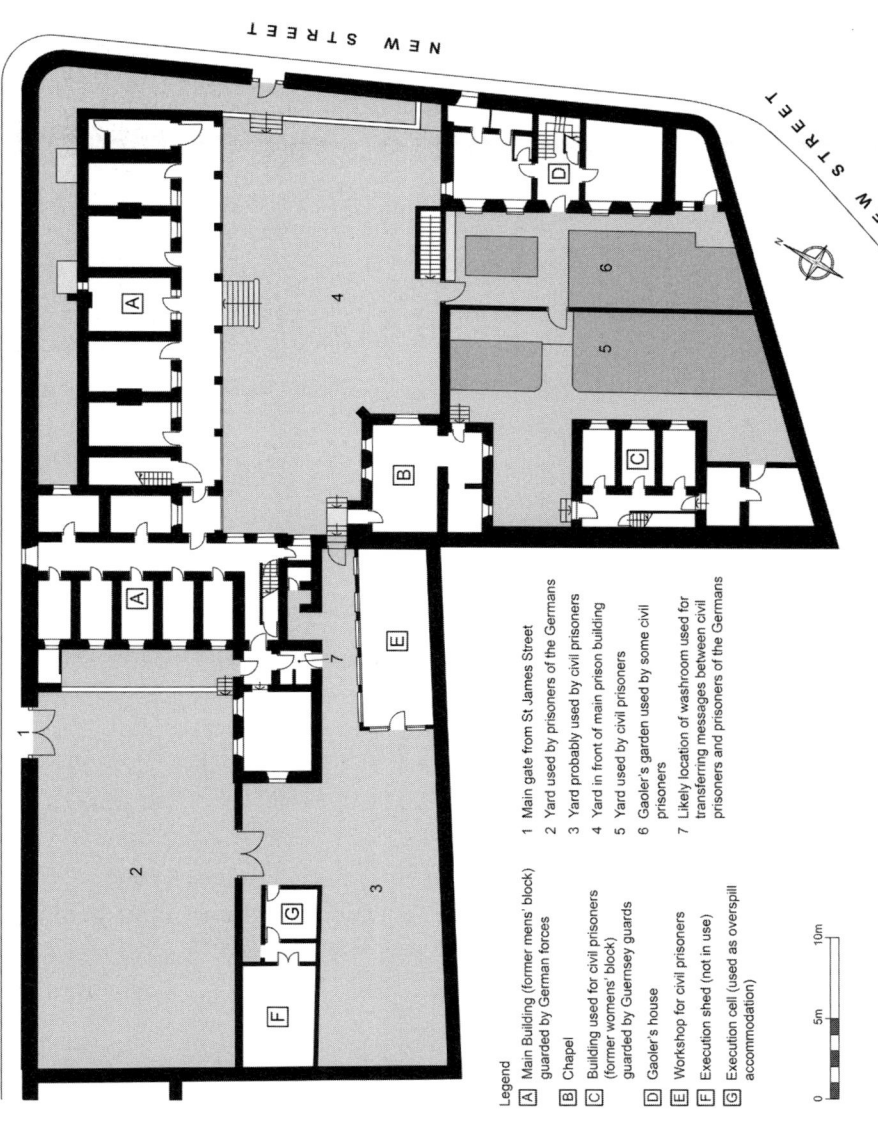

Plan of Guernsey Prison. (Drawn by Ian Taylor, copyright Gilly Carr)

Legend

- A Main Building (former mens' block guarded by German forces
- B Chapel
- C Building used for civil prisoners (former womens' block) guarded by Guernsey guards
- D Gaoler's house
- E Workshop for civil prisoners
- F Execution shed (not in use)
- G Execution cell (used as overspill accommodation)

1 Main gate from St James Street
2 Yard used by prisoners of the Germans
3 Yard probably used by civil prisoners
4 Yard in front of main prison building
5 Yard used by civil prisoners
6 Gaoler's garden used by some civil prisoners
7 Likely location of washroom used for transferring messages between civil prisoners and prisoners of the Germans

Before the Occupation there were four prison warders, but their number rose to eight to cope with the number of additional prisoners.[7]

The subject of the number of prisoners during the Occupation is an important one, as is the related question of which part of the prison was taken over by the German forces, and therefore where the 'civil prisoners' (those imprisoned for non-military offences, as in Jersey) were accommodated compared to prisoners of the Germans.

Left: *Occupation registration card photograph of Harold Blampied.* (Copyright and courtesy Island Archives, Guernsey)

Below left and right: *Occupation registration card photo of Albert Pike and William Ferbrache.* (Copyright and courtesy Island Archives, Guernsey)

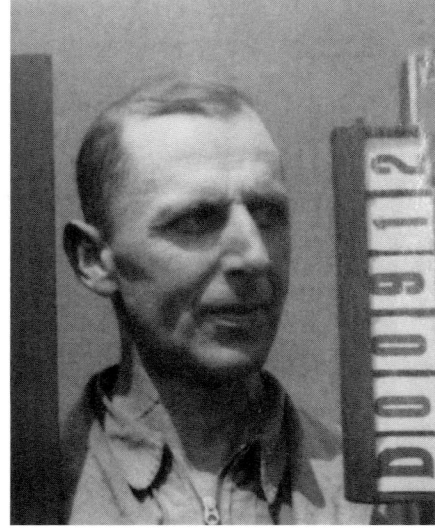

Albert L'Amy, chief officer of the Guernsey police from 1942, later described the situation of the prison when the Germans arrived. The prison, he said, contained thirty-five cells: twenty-nine for men and six for women.[8] This is contradicted by a report dating to April 1946, which lists thirty-four cells for men, twenty of which were in the main building.[9] This is augmented by a letter from Ambrose Sherwill to Dr Brosch at Field Command dated 9 September 1940, stating that the prison could accommodate fifty men and eight women (with no indication of how many were sharing a cell to reach this capacity), but currently held just five men.[10] It seems likely that most prisoners had been moved to the safety of the mainland just in advance of the Occupation.

Although the Germans took over Jersey Prison in an official capacity from 1941, we cannot be sure of the precise date of takeover in Guernsey Prison; surprisingly,

Prison building used for the incarceration of male civil prisoners during the Occupation. (Copyright MOLA)

it is not mentioned in the prison logbook. An August 1945 report written by Mr S. Mainguy from the Receiver-General's office, submitted to Mr D. Cook of the UK Treasury, stated that 'In August 1941 the German authorities commenced requisitioning portions of the Gaol',[11] which gives us a starting date. According to Albert L'Amy, the Germans took over the men's block and left only the women's block for local use. 'All cells had at least three occupants, and there came a time when there was a waiting list . . . [German] Prison warders were soldiers pure and simple, thus coming under the control of the military police, and a large proportion of the prisoners had been put there by the *Feldgendarmerie*.'[12]

The local authorities soon had access to more than just six cells. A letter of December 1941 from the Germans to the President of the Controlling Committee on the subject of 'arrest cells' stated that '11 cells are at the disposal of the civilian population, so that the wishes of the States have been taken into account'.[13] It is unclear precisely where these extra five cells were. Although it has been proposed that they were the five constables' cells in the basement of the men's block,[14] the memoirs dating to 1944 cited later make it clear that the constables' cells were used for prisoners of the Germans. It seems probable that in the earlier days of the Occupation, the constables' cells were made available for local use.

The pressure on space for the accommodation of men was a constant problem. The prison logbook contains a note for 26 May 1942 to say that men were being placed in the waiting cells below the Royal Court because no accommodation was available in the prison; this solution was resorted to again on other occasions.[15]

Further space for prisoners was also found in the Gaoler's house. The diaries of Marie Ozanne and memoirs of Olive Frampton cited later, both of whom had a period of imprisonment in the autumn of 1942, lead us to conclude that the Gaoler's house was used to house women, leaving the former women's block, by implication, to be used by men. This supposition is further substantiated by a note in the prison's admissions logbook which contains a note, dating to 5 March 1942, that, 'owing to the abnormal number of prisoners attained in the prison, prisoner Mary F. was placed in the Gaoler's quarters for sleeping purposes'. This was followed by references to other women being placed there.[16] However, the post-war report by the Receiver-General states that the use by the Germans of 'portions of the Gaoler's quarters' is something that took place from December 1943. This conflicts with Marie Ozanne's placement in the Gaoler's house, as a prisoner of the Germans, a year earlier. We can only assume, therefore, that the use of the Gaoler's house by the Germans did not become permanent until the following year.

A letter from the Receiver-General's office to the Sheriff in December 1943 stated that 'owing to the greatly increased number of prisoners now lodged

The Gaoler's house. (Copyright MOLA)

in the prison necessitating the use of part of the Gaoler's Quarters, I concur with your suggestion that the Gaoler be paid five shillings per week for their use'.[17] With the hindsight of the August 1945 report, we can see that this letter was prompted by the German requisitioning of part of the Gaoler's house.

In any case, that the Gaoler's house was used during the Occupation for the imprisonment of women was not without precedent. Indeed, such placement of prisoners within this building was not uncommon in earlier centuries, where debtors could live in some of the rooms, and the Gaoler was recompensed for each prisoner housed with him. The earliest prison regulations of 1818 stipulated that the Gaoler was to be paid 6*d*. for each debtor living with him – twice that for other prisoners living elsewhere.[18] This also implies that some of the rooms may have been partially adapted for use by prisoners as opposed to members of the Gaoler's family.

It has also been suggested that there was 'no hard and fast division between the German and non-German use',[19] but this seems unlikely and is not borne out by the evidence. Rather, negotiation for space was ongoing and changed over time, but at any one point that space was unlikely to have been blurred. The situation in Jersey leads us to expect a very clear division in the use of space at all times.

We can, however, surmise from the evidence available that Guernsey Prison differed from Jersey Prison in one clear way: after their conviction, prisoners of the Germans in Guernsey were *not* moved to the 'civil side' of the prison, but simply stayed where they were. It is possible that prisoners were moved within the main block of the prison to different floors or wings depending on whether they had been convicted, but no reference to such movement has yet been found within memoirs, diaries or official documents with the exception of one note in the prison admissions logbook. On 11 April 1944, four prisoners convicted of what appears to be minor black-market offences were 'handed over by the German guard [i.e. to the local prison authorities] to complete their sentences'.[20] Similarly, in a reverse transaction, on 24 March 1945 a different prisoner was taken over by the military authorities.[21]

Both events seemed to be unusual enough to merit comment in the logbook, so we can assume that it was not normal procedure and perhaps a reflection of how overcrowded the prison was at that time. It also shows that the German authorities were free to select prisoners to put in their side of the prison if they were so motivated. We can only conclude that it was usual for prisoners of the Germans to stay under German control in Guernsey throughout their imprisonment, and vice versa for civil prisoners. There was certainly little room for shuffling; prisoners controlled by local warders were already squeezed into an impossibly small part of the prison.

Ralph Durand, whose account of the Occupation was published in 1946, notes that the prison was too small to accommodate all who were sentenced to imprisonment, although it is not clear whether he was describing the prison as a whole or just the German or civil side. He informs us that 'several empty houses were converted into use as temporary prisons'. Notes in the prison admissions logbook lists just one of these houses: the nearby 'Annexe North Clifton' (noted elsewhere as the 'Wyatt premises') was used for '6 prisoners being installed for sleeping' from 11 June 1944; the house had been taken over eleven days earlier. By 29 June 1944, thirteen mattresses were loaned to the prison annexe.[22] Durand also tells us that in December 1942, the Royal Court ordained that, at the discretion of the court:

> Terms of imprisonment might be postponed until room in the prison was available, or served in part and part postponed, or remitted altogether if the offender gave bail to be of good behaviour for a specified time. Consequently those guilty of minor offences either escaped punishment altogether or had leisure before they were incarcerated to arrange for their business to be carried on in their absence. On one occasion the question which of two offenders should go to prison was settled by tossing a coin.[23]

By 1944, Durand tells us that the prisons were so congested that it was not practical to punish with imprisonment instead of a fine for buying and selling on the black market.[24] Having access to far fewer cells than needed caused problems for the local authorities. In February 1944, prisoners complained to the prison chaplain, who at that time was also serving as Dean of the Island, about overcrowding in their cells, a lack of proper, adequately lit toilets and a lack of clothing. A letter on this matter from the prison Sheriff to John Leale, President of the Controlling Committee, reveals that not only were the prison authorities now putting three people in each cell originally designed for a single occupant, but that a formal request had been made to the Controlling Committee to ask the Germans if part of the prison might be returned to local control.[25] The result is unknown as there is no record of a reply.

Interestingly, it seems that even though the Germans had taken over the men's block of the prison, the local warders were allowed to retain some storage and office space there – that is, until 5 February 1944, when a note in the prison logbook tells us that: 'the remaining accommodation in the "MENS BLOCK" was handed over to the German authorities, Warders Room, Storeroom, Office, etc. Warders from this date had to use the Kitchen, one Bedroom in Gaoler's Quarters was used for store room. Sitting Room was also used as Office.'[26] It is just possible that this marked the date in which the constables' cells were taken over by the Germans, if they had not done so already at an earlier date. We might also note that prisoners brought in by German authorities were more regular occurrences in the prison logbook before this date, indicating a further step in blocking the local authorities from keeping tabs on local people arrested by the Germans.

Just a couple of months later, in April 1944, we might also observe that the Wehrmacht had definitely taken over feeding local prisoners of the Germans;[27] indeed, we cannot be sure that they weren't doing this from much earlier. The prison provisions logbook indicates that this began in February 1944.[28] Therefore, we can conclude that the requisitioning of the main prison block came with other knock-on implications for the prisoners.

On 17 February 1944, the prisoners made a general complaint to the prison Medical Orderly (MO) about being overcrowded in cells. The MO stated that he would write to the proper quarter. On 25 February, the prison was inspected by the Bailiff and two jurats,[29] Sir Abraham Lainé and Arthur Dorey. There was little that the prison staff could do except move their stores, for a second time in a month, from the Gaoler's house to the cells below the Royal Court. They also made a room (and we can only assume that this was an additional room to that which already accommodated women) in the Gaoler's quarters available to use as a cell for four prisoners. It was noted in a logbook that 'it will be useless to apply to the German authorities for the release of further accommodation'.[30]

Despite this period of shuffling, it seems inevitable that the continued overcrowding led, in October 1944, to an outbreak of scabies at the prison due to the exhaustion of local soap supplies. After a protracted exchange of letters lasting until January 1945, the Germans refused to provide soap for the local prisoners in their section of the prison as 'the heath conditions of the English prisoners' were the responsibility of the 'English prison doctor'.[31] This gives an insight into both the extent to which the relationship between the two sides had broken down, and the conditions in the prison towards the end of the Occupation.

In an attempt to deal with the scabies outbreak, on 16 October 1944 the former women's block was fumigated. In order to cope with the displacement of prisoners, one prisoner was placed in a cell in the German section of the prison for the night, and four others were placed in the prison annexe in North Clifton Street. Thirteen prisoners were taken to hospital for treatment for scabies.[32] Such was the need for the extra accommodation at the North Clifton annexe that from 4 March 1945, ten prisoners were accommodated there[33] instead of the previous six.

In an insight into the number of civilian prisoners held in Guernsey prison on 19 March 1945, a document in Guernsey Archives lists thirteen men held within the six cells in the former women's block (noting that one cell held four men and another held an isolated prisoner), and the condemned cell near an execution shed held three men. A room in the Gaoler's house held two men, one woman was accommodated in the attic and twelve men were held in the prison annexe in North Clifton. In all, thirty-one civil prisoners were held. It is unknown how many people were held by German forces at this time, as this number appears to have been withheld from local authorities.[34]

In February 1945, Ralph Durand tells us that the Germans released all men who were imprisoned for possessing wireless sets, because of the difficulty of feeding them. He tells us that one man with a sentence of four months had been in prison for only four days before he was released. The released men were told to pay a fine of 300 marks within three months, but, fortunately for them, the island was liberated before the deadline expired.[35]

The Changing Geography of Guernsey Prison 129

Although the beginning of the Occupation was not noted in the prison logbook, the end certainly was. Red ink (the relevant text underlined below) was used by the warder to mark the happy day in the following way:

1945
V Day.
This day May 8th 1945 marks the handing over to the Civil Authorities control of Island affairs after the Germans had been in occupation since June 30th 1940.
  Holiday for all prisoners.
  This day whole section of Male Block of Prison was handed back to Civil Authorities and every thing generally found to be in a dirty, dilapidated condition. The liberation also of all civilians serving military sentences was caused by two British Officers. Two French civilians also were handed over to civil prison by the Military to be dealt with by local authorities. May 9th 1945.
  This day 12 German soldiers were made to clean part of the Prison occupied by them. 215 mattresses taken over were this day burnt.
  This day the male bock was disinfected by the Military. 19-5-45.[36]

Following liberation, the medical officer of the prison, Dr Sutcliffe, visited the cells that had been used by prisoners of the German forces, and found them to be 'in a condition quite unfit for habitation. They were filthy and infested with bugs and fleas.'[37]

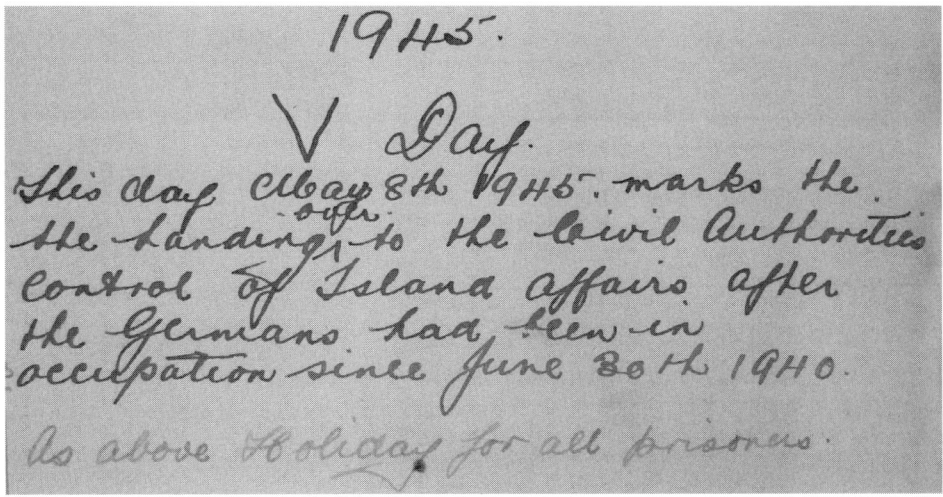

Entry in prison logbook. (Copyright and courtesy Island Archives, Guernsey)

Despite the return of the prison to the local authorities, it was not in a fit state to be used until 8 June 1945; at this time, prisoners from the North Clifton annexe were moved back to the prison. A week earlier, from 31 May, the Gaoler's house ceased to be used for accommodating prisoners.[38] The damage caused to the prison by the German authorities was estimated after the Occupation to be £796 6s. 6d.[39]

Nine different phases of use of the prison during the Occupation can be identified with reasonable confidence as follows:

Phase 1 July 1940 to August 1941: Guernsey Prison warders in full charge of the prison.

Phase 2 August 1941: German forces take over main prison block, allowing local warders use of offices and of five constables' cells in the basement for civil prisoners.

Phase 3 March 1942: Earliest record of female civil prisoners placed in Gaoler's house. Building ceased to be used for prisoners on 31 May 1945.

Phase 4 May 1942: Earliest record of cells beneath Royal Court used for civil prisoners.

Phase 5 December 1943: Earliest record of Germans permanently taking over part of the Gaoler's house for their prisoners, although occasional use seen before this date.

Phase 6 February 1944: German forces take over the rest of the main prison block, including the constables' cells. Local warders' offices relocated to Gaoler's house.

Phase 7 June 1944: North Clifton prison annexe opens for use by civil prisoners; closes 8 June 1945.

Phase 8 March 1945: Earliest record of use of condemned cell in execution block by civil prisoners as overspill accommodation.

Phase 9 9 May 1945: Prison handed back to local authorities.

The location and number of prisoners held by the German forces and local authorities at any one time is a question of high importance. Of even more significance is the identity of those prisoners. Despite the extant logbooks, we cannot be sure that we have the names of everyone. The next chapter addresses this issue.

Chapter 12
The Names and Numbers of Prisoners

The greatest challenge for the researcher is to reconstruct the list of who passed through the prison during the Occupation. For Guernsey Prison, this task is not too onerous if we were to create a list of those convicted. This is because copies of charge sheets from trials[1] were passed to the Guernsey police and recorded in a two-volume logbook, which is still kept in the police station and is not in the island's archives. This covers the whole of the period of Occupation but ends in February 1945 and includes the names of 453 people. However, the author's research has shown many times, during the construction of the Frank Falla Archive website, that some people were imprisoned or deported without trial, or without the details of the trial (and the associated charge sheets) being passed to the local police for notification. This logbook is therefore not an infallible source.

There are, however, other logbooks in existence which can be drawn upon to supplement the charge sheets, although none are records made by the Germans. Although they are excellent resources, they, too, do not give us a full list of prisoners. These logbooks include the 'Prison Identity Book' (which gives the prisoners' basic details, such as name, profession, place and date of birth, address, nationality and passport number)[2]; the 'List of Admissions' (which records name, date of arrival into and departure from the prison, who was responsible for this entry and release, offence, date of sentence and 'general remarks');[3] and a 'Remission of Sentences' book.[4] In addition to some basic information, this last book contains information on prisoner behaviour. One might imagine that all of these logbooks combined would surely produce a complete picture of everyone who passed through the prison. And yet this is not the case. A relatively large number of cases have been identified of inmates who were known to have been in the prison at a certain time, and yet whose names were not present. Nevertheless, these logbooks list a total of 988 prisoners, which includes both civilian and political prisoners. Dates were not always consistent between the various documents, making a time-line of the prisoner's incarceration difficult to construct.

It is important to explain why a list of those in the German-controlled side of the prison might be vital. These prisoners were at risk of being deported without trace. We are already at a disadvantage when trying to identify who from Guernsey was deported. Jersey has a 'political prisoner logbook' which notes who was deported and when, yet Guernsey lacks this information, meaning that we have no official list of those who were sent to Nazi prisons and camps. Surprisingly, no such list was compiled at any point after the war.[5] Such a list has therefore been built from scratch and placed online, on the Frank Falla Archive website. Source material has included family testimony, histories of the Occupation and prison and camp registers from France and Germany. Yet these, too, are not complete records, meaning that an unknown number of people have fallen through the net. Even if we managed to compile a complete list, we have no way of knowing whether or when we have achieved our goal.

And yet we are not entirely helpless in our endeavours to reconstruct any prisoner list for the German-controlled side of Guernsey Prison. In fact, we have four sources which give us glimpses. The first is the memoirs or diaries of prisoners within the German-controlled part of the prison who name other prisoners in cells

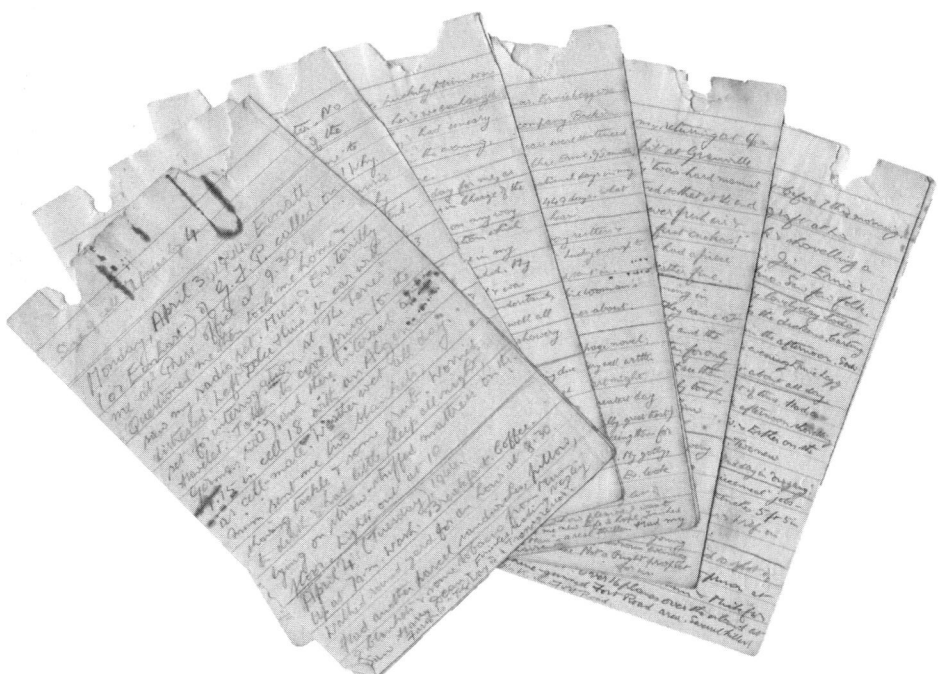

Frank Falla's prison diary. (Copyright and courtesy Sally Falla)

around them; Frank Falla's prison diary is especially useful for this, although the number of names is small.

Prisoners were aware of the identities of those with whom they were incarcerated, and their records of others are valuable in helping us reconstruct who was imprisoned with whom, and when. On only his second day in prison, Frank Falla saw a face he knew, publican Harry Dean, most likely while doing his 'promenade', i.e. walking in the exercise yard. Dean was in prison for wireless offences and owning a camera. Falla's prison diary also makes it clear that prisoners were told – truthfully, in each of the cases cited by Falla - to which prison they were about to be deported. To give just one example from the eight specific references in the diary, on 19 April 1944, Falla was 'distressed at the fact that my "prom" [i.e. promenade] mate Harry Dean was leaving for France at 8.30pm tonight. He is to go to a place called St Lou [i.e. St-Lô Prison] near Granville. Myself more lonesome than ever. Mrs Garland and "Smiter" Gallienne[6] also left for France with HD'.[7]

Neither the deportation date, nor the first place of deportation, of these three was known before Falla's prison diary was uncovered in 2019. Because prisoners deported together were usually sent to the same location, Falla's reference tells us that Garland and Gallienne also went to St-Lô Prison with Dean. The reference to Evelina Garland is especially poignant because, not only was she one of the few women to have passed through Guernsey Prison during the Occupation to begin a long sentence of hard labour at many Nazi prisons on the continent, but other prisoners refer to hearing her cry, her sobs resounding around the prison. References to her being held with the men also tells us that by this date, female prisoners of the Germans were not necessarily held only in the Gaoler's house.

Garland was given a sentence of two years and three months on 28 March 1944 for 'failing to deliver an anti-German leaflet [i.e. for not surrendering it to the German authorities], and for making and spreading the leaflet'. In fact, she had composed alternative, anti-German lyrics to the song 'Bless them all', which other islanders delighted in whistling to each other in public.[8] Hayes also referred to Garland in his memoir, writing that there was:

> At least one unknown woman from whom we were kept separate and whose distressed sobs could be heard all over the prison. It was rumoured that she had been given a long sentence for having been involved in some scurrilous versus about Hitler and at first took it very badly. Later, we heard her singing over and over again

the Prisoner's Song ('If I had the wings of an angel, over these prison walls would I fly . . .') and then she vanished though whether back to her home or elsewhere we never knew.[9]

A few days later, Falla referred to seeing 'Chas' in prison, i.e. Charles Machon, his colleague in GUNS. He also recorded that 'CM lent me a novel', indicating that those within the German side of the prison were able to exchange items, although we do not know how clandestine this practice was.[10] On 13 May 1944, Falla noted in his diary that he and Ernest Legg moved into the next door cell, cell 17, where they would share the space with Charles Machon. Falla noted that 'His previous mates, Jack Le Caer and Cliff Tostevin (with young Hockey and Ferbrache) had left by boat the previous evening for imprisonment at Dijon, France.'[11] Gerald Domaille's memoir also makes clear that he was told where he was going: 'I was taken to the prison office and told "tomorrow you will be sent to a German prison in Frankfurt-am-Main; you will be given the day to go home and settle your affairs. You must be back by six pm."'[12]

The second source of names or makeshift prisoner list comes from an unexpected source: records held in the Island Archives in Guernsey include a series of German documents, sent to the local authorities weekly or more often, whenever new prisoners were brought into the German-controlled part of the prison. Rather than a system of letting the authorities know who had been arrested, these documents were actually requests for the ration cards of named prisoners to be confiscated. This is further elaborated by an English translation of just one of the documents, which includes a post-script to say that these prisoners were instead being supplied with food by the Wehrmacht.[13] These documents date only from 16 April 1944 onwards, although the prison's provisions logbook indicates that the Wehrmacht began taking over the feeding of its prisoners from February 1944, as from this date the number of 'military prisoners' is no longer recorded.[14] In any case, only a very tiny number of these prisoners' names can be found in the prison entry logbook, indicating that prisoners of the Germans were *not* also registered in the prison logbook alongside their civil prisoner colleagues. Where these prisoners' names *do* appear in the logbook, the reason for their incarceration is given simply as 'military'. The offences of civil prisoners, on the other hand, are listed as specific offences such as 'stealing', 'breaking and entering', 'fraud', etc.

We might also observe that for some (though by no means all) prisoners brought to the prison by the Germans around and after this time, their entries in the logbook, where present, are sometimes squeezed in between rows, or given the same entry number as the previous person with an 'A' added afterwards. For example, there are two prisoners listed as the 46th entry in the prison for 1944, and a prisoner 53 and 53A for the same year. This acts as another clue to inform us that prisoners of the Germans were sometimes added ad hoc, perhaps when spotted by local warders rather than through official channels, or after information provided by local police of their sentences. Notes in the margin of the prison logbook suggest that the very few prisoners of the Germans whose names appear in both the logbook *and* on the notices relating to the confiscation of rations were handed over to the military for detention just after their arrival in prison.[15]

Whatever the reason for a tiny percentage of German prisoners appearing in the prison logbook, a comparison of the names of prisoners whose ration cards were being confiscated with charge sheets reveals that most (although not all) are accounted for. In total, the 37 documents listing those whose ration books were to be confiscated amounts to 129 names over a 1-year period – quite possibly the full list. This list of names is also a very useful way of making sure that no names have been omitted in our search for islanders who were deported, noting that those in prison in Guernsey from July 1944 were almost certainly safe from deportation because of the progress of the Allied invasion of Normandy. As these prisoners of the Germans were political prisoners, we can add their numbers to those listed in the police logbooks mentioned at the start of this chapter, bringing this total to 582 people.

Our third source relates to absolute numbers, rather than names, of prisoners in Guernsey Prison. The prison's provisions logbook records (among other things such as weights of different foodstuffs allocated to prisoners each day) prisoner numbers between April 1942 and December 1945.[16] Although much information is lost through not having the data from June 1940 onwards, we can observe that records combine the number of civil prisoners and prisoners of the Germans ('military prisoners') from April to July 1942, and then specify the separate numbers of each of the two groups until January 1944. From February 1944 onwards, when the Germans took over feeding the military prisoners, the numbers of these prisoners are no longer provided, which (no doubt deliberately) acted as a screen to prevent the local authorities from knowing how many local prisoners the Germans had – and were deporting.

Bearing in mind that the prison was designed to hold around fifty prisoners in total, numbers regularly hovered around a maximum number of seventy. Although records show how many prisoners were present on each day of the month, numbers were totalled each month to show how many 'prisoner days' (or meals) were provided. These figures show us that the average number of prisoners on the civil side of the prison grew as the Occupation progressed, with distinct peaks and troughs which are less easy to interpret. After the Occupation, it took until the end of 1945 for numbers to drop significantly, showing the high levels of lawlessness caused by the military Occupation and its legacy.

Similarly, the number of military prisoners fluctuates, climbing steadily from August 1942, when the data begins, reaching a peak in the third quarter of 1943 before dropping a little between then and January 1944. In order to fully understand these figures, one would need to identify each of these prisoners and their offences and to correlate them with what was happening in the Channel Islands' Occupation at that point, and in the war more generally. Acts of protest, defiance and resistance have been shown to be reactions to events in both Europe and the islands over time.[17] It is extremely frustrating that the counting of military prisoners ceases in January 1944. If they had been available until July 1944, we might have been able to observe a dramatic drop in the military prisoner population caused by the rushed deportation of military prisoners prompted by the Allied invasion of Normandy. Such prison evacuation is seen in Jersey at this time, which alerts us to potentially similar actions in Guernsey, although further research by the author has found no evidence for this. It is probably that the greater proximity of Jersey to France facilitated such action in one island only.

In terms of the ratio between civil and military prisoners, figures are available from August 1942 to January 1944. While the ratio was more or less equal for August to November 1942, we see double the number of prisoners of the Germans to civil prisoners from December 1942 and more than triple in February 1943. The ratio then fluctuates between 2.5 and 3.5 until September 1943, before staying at a ratio of 1:2 until January 1944, when comparative data ceases. These figures surely reflect the increasing severity of the Occupation, when it took very little perceived wrongdoing to get arrested.

Our fourth source of names and numbers of prisoners takes the form of an intriguing report which refers to a logbook not yet located and thought to no longer exist. Kept in the Imperial War Museum, this report forms part of the archives of Captain J.R. Dening, an intelligence officer attached to Force 135, which liberated the Channel Islands. The report is entitled *The Feldgendarmerie – Guernsey*, and follows an earlier report on German judicial records. Tantalisingly, it seems that intelligence officers had access to German prison and court records in 1945; records which no longer survive, indicating post-war destruction. The report on the *Feldgendarmerie* contains a criminal case list from the military court of 319 Infantry Division of both civilian and military crimes.[18] This comprises a typed list of selected names, although we do not know on what basis the intelligence officer concerned picked the names from the original source. This list runs to eight pages, and gives the accused's name, charge, sentence and date of sentencing. This list indicates that at least 1,834 local people were tried by this military court, although we now have no way of knowing how many of them spent time in Guernsey Prison. It also provides a reference number for each person which does not tally with any known extant list of convictions from any of the sources listed above. Further, many of the names and charges do not tally with any list of convictions of Guernsey citizens. Although the intelligence report states that all of those with a sentence longer than three months were deported, there is no indication of whether this was actually carried out for the listed people.

In order to supplement the list of names of deported islanders, which in itself is a sub-set of all prisoners held by the German forces, extant French and German prison and camp records have been consulted by the author, where they still survive. Some continental prison logbooks have been found to contain names of deported Channel Islanders, even where no record exists in the islands of a person's offence against the occupying authorities. There are also plenty of cases where islanders were known to have been sent to certain prisons, yet the prison logbooks do not list their names. These are just some of the reasons why drawing up complete lists of deported islanders is an almost impossible task today.

Having established the significance of counting and naming those who were prisoners of the Germans, it is important to establish the conditions under which they were held, and whether there was a difference between their experience of imprisonment and that of the civil prisoners. The next chapter therefore looks at daily life in Guernsey Prison during the Occupation for prisoners of the Germans.

Chapter 13
Daily Life in the German Side of the Prison

One of the more interesting documentary sources for finding out about day-to-day life in the prison comes from the admissions logbook of the prison.[1] In the right-hand column of the book, the Guernsey warders kept notes akin to a diary of daily entries of occurrences at the prison. Before the arrival of the Germans, this column recorded such items as the swearing-in of new warders, the absence of existing warders due to sickness or holidays, the transfer of prisoners to solitary confinement and corporal punishment. Although the start of the Occupation is not mentioned, on 12 July 1940 a note records that the prison was 'visited by officer of the German army of Occupation in the island of Guernsey'. Three days later, we learn that 'a German Soldier under military escort was placed in prison by order of the German Military Command.'

On subsequent days throughout July 1940, British soldiers trapped on the island by the Occupation were brought into the prison. As the summer of 1940 progressed, there are records of islanders being brought to the prison 'by order of the German military command'. Slowly, things begin to move to a new normal. Civil prisoners are taken away 'by the German Military Command', presumably to be deported to prisons on the continent. Although to begin with, the temporary removal of prisoners by the Germans (presumably to be taken for interrogation) is recorded, this ceases quickly, presumably either because of its regularity (and lack of space in the logbook) or because the warders were asked to stop recording the removal and return of prisoners. Perhaps they were no longer informed.

One of our earliest insights into the treatment of prisoners of the Germans comes from two letters and a diary written by Henry Marquand, imprisoned for his role in helping to shelter two British commandos. He and fifteen other members of the families and friends of the commandos, along with the commandos themselves, were deported to Caen and Cherche-Midi prisons in France after a short period in Guernsey Prison in October and November 1940.

Of his arrest on 9 November 1940, Marquand wrote that he, 'Received message 5.00pm at office, wanted at home. Arriving home, Herr Wölfle and Herr Felte informed me I was required to go to Paris for further interrogation and would have to sleep at prison that night . . . Packed bags and was taken to prison about 8pm.'[2]

Helpfully for us, Marquand itemised precisely the food he was served in prison. We assume that this food was provided by local authorities, but we do not know whether these sixteen people were given favoured treatment given their high profile and later use in propaganda photos, or even whether the standard of food was normal at this early stage in the Occupation. We might also suggest that the quantity of food was increased because of local sympathies with these prisoners, or even supplemented by others.

For breakfast, Marquand was given two pieces of fish with fried bread, bread and butter and marmalade. At lunch he was served vegetable soup, stewed steak, boiled potatoes and Brussels sprouts, followed by tapioca pudding. For dinner, he had tinned salmon, lettuce and bread and butter. Compared to the watery soup and ersatz coffee given to prisoners of the Germans in 1944, as mentioned by several of our memoirists later on, this was nothing short of luxurious. Even Marquand wrote that 'the meals are good and plentiful' and sometimes was unable to finish all that he was given. A month later, in prison in France, his meals consisted of soup, with bread, butter and cheese for dinner.[3]

Although only in Guernsey Prison for a few days, Marquand was eloquent about how it felt to be locked up: 'the loneliness and inaction I find very trying. I used to think I was fond of my own company, but now I don't like myself so much. Oh for a chat or a game of cards!' Later on, he remarked, 'By jove, freedom is a valuable thing and is not really appreciated until one is deprived of it. To think that you can't just open the door and go out when you want to is not a pleasant experience . . . I do find the time dreadfully long and reading becomes monotonous.'[4]

Despite this, he soon became accustomed to prison life. 'The sentries are up and down, day and night, clank, clank, clank on the stone floor. It was a bit trying at first but I am getting used to it . . .' Marquand was visited by 'Lt Wolff and Herr Felte', at least one of whom [Wölfle] we recognise as a *GFP* man. Surprisingly, given what we know of Wölfle's later character, his behaviour was very different towards Marquand in November 1940: 'They were very kind and expressed regret that this confinement must continue.'[5]

After Marquand's letters of 1940, we must leap forward three years before we gain an insight into the experience of another male prisoner of the Germans in Guernsey Prison. Norman Dexter, imprisoned for illegally withholding his radio set after the June 1942 confiscations, sketched his prison cell. This remains the only known piece of Occupation-era artwork to have emerged from Guernsey

Prison. Sketched on 9 September 1943, a close examination of the now-yellowed paper reveals his bedding propped up against the wall and somebody else's on the floor, indicating at least two-person occupancy of this cell. In terms of furniture, Dexter drew a table and two small wooden stools, one of which has a book placed on top. Rather than a spartan cell, the table and small shelves are bursting with objects. We can identify prison-issue towels, a sketch and a calendar on the wall, a cup (perhaps a pail) and dish on the floor, cutlery and a plate on the shelf, a shaving kit, a thermos flask and his suitcase. On the table, where he is sitting, are a lighter and a tobacco pouch. Such items may have been typical of the average prisoner's possessions behind bars, and also give us an insight into items allowed to prisoners of the Germans. Pencil, paper, tobacco and reading matter, available, on display and even sketched by a convicted prisoner of the Germans tell us a little about what was and was not considered contraband at that stage in the Occupation, or perhaps what contraband was depicted in the drawing as a small act of defiance.

Six months later, we hear from schoolteacher John Hayes. Since Henry Marquand was in prison, times had changed, although Hayes' experience seems not to have been too traumatic. Hayes was taken from his home in March 1944 for

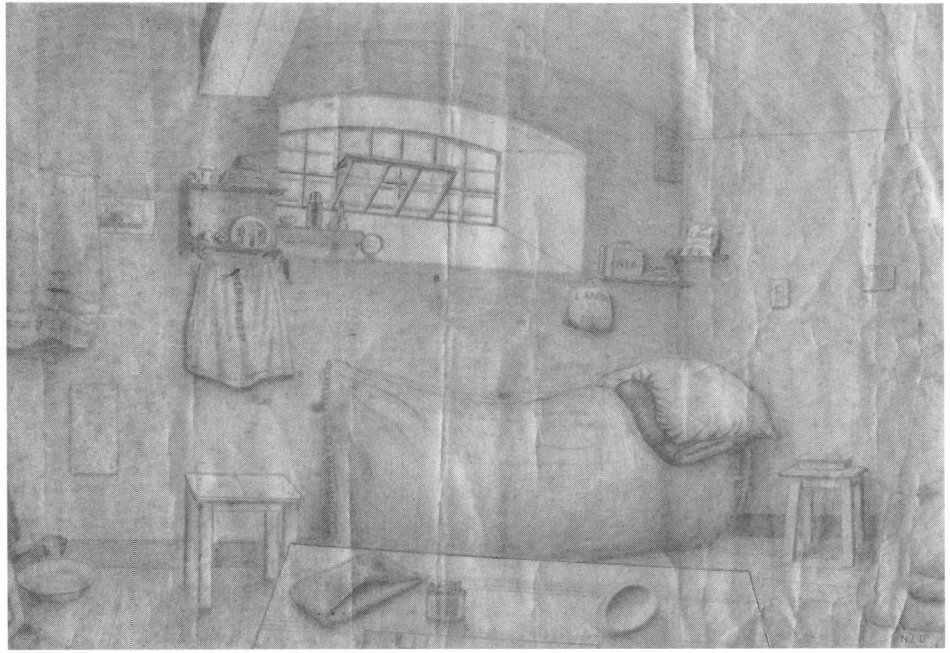

Sketch of his prison cell by Norman Dexter, 9 September 1943. (Copyright the family of Norman Dexter)

Photograph of prison cell taken in 2003. (Copyright MOLA)

possession of a radio. After his arrest, he was first taken to the headquarters of the *GFP* which, at that time, was in a building called 'The Terres' at the bottom of Havelet, a street in St Peter Port. After interrogation he was allowed to go home to look after his two daughters, who had been left alone while their mother was in hospital.

After some weeks went by, he was picked up once again by the *GFP* and taken to 'the German side' of Guernsey Prison with a bundle of bedding under his arm. He was first taken to the prison office, where he was put before a man who he described as one of the 'German troops who spoke Russian . . . from the occupied territories to the east'.[6] He described his admission into the prison as 'very informal'. He was not searched and nothing was either given to or taken from him. This much was confirmed in the memoirs of Frank Stroobant, imprisoned for two days in March 1942, two years earlier, for suspected black-market dealing in cigarettes.

Stroobant commented how surprised he was 'how easily one could be introduced into a German prison. There were no formalities of any kind such as one might have expected from so orderly a people as the Germans.'[7]

During his entry to the prison, the Russian military guard wrote Hayes' name 'in a book' and 'added another small cardboard square to those already fixed to the wall behind his desk',[8] which we can assume was some sort of tally system or indication of filled cells for prisoners held in this section of the prison.

He was then taken back outside the prison and to the end of the building, to 'one of two unheated dungeons built side by side at ground level into the base of the building at the back', where he was to spend three months of incarceration. We can readily identify these cells as those in the basement of the main prison building. Hayes described his cell as cave- or cellar-like. 'The sole opening for light and air was a barred trap, about twelve inches square, in the door . . . Just a few feet in front of the door was the high perimeter wall of the prison so that very little light came into the cell.'[9]

The cell was filled with a large double bed and his fellow occupant: Cecil Duquemin, a member of GUNS who had already been in the cell a few weeks, and who in his memoirs referred to the 'dungeons' as the 'drunks' cell'.[10] Apart from the bed, and a 'grubby wash-basin in the only accessible corner', there was barely enough room for the two of them to stand at the same time. The toilet was in the corridor outside the cells. Duquemin possessed a large knife, which he used to push through the grating in the door to reach the light switch outside the cell, so he could operate the light at will.

Before Hayes entered Duquemin's cell, the latter's previous cell-mate had been Gerald Domaille, imprisoned in February 1944. Domaille's impression of the room was less glamorous than Hayes had painted it. He described it as:

Very small, about ten feet by eight, two thirds of this area was taken up by a wooden bench which was covered by straw; it was just large enough for two people to sleep. In the corner was a tin container as a toilet. There were no washing facilities at all, and you were not permitted to take a walk in the fresh air. Conditions were really terrible . . . the amount of light coming through the small window in the door was so bad that you couldn't read a book. The warder, a very simple German soldier, came in with our three daily meals . . . but it was really a starvation diet.[11]

Around the same time, or very soon thereafter, the occupant of the next-door cell in the 'dungeons' must have been Hubert Lanyon, the member of the GUNS team from the island of Sark. After his arrest and interrogation by '*Feldwebel* Einhart' (probably the man referred to by others as Einert) of the *GFP*, he was put in Guernsey Prison, in an 'underground cell' on 8 April 1944. It was to be another forty days before he was sentenced. In his short memoir, Lanyon wrote that he was:

> Not allowed visits, letters, or communication with the outside world. If weather was fine, I was taken into a yard for exercise, or what they called 'promenade', for about 15 or 20 minutes, then back to underground cell for 24 hours. It was a bit hellish, no reading material allowed but I smuggled some in, through fellow jail birds.[12]

We do not know whether the prisoners under German control were allowed – or dared – to complain about their cells or the circumstances under which they were imprisoned. There was nobody to whom they could show their cells. A letter of August 1941 to Agnew Giffard, Dean of Guernsey and prison chaplain, from the tribunal of the *Feldkommandantur* 515 makes it clear that he was denied a permit to visit the 'English prisoners interned in the prison by order of the Army authorities', indicating that no succour to the imprisoned or those soon to be deported was allowed to be dispensed within cells.[13] At this relatively early stage in the war, the Germans were starting to prevent others from seeing the circumstances in which they housed their prisoners.

A surviving document in Guernsey Archives dating to December 1943 tells us that visiting times at the prison were relaxed in accordance with 'Article 70' of the prison regulations (which have not been traced). This article stated that 'Prisoners under sentence be permitted to see their relations or friends after the expiry of one month of their sentence and that this privilege be afterwards augmented to a visit every fortnight. This privilege to be withdrawn by the Sheriff from any prisoner who might commit himself through misconduct or infraction of any of the Prison Regulations whilst in Prison.'[14] Given that this document was written by the Guernsey authorities, it seems likely that this regulation was for civilian prisoners rather than political prisoners. In any case, it might provide some insight into why some referred in their memoirs to visits that were denied to others. It seems likely that parcels from friends and relatives were also controlled by similar regulations.

Although Hayes was allowed to receive food and cigarettes handed in by his wife, it seems that Lanyon was treated more harshly (perhaps because of his offence), although possibly his treatment improved after sentencing. Also in prison around the same time, in cell 18, Frank Falla's diary shows that he received parcels containing clothes, cigarettes, bedding and food from his mother and girlfriend, and was allowed reading material but no regular visitors.[15] He was also, in common with other prisoners on the German side of the prison, not allowed to attend services in the prison chapel.[16] It is possible that this is because the chapel was on the side of the prison controlled by local warders, or because the prisoners of the Germans might be seen and identified.

Cell 18 was '7 paces by 4' and had a 'water tin' or makeshift toilet in one corner, which smelled so bad that it made Falla's eyes water and took some getting used to.[17] Falla also recorded the treatment of a prisoner with whom he shared his cell, who was dealt with in quite a different way. An 'Algerian who had fallen foul of the Nazi labour corps' was 'allowed neither fork, spoon or knife with which to cope with his tough prison food. When he had it on his plate he just had to get down to floor level and lick the whole plate for he was also handcuffed all this time.'[18] We might question whose experience in the German-controlled prison was the most out of the ordinary here for occupied Europe: the Channel Islanders' or the Algerian's.

Food in the prison and the daily regimen was often a subject worthy of description for Falla. Food brought in by friends and family made a great deal of difference to those incarcerated, as did non-edible gifts. After going several days without a parcel from home, Falla wrote that 'Joy of joys! The sun shone, for Mum sent me in a parcel of clean clothes, a couple of books and some tobacco and matches. I live again! Bless her.'[19]

The daily prison regimen, according to Falla, was reveille at 7am, after which they washed and swept out their cells. Breakfast with coffee was served at 8am, which was followed (depending on the weather) by a walk around the prison yard for an hour, presumably in shifts. This gives an insight into the possible use of shared space with the civil prisoners. Lunch was at 1pm and consisted of a bowl of soup, which Falla gave to his Algerian cell-mate, who 'revelled in it'. At 2.30pm, Falla was 'given a hunk of German bread 1½ inches thick and a piece of "butter". This constituted my tea with a cup of "coffee" delivered at 6pm',[20] the ersatz nature of some of these foodstuffs indicated by inverted commas. Falla passed the rest of his time in reading books brought in by his mother. Despite the forced labour encountered by many, as discussed later, proper access to washing facilities (other than a small sink) seemed rare. It was only after three weeks in prison that Falla was allowed a bath.[21]

After his sentencing, Falla was allowed a 20-minute visit in the guardroom from his mother and girlfriend. Despite it being a day after his trial, he described it as 'quite easily the greatest day since I entered prison'. The two women brought him 'a lovely lot of good things . . . they gave me new life and hope'.²² Hayes, however, remarked that, as there was no system of permits for visitors, 'visitors just came to the prison and asked to be admitted which they usually were'.²³ As this was not Falla's experience, it seems more likely that Hayes had preferential treatment, perhaps because of the lesser severity of his offence. One might be tempted to suggest that Hayes was misremembering his period of incarceration, and that only after sentencing were people allowed visitors, as at Jersey Prison. However, he noted that his wife visited him in prison 'three times during the first week and later she even visited me twice in one day as I noted in the brief diary that I kept and which I still have'.²⁴ Visits took place in the prison office in the presence of:

> Whoever happened to be on duty but there were no restrictions of any kind to bother us and the visit usually terminated when we ourselves decided that it should. We exchanged food-containers, laundry bags and books with only the most perfunctory pretence at inspection. There must have been prison rules known to somebody but I never knew what they were.²⁵

This seems very much at odds with the situation on either the civil or military controlled side of Jersey Prison. In fact, Hayes commented that, 'We all had knives and many of us collected tool-kits, hoping that if it became necessary we would be able to make our way out.' When his wife needed to go into hospital, he asked for a month's leave. A call was put through to Jersey and the leave was approved immediately.²⁶ Hayes was a fortunate prisoner indeed.

Our insight into the prison two years earlier, in 1942, is provided in a snapshot given by Frank Stroobant, who was imprisoned for just two days in March of that year. He was not put in the 'underground' or drunks' cells. Instead he was put into a cell on the first floor of the prison, sharing with one of the policemen who were imprisoned at this time, charged with stealing food from German stores. Stroobant was provided 'with a sack of straw for a mattress and two blankets'. As he and his cell-mate chatted into the early hours and were told off by a German guard, we learn that he had been placed into the German-controlled part of the prison.

He remarked that there was 'a gap under the door almost wide enough to crawl through' which he tried to plug with his mattress, but, as he had to sleep on the floor he woke up freezing. As for the food, he remarked that his breakfast was 'so abnormal in quality that only the fact that I had had nothing to eat since the previous day's lunch stopped me from refusing it . . .'.²⁷

Hayes also described the civilian prisoners' situation in the German part of the prison:

[They] were not separated from the German troops who were in the prison though we did not share cells with them; or from the few women who from time to time appeared among us. After I had been moved from the dungeon there was a young Frenchwoman in the cell next to mine for ten days or so and I was able to chat with her at length. She was allowed more freedom within the prison than the rest of us and she did sewing and ironing for the prison guards in exchange for this freedom.[28]

This reference shows us that the conditions of one's incarceration within Guernsey Prison could be negotiated by the right person with something to offer.

In addition to the Russian in German uniform who processed Hayes into the prison, it is interesting to note the presence of other nationalities in the prison, including a Georgian prison barber, a Russian civilian who was the 'longest serving resident' in the prison who 'had the run of the prison and spent his time sweeping and fetching and carrying. He was able to pass notes round and in a limited way keep us informed.'[29] Hayes also made notes on the identity of the German prison guards: Alois Horak, an Austrian; Hermann from Frankfurt; and 'Long Tom' from Stettin; all 'colourless types' judged by the prisoners by how they ladled out the soup: either from the bottom, where the soup was thick, or from the top, where it was very thin.[30]

Women's experience of imprisonment in Guernsey does not concern itself with food, although our sources are brief and few. In fact, our knowledge is based almost entirely on the diary of Marie Ozanne, supplemented only by Olive Frampton (née Allo)'s single night in prison; both women were incarcerated in 1942. Interestingly, Ozanne recorded that both a Guernsey policeman and a German came to take her to prison; it is unclear how typical such collaborative action was in arresting prisoners, or whether the Guernsey policeman attended to make sure she was well-treated.

At first, Ozanne was placed in an unknown prison cell. A few days later, she was moved to 'a Guernsey policeman's house in room with Miss Nicolle'.[31] Marie Louise Nicolle was serving a six-month sentence for 'insulting the forces and attempted corruption with abuse'.[32] It seems likely that the 'policeman's house' was actually the Gaoler's house. It is clear that Ozanne was actually inside the prison, because not only does she preface her diary pages with the word PRISON, but she refers to regularly attending prison chapel services, to prison exercise (presumably in the prison yard) and to her German guards, for whose salvation she prayed. She also expressed anxiety about those prisoners kept in the underground cells elsewhere in the prison, and passed a note to her guard about this.[33] She heard about other prisoners entering the prison, sometimes mentioning them by name or by their offence, even writing to one of them,[34] and was well informed about the Guernsey warders on the prison grapevine, as she referred to praying for the chief warder, Mr Pike, when he was ill.[35]

Ozanne was a devout Christian who spent her time in prison praying, reading the Bible, writing letters to the German authorities to criticise their regime, composing religious articles and knitting. She also prayed for the souls of those imprisoned alongside her and tried to initiate conversations with fellow prisoners about their faith, feeling concerned that she was 'the only converted one here'. Evidently Ozanne was a shy woman, as she prayed for the courage to speak to others about their beliefs,[36] but she evidently valued her time in prison because it gave her time to focus on her faith. In fact, when her release was announced, she wrote that 'In my prison experience have I found joy in communion with the Lord; anxious now about life outside prison.'[37]

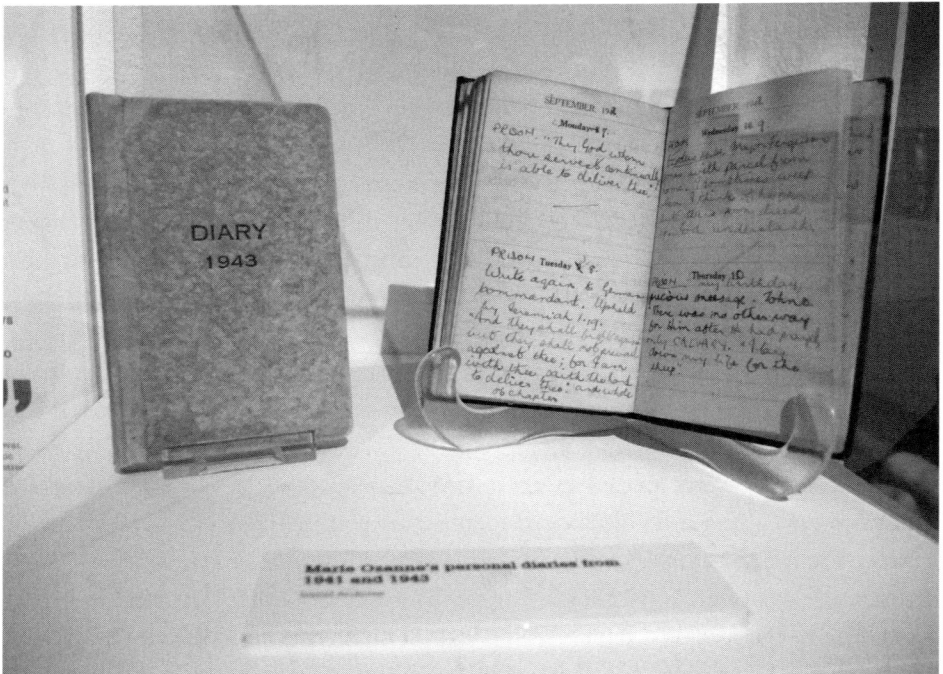

Marie Ozanne's diary on display in Guernsey Museum. (Copyright Gilly Carr)

Ozanne was not short on news of what was happening in Guernsey outside the prison, such as the deportation of many hundreds of Islanders to civilian internment camps in Germany in September 1942. This information is most likely to have come from her mother, who visited her regularly. Ozanne also received gifts of food from family members and neighbours, who clearly thought highly of her. She was also free to send and receive letters, although presumably this was done through an intermediary such as one of her visitors.

Ozanne was treated well in prison by her German guards. When she asked to walk in the prison garden for an hour, she was given 2 hours. When she asked for permission to have a typewriter, it was granted.[38] In summary, there are only a few differences that we can glean from Ozanne's diary in terms of the way female and male prisoners were treated in prison by the German guards. We might note that Ozanne did not carry out any forced labour, unlike the men. She appears to have also been allowed regular visits, letters, plenty of exercise time and even a typewriter. The noise of such a machine must have been heard across the prison to the annoyance of those without such privileges.

Because Ozanne is our only female prison diarist, we cannot say whether she was favoured with such treatment because she was female or because her offence was not considered to be sufficiently grave. There are, however, two small pieces of information that can provide a little insight here. The first comes from a single sentence within the compensation testimony of Julia Brichta, who was deported in the early months of 1944 for black-market offences. In her application for disability compensation, in answer to the question of when she first began to suffer from her disease or injury, she wrote that it 'started with the first beating in Guernsey'.[39] Although we might be inclined to dismiss such a statement as a clear lie, made only for the purposes of obtaining compensation, the experiences of the Guernsey policemen, discussed later, gives us ample pause for thought. It also suggests that women were not immune from bad treatment.

The second piece of evidence which helps us understand Ozanne's experiences comes from the memoir of Olive Frampton. After attending a party at which patriotic songs were loudly sung, Frampton was one of many young people rounded up by *Feldgendarmerie* and found to be without her identity card. Sixteen young women were marched to the prison, and when they arrived:

> The prison warden was very worried; he said he didn't have any cells to put us in and didn't quite know what he was going to do with all of these people . . . all the girls

were put into this warden's sitting room for the night and there were not very many places to sit. There were sixteen of us so we had to lay on the floor . . . But when the next morning came they took us upstairs somewhere to where the women were imprisoned and gave us a big chunk of bread and a cup of tea in a great big enamel mug covered in chips and even though I was hungry and thirsty and frightened, I didn't want mine so I gave mine to the women prisoners and they were chuffed because they didn't have much food in there.[40]

The main piece of information we can extract from Frampton's memoir is that she confirms Marie Ozanne's words that at least some women were imprisoned upstairs in the Gaoler's house in 1942; Ozanne's reference to a 'Guernsey policeman's house' is likely to have been a simple mistake or incorrect guess as to where she was. Given that Ozanne was guarded by the Germans and Frampton by local warders, we can only imagine that the Gaoler's house was considered either to be shared space, or a place where different rooms (and prisoners) were guarded by different guards.

In any case, while Ozanne was free to write, send and receive messages within and outside the prison, the male prisoners on the German side of the prison had to resort to what Hubert Lanyon called 'underground methods', which enabled him to get a copy of the *Guernsey Press* newspaper nearly every day. He was also able to smuggle a message out to Sark through a local prison warder, to let two acquaintances of his know that they were suspected of possessing banned radio sets. During his interrogation he was left alone in the room for 10 minutes and was able to look at papers on the *GFP* officer's desk.

Lanyon described how the German side of the prison was divided from the rest of the prison by adjoining doors. These were opened to allow a lorry to pass through carrying timber, which the prisoners were to turn into boxes as part of their punishment. As the lorry passed by a local warder, Lanyon was able to mutter the message, which was passed on. Frank Falla also refers to the same lorry in his memoirs, but used the lorry driver to deliver a message to his mother by throwing a letter in through the open window of the cab.[41]

Lanyon also managed to receive the radio news every night through a Russian prisoner, who was sentenced to fifteen months' imprisonment for stealing bottles of cognac from the store of the Organisation Todt, no doubt to sell on the black market. Like the Russians in Jersey Prison, this man was used by the Germans as their prison servant.

Lanyon is a source of detailed information about how messages were smuggled around the prison by this prisoner. The Russian prisoner was:

> Allowed to work around the prison, cleaning and bringing meals around. He also carried messages to fellow prisoners from me, concealed in a double top of his rubber boots. These boots were in a worn out condition, every day he had wet feet, because his work consisted of washing down the kitchen . . . he put up with this great inconvenience so as to carry messages he concealed in them. He passed around the prison all the latest inside information concerning the movement of prisoners, who was the new arrival, and who was to be sent to France, etc. He passed out many an underground letter for me, and brought in those I received. He was ably backed up by a fellow on the civil side of the prison. They would whistle a few bars from that song 'Oh I wish I had someone to love me' when either wanted the other. A few minutes later they met at their rendezvous and the message had passed in or out.[42]

The location for the rendezvous was the wash-house window, and the methods of passing on messages through the prison seems to have been every bit as devious as those employed in Jersey Prison. Lanyon also recalled how he threw letters into the bucket used by the man employed to sweep the yard; these were posted or passed to members of working parties – prisoners who were employed in forced labour, and who will be discussed in the next chapter.

Chapter 14
Forced Labour

Forced labour is an interesting subject, because political prisoners in Jersey did not carry this out yet it was standard in Guernsey. While forced labour was a widespread phenomenon for prisoners in Nazi Germany, its use in the Channel Islands, under the description of 'hard labour', had been a normal activity for prisoners since the nineteenth century.[1] We might recall the experiences of Jersey's Anthony Faramus in the stone yard in the early years of the Occupation as a civil prisoner. Working in the stone yard was normal prison labour in Jersey; in Guernsey, stone-breaking had been phased out and prisoners before the Occupation were engaged in making wooden boxes for tomato packing, for the island's tomato industry.[2] A workshop in the prison grounds was used for this kind of industry before and during the Occupation, and there are references to wood being delivered to the prison in prisoner memoirs.[3] The prison logbook also records civil prisoners fetching 'thalassol',[4] a disinfectant, probably made locally from seaweed, for use in cleaning the prison.

In terms of forced labour during the German Occupation, there is evidence that the local authorities in Guernsey themselves asked for this kind of work for the prisoners under German control – or rather, for something to help them 'pass the time while incarcerated'. A letter from John Leale, the President of the Controlling Committee, to the German field command, dated August 1941, gives insight here. Leale stated that he had received a letter from the prison Sheriff for:

> Permission to give persons undergoing German sentences in HM's Prison some kind of work to occupy their time, and I would be obliged if you would pass this request on to the appropriate German authority. The work normally given to prisoners includes stone-breaking, wood-breaking and sawing, in the case of male prisoners, and laundry and sewing in the case of females. [5]

One can only imagine what the reactions of the prisoners would have been had they learnt that their own authorities had effectively handed them over as forced labour. Perhaps this was not quite what the Sheriff had in mind when he made the suggestion; indeed, earlier letters of his enquiring about 'Hard Labour' stressed the point that 'Prison "Labour" includes the ordinary work done in the Prison . . .'.[6]

In order to discover what kinds of forced labour was normal in Guernsey, many of the diarists and memoirists wrote about their work. It seems that the Sheriff had not been too out of step with the prisoners in asking for this kind of work. Most prisoners seemed pleased to get out of their cells and did not find the work too arduous.

Hayes wrote that 'Going out to work was much better than being cooped up all day in our cramped black hole . . . particularly since when working we were entitled to, and for a time actually got, worker's rations and three cigarettes a day'. When working in the garden of a vicarage, now taken over by two men of the *GFP*, Hayes and Duquemin were left unsupervised and told to prepare the ground for the planting of potatoes.[7] On such days Hayes was able to visit his home with the connivance of a Wehrmacht soldier who was giving him a lift to the vicarage.[8] On other occasions, he was visited by friends who gave him cigarettes.[9] This laxity was further in evidence when one of the *GFP* men told the men to 'Take it easy boys: there's plenty of time'. Hayes recorded that, somewhat incredibly, the *GFP* men themselves joined in the work alongside them.[10] On another occasion, while working on bunker construction, a 'conscientious guard from Darmstadt sometimes thought we were working too slowly. He would strip to the waist, take a pick from one of us, discard it as too light and then, having found a really heavy one, he would ferociously attack the side of the hole we were excavating and knock down in a few minutes as much earth as the six of us would shift in an hour.'[11]

Gerald Domaille's memoirs detail his forced labour, which took place after his sentencing:

> We were taken to Granville Mount barrack to prepare a large dining room for officers for a meeting and afterwards for a buffet. Really our job was to help in building an air raid shelter in the garden of a house across the road . . . It was very hard work moving large granite lintels. It took six of us to move each lintel into position. We never finished the job because we were directed to Government House in Queen's Road to beat large carpets with sticks, a much easier and lighter job than the previous one.[12]

Duquemin's memoirs record forced labour that involved 'peeling potatoes and other vegetables' and 'doing a garden',[13] which is where he met Frank Falla. Falla, too, was put to work during his period in prison. In his memoir he records that he 'got more enjoyment than he expected' from his imprisonment, during which he was:

> Compelled . . . to dig trenches, help build bunkers and air raid shelters, load sand onto lorries, peel potatoes and pod peas for the Wehrmacht. Unfortunately for me when I was podding peas the Germans discovered I couldn't resist eating as many peas as I podded, so I was shifted onto less edible potatoes. The choicest job the Germans put me on was . . . sweeping horse-dung off the road near the German officers' quarters at Mount Durand in St Peter Port . . . Not many people in Guernsey can claim the doubtful honour of sweeping horse-dung from the streets for the enemy.[14]

Like Hayes, who found constructing a bunker to be 'enjoyable work for me in very pleasant surroundings'[15] where his wife visited him daily, Domaille, too, realised that it 'relieved us of the monotony of remaining in our cell the whole day long'.[16] Falla also appreciated the benefits of being away from the prison. His mother found out when he would arrive with a broom and shovel when on manure duty, and would stand in a concealed gateway to hand him a parcel of food to stuff up his jumper.

Yet the humorous anecdotes of outwitting the enemy in the published memoir belie the realities behind forced labour. After his first day of it, Falla wrote in his prison diary, 'My golly, 'twas hard manual labour to which I was unaccustomed so that at the end of the day I ached in every limb. However, fresh air and green scenery was welcome . . . we were searched on return to prison.'[17] A few days later, Falla wrote that 'We had a real hard day's work today with no respite. Left prison at 8.30, not returning until 6.30 to cold soup and coffee.'[18] Later reports of 'real hard graft' and having to work 'like the dickens'[19] from Falla suggest that Hayes had either forgotten how hard the manual labour was, or was simply treated differently to Falla. As neither man had worked in manual labour before the war and both were almost the same age, there is no reason why their experience of the work should have differed.

Hubert Lanyon was not deported, but kept in prison after the Allied invasion of Normandy. Interestingly, he commented that the treatment of prisoners changed after this date. He was working on 'pick axe and shovel work, which, after D-Day, was speeded up, for we were taken out at 7am, allowed ½ hour for mid-day break, to partake of a meal consisting of "Atlantic soup": one cabbage drowned in a bucket of water, and knocked off at 7pm. I can assure you my hands were terribly blistered.'[20]

Hayes and Falla's reports – of smuggled messages and food, of taking it easy while working, and of eating the Wehrmacht's food – seem to speak of a wider culture of German guards going easy or turning a blind eye towards Guernsey prisoners (or at least some of them). Hayes writes of often being 'abandoned' after passing through the prison door, and of 'being expected to let ourselves in'.[21] He also recorded that he once refused an order at another work site in St Peter Port, telling the 'bossy sergeant . . . that I was not in the Wehrmacht'. He was sent straight back to the prison but there were no repercussions of any sort and his wife was still allowed to visit him.[22] After the Allied landings in Normandy on 6 June 1944, an RAF attack on the harbour in St Peter Port shattered the glass windows of every shop in the harbour. Hayes was sent, unsupervised, to sweep it up, and his wife found out where he was and came out to chat to him.[23]

Hubert Lanyon also found that some forced labour could be easy:

In the middle of July [1944] I worked in one of their kitchens in the Channel Islands Hotel, and here I made up for the expended energy in the previous months. This was a peach of a job, with better food, a good chef, and a chummy 'underofficer'. Our guard . . . spent his days sleeping, and he had full confidence in us. We had a cushy time.[24]

Hayes' memoir was written in the early years of the twenty-first century, nearly sixty years after his release from prison. One wonders whether his somewhat easy prison life was really as un-stressful as he made out. Frank Falla, imprisoned at the same time, was suffering from bad nerves, uneasy days and nights of constant worry and depression which are conveyed only in his prison diary. Was the difference of experience down to prisoner personality or the failure of memory after the passage of time? Hayes remarked, of his prison experience, that 'I cannot regard it as a grim experience and I well remember that that is how I felt at the time . . . In prison we were not overfed but neither were we overworked and I felt no physical or psychological stress.'[25]

Although we have few diaries and memoirs upon which to draw to compare the treatment of prisoners, we might note that Hayes and Lanyon both had a six-month sentence but were not deported; but Hayes seems to have been treated a little more leniently than Lanyon. Both men were clearly treated much better than the Algerian prisoner. Despite the small sample size, this might indicate that the Germans were prepared to treat English prisoners slightly better than indigenous Channel Islanders, although neither seemed to be kept on a short leash. The difference is striking, however, between the tales of ease from prisoners in Guernsey and the experience of those same men in continental prisons, as we shall see later.

Chapter 15

Interrogation and Trial

In light of the violence visited on some of those interrogated in the Channel Islands, it is interesting to see how a non-violent interrogation was conducted in Guernsey, and what methods were used to deal with frightened prisoners whose offences or behaviour did not warrant beatings.

John Hayes' interrogation was at the hands of two *GFP* officers identified by him as 'Schmidt' and 'Sievers'. After finding Hayes' illegal radio, he was immediately taken to *GFP* headquarters, 'The Terres', and questioned. He sat at a table and was questioned while Sievers typed his answers to mundane questions about his personal details. 'Through the open door I could see a Guernseywoman preparing elevenses. She came into the room with coffee and biscuits but all I got from her was a completely emotionless unblinking stare'[1], which rather implies that the refreshments were not shared with him. The experience appeared to be unstressful. It was 'all very polite, almost relaxed'.[2] Because his case was 'uncomplicated', Hayes was interviewed only once. Others were interrogated over a longer period of time, such as those involved in GUNS.

In his published memoir, Frank Falla does not claim that any physical violence was used on him or his colleagues. Instead, he refers to interrogation as 'grilling'. We are told how, after their initial 'grilling' by the *GFP*:

> Machon and Duquemin were closeted in the local prison and on subsequent days each was in turn taken to Gestapo [i.e. *GFP*] headquarters for questioning. Machon . . . was really put through it. He was a brave man, but it was just a case of how long he could stand up to this treatment. They would haul him from his cell to their headquarters, grill him and, at the end of each day's performance, tell him, 'Well, Mister Machon, you have told us some more of the truth, but not yet all of it. You will go back to your cell to think more about it and we'll speak again tomorrow.' This went on intermittently for a couple of weeks with Machon valiantly trying to hold out but gradually cracking.[3]

Machon had an ulcerated stomach and needed special food, which was denied to him in prison. After they threatened to imprison his mother, Machon finally told his interrogators what they needed to know. Falla was arrested at work by a *GFP* man he named as Einert and taken home to retrieve his hidden wireless set, then taken to *GFP* headquarters.

> Einert escorted me to a large room on the ground floor where another Nazi was sat at a desk, glancing through some papers. He stood up and he and Einert adjourned to the next room for a private talk. This over, Einert left and my interrogator resumed his seat at the desk. Warm day though it was outside, the room was made unbearable by the heat from an almost white-hot stove . . . 'Well, Falla, you know you are liable to be shot for this?' I could only meekly answer 'Yes', but my heart sank. Then the grilling got under way. The questions fired at me were spaced out, but crisp when they came. I was getting hotter and hotter. The Nazi saw my discomfort but ignored it.[4]

Falla was informed, before he left, that it had been fortunate for him that he had spoken the truth, otherwise 'it would have been harder for you'. It was, indeed, somewhat harder for Gerald Domaille, who was taken to *GFP* headquarters where he was:

> Really grilled. I was told that my story was a pack of lies; I was told that my sister who was in prison had told them a different story. I remonstrated with them that I knew what they had told me was untrue, whereupon my chief interrogator picked me up by my jacket and just threw me across the room. What could I do? His name was Statsfeldwebel Kuhn, he was a big fellow, about fifteen stone; he was wicked.[5]

From these accounts, we can begin to observe *GFP* behaviour towards those accused of offences such as illegal retention of a radio, distribution of a newsletter, and suspected theft of cigarettes. The men involved ranged from compliant, respectful and truthful (Hayes and Falla) to refusal to tell all immediately (Machon), to argumentative (Domaille). The treatment they received was straightforward – albeit with the heat turned up (Hayes and Falla), drawn-out, intensive and with threats made (Machon), and coupled with minor violence (Domaille). Beyond this, it is difficult to draw out patterns without further evidence from witnesses. Later we will see what happened to men involved in more serious, large-scale group resistance that threatened to make the occupiers look like easily duped fools. For such people, all pretence at what Hayes had referred to as a 'polite' or 'relaxed' manner was gone.

It is worth following up our insight into interrogation techniques by observing what happened during the trial of these men. First, Hayes' memoir adds weight to the impression, based on missing records, that some islanders were imprisoned or deported without trial. He notes that instead 'they were just taken to the HQ of the *Feldgendarmerie* and told their sentence by a mysterious British girl who, it was rumoured, had been brought from Jersey'.[6] It seems likely that this method of sentencing was that later explained by Albert L'Amy, chief officer of Guernsey police from 1942. He noted that in cases of a:

> Mild character, statements were taken from all concerned, submitted to a Tribunal outside the Island and eventually the culprit received a notice in German stating that he had only been fined so many Reichmarks or sentenced to a term of imprisonment. He had no opportunity of defending himself and was told he could appeal if he liked, but they advised him not to do so because invariably the sentence was doubled.[7]

Hubert Lanyon decided to try his luck, despite this knowledge, and appealed against his sentence. He was told that if his appeal failed, he would 'get 12 months and sent to a concentration camp in Germany. I decided to take the risk and was lucky enough to have 2 months knocked off.'[8]

'The Terres' (GFP *headquarters in use 1944), as it looks today.* (Copyright Susan Ilie)

Hayes was unlucky enough to face trial in the Magistrate's Court, and the experience is worth quoting at length:

> I was escorted to the court building to appear in what I suppose was the Magistrate's Court before a colonel, a major and a corporal . . . My three judges were sitting on the bench below the Lion and the Unicorn and standing facing them was another corporal, the prosecutor. An interpreter there was *Sonderführer* Krefft . . . There were just these six of us in the courtroom which was otherwise completely empty. The proceedings began with a declaration by the presiding colonel: '*Im Namen des deutschen Volkes*', 'in the name of the German people'. . . . The prosecutor then read out the charge, i.e. radio retention . . . I pleaded guilty to the charge, and without more ado the prosecutor then asked for a sentence of eight months which did not please me at all since I knew that sentences of six months or more were served off the island, in France or even in Germany . . . The presiding colonel asked me if I had anything to say . . . but the facts were not in dispute so I had nothing to say. The tribunal then withdrew to confer and came back moments later to give me six months.[9]

Records show that Hayes was sentenced on 28 March 1944.[10] It is unclear why he was not deported. His memoir states that he was polite during the trial and that

The Magistrate's Court today. (Copyright and courtesy Jon Torode)

he was wearing a neat suit provided by his wife. Historian Paul Sanders, who has written about the fate of the Jersey 21, has noted that a belligerent or argumentative attitude at the trial could worsen the outcome and result in a longer sentence for the Channel Islander in court. This affected the fates of William Marsh and Frederick Page in Jersey,[11] for example, for whom a lengthier sentence made the difference between life and death. Hayes had other ideas about the 'special favour' of being allowed to stay in Guernsey Prison: he believed that it was because he was one of only twelve trained schoolteachers left behind in the island after the evacuations of 1940, which resulted in 196 teachers leaving the island.[12] If he had been deported then he would not have returned before the end of the Occupation, if at all.

It rarely occurred to the accused to question the competence of the court or the legality of the conviction. Hayes noted that he was 'satisfied with its fairness'. Islanders were rarely represented in court by a local lawyer; Hayes felt that it would not have given him 'any significant advantage'. The trial, he felt, was simple and needed no legal interpretation, and that he was quite capable of conducting his own defence if he had needed to plead not guilty. He also noted that as his offence could incur severe punishment up to and including death, he never felt any resentment against his own lenient treatment.[13]

While Hayes seems to have gone through the experience with apparent calmness and equanimity, the same could not be said for Falla, for whom more was at stake because of his more serious offence. Whether the impression of calmness was the effect of a memoir written decades after the event or because the two men were of different characters is difficult to say. In any case, Falla's experience, according to his prison diary, was as follows:

> My God, what a day! The day of our trial before a German Tribunal in the civil Police Court. It started at 9am and finished at 12, and was carried out in the German language with an interpreter before Judge Stolz. The sentences of the court were as follows: C Machon 2 years 1 month; Duquemin 1 year 11 months; E Legg 1 year 10 months; FW Falla 1 year 4 months; J Gillingham 10 months. This is to be ratified by the Supreme Court in Jersey, so there's little hope of reduction. Pleaded that I be allowed to serve sentence here instead of France for Mum's sake – but no hope . . . Ernie Legg was put with me in Cell 18. Am grateful for company. Back in cell for dinner . . . 'Prom' 5.30-6.30 with Chas, Ernie, G. Domaille, J. Le Caer and Tostevin. So ended one of the most sensational days in my life with me a 'criminal' and 18 months' time to do – 449 days. What an awful shock this will be to mum when she hears.[14]

In his published memoir, Falla gave more detail about the trial of the five men in his GUNS group. After twenty-three days in prison, two members of the *Feldgendarmerie* marched the men to the Magistrate's Court in the Royal Court buildings – the same building in which Hayes had been convicted. Falla described the military tribunal, which took place before the judge, who sat behind a swastika flag which covered the royal coat of arms.

> Of course, according to Nazi, and in direct contrast to British, law we five were guilty before proceedings even opened, and had to prove our innocence. The court consisted of a judge, a major, who spoke fairly good English, a ranker from the German Army, the Prosecutor, a miserable, sour-faced *Obergefreiter*, and a German interpreter. We were not allowed a defending counsel . . . we were refused and the civilian authorities did not bother to insist on what, after all, was a common right of an accused person under international law . . . Before the trial opened the last person to enter the court was the Prosecutor . . . Plainly to be seen at the back of the wad of papers in his hand was one foolscap sheet which bore, not only our names, but the sentences he was recommending the court to pass on us.[15]

Unlike Hayes, Falla was very critical of the way the trial was conducted, although there was no sign of this in his prison memoir. Falla's subsequent experience in Nazi prisons, followed by twenty years of being a 'guardian of memory' for political prisoners, coupled with his hard work in getting compensation for the Channel Islands' victims of Nazism, had certainly politicised him. His memoirs, written in 1967 at the culmination of this process, had taught him how to identify and highlight the illegitimacy of the Nazi trial.

Chapter 16
Violence and the Case of the Guernsey Police

A comparison of Guernsey Prison with Jersey Prison and the treatment of its respective prisoners by the German authorities might thus far give the impression that the former was much more lax and permissive. This is despite the fact that all of the writings from the prison that survive today were penned by those guarded by the Germans. Superficially, conditions were similar in both Victorian prison buildings. The quality of the food was likewise poor, needing to be supplemented by friends and family on the outside. One might be forgiven for thinking that, apart from the healthy exercise and opportunity for speaking to friends afforded by forced labour on work parties away from the prison, being imprisoned in Guernsey Prison was not a real hardship. One cannot help but observe that narratives of violence, real hunger and ill-treatment at the hands of the *GFP* and the guards in Jersey Prison are thus far entirely absent from Guernsey Prison. Such narratives do, however, exist, but we need to move to a different set of records and a different case study in order to discover them.

In March and April 1942, eighteen members of Guernsey's police force were arrested and imprisoned for stealing food and alcohol from German stores. It was one of the biggest and most notorious trials in the Island of the entire Occupation. The treatment of the policemen has been narrated in the post-war period by most of the men in a variety of different forms: through their compensation testimonies, through their post-war affidavits, and through a memoir written in 1958 by one of them, Kingston Bailey, supplemented by Frank Tuck, arguably the two policemen most deeply involved in what they saw as a the resistance operation.

These documents together show a very different side of the *GFP* in Guernsey. From the moment that Bailey and Tuck were caught by the Germans in one of the stores, the ill-treatment began. Their houses were ransacked, searching with only minor success for the stolen tins of food. As the *GFP* shouted at them to reveal the hiding place of the food, Bailey states that he was struck across the face. This marked the beginning of their maltreatment. At the start of the interrogation, Bailey was again struck across the face and told that he would be given 'only a little food until you tell us what stores you

Occupation registration card photographs of Kingston Bailey and Frank Tuck. (Copyright and courtesy Island Archives, Guernsey)

have been in, where the food is, and who else went in the stores with you'.[1] He was then taken to the German side of Guernsey Prison on 5 March 1942, where he was joined by the rest of his police colleagues over the following five days.[2] Of this period, policeman Jack Harper later wrote that 'In consequence of threats of the firing squad and other tortures to which these officers were subjected by the Gestapo and statements made by these officers under remorse and extreme pressure, the whole Guernsey police force were taken into custody and detained.'[3]

Bailey described the cells in Guernsey Prison as follows:

> We were put into separate cells, which were in a filthy condition and swarming with vermin. The food was terrible, consisting of a small plate of vegetable soup, with one slice of bread for dinner; for breakfast and tea we had the same quantity of bread with a piece of margarine and ersatz coffee without milk or sugar. The cells were terribly cold and one had to sleep fully dressed to keep warm.[4]

On the second day of their imprisonment, the policemen were taken to Grange Lodge in St Peter Port, the headquarters of the *GFP* in 1942. According to

Bailey, they first had to be signed out of the prison, indicating the existence of another prison logbook which no longer survives. Waiting for them there were two *GFP* men, named as 'Ogier' (probably Sergeant Major Oeser) and 'Wolff' (Wölfle), both of whom are listed in Captain Dening's records now in the Imperial War Museum,[5] and the latter of whom we know also operated in Jersey.

During questioning, Bailey testified that, when he denied knowledge of the robberies, Ogier/Oeser 'flew into a rage, striking me across the face and yelling: "English pig! You are a liar. We will make you talk very soon. Stand to attention. You are talking to a German officer."[6] Bailey was sent back to his cell to give him time to 'remember what he had done'. He was told that he would be given less food each day until he 'remembered the truth'.[7] Bailey was marched back to the prison, but 'already I knew what it meant to lose one's freedom. I was dirty, unshaven, and had not washed or undressed for two days. Several passers-by stared at me . . .'

Bailey's colleagues were each taken to Grange Lodge for questioning. Of his own interrogation, police Sergeant Jack Harper later wrote, in a compensation testimony of the mid-1960s, that:

> All of the officers detained were taken separately to Nazi head quarters and were questioned by 6 members of the Gestapo [i.e. *GFP*] and each officer was treated with the utmost brutality. I was the last officer to be interviewed and interrogated by the Gestapo and during this time I was knocked to the floor, kicked in the stomach by the Jackboot and my face was spit on and I was called a bloody liar by the Gestapo chief in broken English. They accused me of sabotage, and holding meetings with other officers in my home with a view of wrecking the efforts of Hitler's armies of the Peoples Third Reich; all of which I denied.[8]

Writing about his own interrogation immediately after the war, in an affidavit for war crimes investigators, police Sergeant Alfred Howlett stated that:

> On 10th March 1942 I was taken from the prison by car to the German Military Headquarters at Grange Lodge, and I was there interrogated by OESER,[9] who employed a member of the Gestapo named Wolff as an interpreter. On my again denying any knowledge of the stores, OESER struck me in the face with his fist, knocking me off my stool into a fireplace. I was then taken back to prison.

Grange Lodge today, headquarters of the GFP *in 1942.* (Copyright Susan Ilie)

Howlett then proceeded to write that when the *GFP* drove him to his house to make him confess where he had hidden foodstuffs, they kept him in the car while they dragged his wife across the yard and into the kitchen, while he watched helplessly from the car. He heard Oeser tell his wife to get ready to go to prison, and so he confessed and the foodstuffs he had hidden were retrieved. He was driven back to Grange Lodge, where Oeser accused him of breaking and entering a store four months previously. When he denied doing so, Oeser:

> Picked up a field-boot jack and pinned me by the neck with this against the wall. While I was in this position he struck me two or three times on the head. On releasing me he struck me again and I fell into the fireplace. During the assault my top dentures were broken. I was then returned to the prison.[10]

Police Constable Frederick Short later wrote in his compensation testimony that 'These interrogations would last all day from early morning until late at night without food or drink. I got beaten up, kicked and knocked unconscious several times during these interrogations which went on for several weeks . . .'[11] Guernsey historian William Bell later interviewed Short about the experience, which he summarised as 'a nightmare of pain and torture'.[12] Bell reproduced a number of interviews he had conducted with the policemen, and their memories of their period of interrogation and imprisonment included Frank Tuck, who stated that:

> During their interrogation the German Police beat me up with various objects, punched me and kicked me when I was lying on the floor. They lugged me up again and repeated the process. They then threw me into a bare cell and left me there for several days without being able to wash or shave and with only bread and water. When this process had been repeated on several occasions, they presented me with documents written in German which they told me were statements from my colleagues, implicating me. They then told me what was supposed to be in the documents. I disagreed and they invited me to sign under the threat of a repetition of the former treatment. A revolver was thrust into my ribs and I signed.[13]

It was not until ten days after his initial interrogation that Kingston Bailey was taken from the prison again. During this time he was not allowed to wash or shave, nor speak to any person, nor communicate with his relatives. His cell grew dirtier but he was not allowed to clean it. His straw mattress seemed to disintegrate into a sack half full of straw dust and half full of fleas. He chose instead to sleep, fully clothed, on the floor of his cell to avoid the fleas, and given only one worn and dirty blanket.[14]

One day, Frank Tuck returned to the prison. As his and Bailey's cells were adjacent, when the guard was at the other end of the passage, they were able to exchange a few words. They discovered that the *GFP* were trying a different tactic. Tuck was shown a signed confession alleged to have been made by one of the police involving him in the robberies. When he denied the allegation, he was beaten up.

At this point, the memoir of Frank Stroobant becomes relevant. Imprisoned for two nights, from 19 to 21 March 1942, and placed in a cell with one of the policemen, it seems that the other police had learned about the alleged signed confession, believed its veracity and were all blaming each other for implicating each other. 'As a result, for the rest of the day the prison resounded with threats and abuse shouted from cell to cell. By evening the noise had become so great that the German guards threatened to shoot the next man who made a sound.'[15]

Stroobant's memoir shows us that the *GFP* had succeeded in sewing discord and distrust among the policemen, turning them against each other. Bailey confirmed in his memoir that 'we were all slowly getting utterly confused . . . we could not tell what was truth and what was lies . . . Through lack of sleep, bad food, beatings, lies, and alleged self-made confessions, the Gestapo interpreters gained their object.'[16] Believing that his comrades had already confessed, Bailey admitted the charges against him. Once back in the prison, he was amazed to hear that his comrades had gone through the same charade, believing that Bailey had been the one to write a confession, and admitted their guilt. 'By this cross-questioning, and through continual brutality, the Gestapo obtained sufficient evidence to stage a first-class propaganda trial.[17]

A statement made by PC Bill Burton in 1947 shows the multiple avenues the *GFP* were trying in order to extract information about the men's activities. He wrote that, during his interrogation, an officer of the *GFP* offered to release him and send him back into the local police force if he agreed to keep them informed about resistance-related activities going on in the island. This, Burton refused to do. 'For that reply I received a blow in the mouth, whereby I lost five bottom teeth.' During another bout of interrogation, Burton was defiantly proud about having fought with British forces in the First World War. As he spoke, a lieutenant started striking him on the side of the head and he ended up on the floor. As he got to his feet, ready to fight, the men in the room drew their revolvers and pointed them at him; he was told that if he struck the man, it would be the last thing he would do. He was then 'bashed all over the room until I fell exhausted on the floor'.[18] He was then returned to the prison by car so that no members of the public could see his beaten face. A few days later he was taken back to Grange Lodge, where seven men were waiting for him. He was given a last chance to tell them what he knew. After repeating that he knew nothing, the seven men beat him up and told him to sign a confession, written in German. He had no choice but to sign.[19]

Bell also interviewed other policemen. William Quin was 'hit about, knocked about and threatened generally before I signed the statement'. Charles Friend was:

> Hit severely about the head and face and . . . spent a great deal of time on the floor . . . I was . . . threatened with revolvers and they stated that it would be easy for them to kill me accidentally. They also said that if I did not plead guilty and give them a full admission to these various charges, then they would fetch my mother and those nearest and dearest to me and torture them as well.

Frank Whare was hit on the face, spat in the face, knocked to the ground and, with his arms held back by Germans, 'kicked in the back, abdomen and thighs until I began to vomit'. Jack Harper was 'brutally bashed about and almost lost my senses'. Fred Short was taken to a house next to Grange Lodge, where they 'battered the hell out of me. They ripped my uniform, kicked me in the face, splitting my lip and smashing my false teeth.' He was beaten with a rifle butt, grabbed by the hair and his head smashed against the wall. He was also beaten up in his cell. 'Three times a German stuck a revolver against my side and threatened to press the trigger accidentally if I didn't say "yes" to something they wanted me to admit. In the end, like everyone else, I confessed . . .' The statements of brutality recorded by Bell concluded with a testimony by Archibald Tardif, who was 'punched, kicked, hit with a wooden ruler . . . stretched over a stool and my head bashed against a wall'. He was told to sign the typed confession or he would be shot.[20] All of these statements stand in strong contrast to the accounts of men like John Hayes and Frank Falla, and if it was not for the existence of both sets of records then a very unbalanced and incorrect impression of the regime of Occupation in the Channel Islands emerges.

After the *GFP* had assembled their 'intelligence', the policemen were moved, on 26 March 1942, to a military prison at Fort George, an old military barracks which today is an exclusive estate of large houses for the wealthy. Before the Occupation it was used by British troops, and when the policemen arrived they found that a building had been specially prepared for their arrival. This was the beginning of what Bailey called 'really excellent propaganda'.[21] The men were put two into each room, and each given their own clean bed with several blankets each and a new, clean straw mattress. The windows of each room were unbarred. They were allowed to receive cigarettes, letters, food and parcels from friends and family, and told that visitors would be allowed after the trial. Responsibility of feeding them was left to friends and prison staff.[22] Bailey recorded that:

> The chief of the German police even had the audacity to visit us, asking if we were quite comfortable; and this so soon after the long weeks of brutality, from which some of us still bore the marks inflicted by this same person. I hated him . . . he was only about twenty-eight years of age, and had struck one of my comrades across the mouth with a wooden shoe-tree, breaking his false teeth.[23]

The men were kept in Fort George for four weeks and, thanks to the food provided by their own families, some of which was food that the police had taken from German stores, they were able to rebuild their strength, recover from injuries and regain the weight they had lost. This meant that the men looked fit and well for what was to be their show trial, with all that this implied to the public about their

*The entrance to
Fort George today.*
(Copyright Gilly Carr)

treatment in custody. One might observe that none of the men's physical injuries were permanent. Despite the severe beatings and ill-treatment, it seems likely that those who administered the blows knew what they were doing and how far they could go. No claims of broken bones, internal injuries or fractured skulls emerged. The *GFP* men achieved their aims while having fit and well men to put on public trial – all it seems, except Herbert Smith, who was on the verge of a nervous breakdown after his treatment at their hands. Frank Tuck later recalled that Smith 'lost his head . . . Somebody took a knife away from him at Fort George. He tried to cut his wrists . . .'[24] As Smith was the one policeman not to survive his punishment of hard labour in German camps, we might be correct in wondering whether his treatment in Guernsey was enough to lower his mental and physical reserves to the point that he was weakened to a greater degree than the other men before he even left the island.

On 24 April 1942, the policemen were taken to the police court, where a 'large crowd' had gathered outside, calling out supportive comments to the men.

They were taken to a small side room (to what is today the Magistrate's Court) rather than the main court room, and noticed that a swastika flag had covered the British coat of arms and was hanging behind the presiding judge's seat. Ralph Durand tells us that the judge and his two assessors gave the Nazi salute as they took their seats.[25] Members of the public were allowed into the gallery[26] 'to see the fairness of German justice; to see also the healthy condition of the prisoners after four months[27] of German imprisonment'.[28] The trial was described by Bailey as a 'farce':

> Everybody, prisoners and public alike, were astounded by the sentences imposed, which ranged from eighteen months to four and a half years. So we left the court-house and, for the first time, and indeed the last, we were sentenced in a British court, decked out with a Nazi flag, in the name of the German people . . . What fun, they must have thought, to cover the British Crown with a Nazi flag and humiliate these English dogs in their own justice court.[29]

Most of the men were given sentences of several years' hard labour; Harper, Smith and Quin were given four years or more. Former Attorney-General, Ambrose Sherwill, who represented the men at the trial, later commented that he visited the men alone, before their trial. He saw that 'A number of them had been beaten up to secure admissions of guilt but it was clear that, however much I deplored the method of obtaining such admissions, those admissions were in accordance with the truth.'[30] Such a statement seems shocking today in the light of the way the policemen were treated, and indicates Sherwill's lack of sympathy for these men.

But this was not the end of their court appearances. They were kept at Fort George between their Nazi trial, which lasted from 22 to 24 April 1942, and that at the Royal Court, at the hands of the Guernsey authorities, on 1 June 1942. During this period, more statements were collected from the men by the local authorities and advocates in readiness for the second trial. It appears that the men were returned to the prison after their second trial as the prison logbook of admissions states that the men were removed from the prison on 13 June 1942, when they were deported.[31]

This second trial was to make the men answer charges of breaking into civilian stores in addition to German stores. Bailey informed us that 'the evidence was German and we were informed that, if we denied the evidence, the Germans would take over the trial and we were liable to be shot for sabotage . . . On the day of the trial, the court was full of German police in case anything went wrong.'[32]

Although the policemen felt, so Bailey tells us, that the Royal Court should have refused to take the trial, it went ahead. They were advised to plead guilty as it was clear that the local authorities were scared of the Germans. The policemen knew that the evidence had been faked by Sergeant Major Oeser, who had forced the men to sign confessions, but there was little they could do. They were sentenced by the Bailiff, Victor Carey, whose address to the men at the end of the trial is worth repeating in detail:

> As Police officers . . . you must realise that you have brought shame and humiliation on every single soul in the Island from the Royal Court downwards . . . Clothed in the uniform of the Police, you were given certain privileges by the German Army of occupation in being allowed out after curfew. No one else was allowed out after curfew, you alone, and what have you done clothed in the uniform? You have broken into our own property, you have stolen and carried on with the most terrible way and you deserve everything that you can possibly get and you will be looked upon with contempt by the whole of your fellow Islanders. I can assure you that I am filled with shame that such a thing should have occurred in this Island of Guernsey. I have nothing further to say except to say how much I regret having to speak to you all in this way.[33]

Such words strike us today as offensive given what we know about the men's treatment after arrest and their fate after deportation. Perhaps Carey's choice of words was indicative of how well the Nazi propaganda had worked. The police were taken back to Fort George and, on 13 June 1942, were assembled and told that they would be shot if they tried to escape. They were then handcuffed in pairs before being marched through the High Street, at the height of its shopping hours, in order to publicly humiliate the men, en route to the harbour for their deportation to France.[34]

After spending a month in Caen prison, most of the men were moved to Fort de Villeneuve-Saint-Georges prison on the outskirts of Paris, after which they were divided up. Many were sent to a series of Nazi prisons and forced labour camps in Germany thereafter. Kingston Bailey was sent to Dachau concentration camp; six of the men experienced Bernau forced labour camp, where they dug a canal; four went to Neuoffingen forced labour camp, where they were forced, with other prisoners, to build a railway. All of them were severely ill-treated and starved to a far greater degree than they had experienced in Guernsey; they were also targeted for ill-treatment by guards for being British, and were in a minority wherever they went. All, however, managed to survive, except Herbert Smith, who was murdered by a camp guard at Augsburg prison.

When the surviving men limped back to Guernsey after the war, they were not reinstated in their old jobs and they were denied their pensions. Many of them left Guernsey to start afresh elsewhere. Nearly all of them suffered with Post-Traumatic Stress Disorder (PTSD) and the legacies of their time in Nazi camps, such as tuberculosis and other long-term physical injuries. Although a number received compensation as victims of Nazi persecution in the mid-1960s as part of the Anglo-German Agreement of 1964, their conviction by the Royal Court of Guernsey was never overturned, despite several attempts. That conviction – and a good deal of the Nazi propaganda which aimed to destroy the men's reputations – remains in force today.[35]

Chapter 17

Conclusion: A Comparison of the Prisons in the Channel Islands with the Nazi-Controlled Prisons in Europe

Quite how representative Guernsey and Jersey prisons were of other prisons in German-occupied territory is difficult to say given the hundreds if not thousands of places of incarceration across occupied Europe and the degree to which they differed from each other and changed in severity over time. The islands' prisons were probably similar in some respects to prisons in occupied Western Europe. Accounts from islanders who spent time in the Normandy prisons of Caen or St-Lô suggest they were treated better than those in, say, the Parisian prisons of Villeneuve-Saint-Georges, Fresnes or Romainville, which were often stepping stones to concentration camps. Conditions in Fort d'Hauteville in Dijon and Haut-Clos Prison in Troyes, which housed 41 and 19 islanders respectively, were notable for their verminous and foetid living conditions, and food that was poor in quality and quantity.

There are at least six key elements which dictated the experience for prisoners: the quality and quantity of food; the comfort of their cell (or lack of it); prison architecture; treatment at the hands of the guards; the arduousness and conditions of forced labour; and the behaviour of the prisoners towards each other. These elements could vary for a prisoner depending on their offence and their behaviour while incarcerated; both of these could influence where in the prison they were placed, how they were treated and what food they were given. Even the personality and disposition of the prisoner could influence how they coped with imprisonment. Therefore, there is no easy way of ranking Guernsey and Jersey prisons within the range of others in Europe under the control of German forces.

Food is always an important yardstick when comparing prisons. If the friends and family of a prisoner lived near the prison, they were often able to take food to the prison for the prisoner's consumption. If a prisoner was deported abroad, as many Channel Islanders were, they would have little opportunity to receive food parcels. Food rations in prisons in one occupied zone varied from those in another. Different prisons in different zones also had different regulations about what prisoners should be fed. When in Guernsey Prison towards the end of 1940, when conditions might still be considered fairly good, Henry Marquand was fed a great deal better than in Cherche-Midi in Paris, and consequently lost much weight while in France.

Prison architecture certainly had an impact on the prisoner experience. The survey carried out of Guernsey Prison in 2003 concluded that the old prison building was 'probably unique in the British Isles as a small, urban, multipurpose prison that had survived into the twenty-first century. Similar small prisons were common in England around 1800, but by the end of the nineteenth century they had all been closed and demolished in the UK.'[1] Although no similar survey was carried out of Jersey Prison before its demolition, we know that its original buildings, too, survived until their destruction in the 1970s. The impact of living in old buildings which were badly equipped for basic provisions such as light, heat, washing and toilet facilities took its toll on prisoners in the Channel Islands just as it did for those held in old fortresses and prisons on the continent. As we have seen, Guernsey and Jersey prisons were cold and unforgiving Victorian structures, with condemned cells brought back into use in Jersey during the Occupation. Guernsey's underground cells provided a dark and depressing atmosphere for those imprisoned within them. These were only tasters of what awaited those unfortunate enough to be deported.

Jersey and Guernsey prisons were sub-divided into blocks or areas controlled by the German military and by local warders. As Jersey and Guernsey had only one prison each (although other buildings were used for other kinds of prisoners), this sub-division was deemed necessary in order to separate the 'ordinary criminals' and the political prisoners. This was important because political prisoners were considered dangerous, and their resistant behaviours and mentalities might have spread to other prisoners. The Germans also wanted to be able to control, separate and watch their prisoners; they needed the freedom to enter the prison at any time of day or night and to treat prisoners as they wished, beyond the eyes of those who might have reported their activities to the outside world. The majority of the ill-treatment and beatings were carried out, however, in the headquarters of *GFP*, where the cries of prisoners could not be heard by others. Similar sub-divisions are likely to have taken place within continental prisons, and deported Channel Islanders often referred to their guards in terms of nationality rather than their status (such as Gestapo, etc.), with the implication that we cannot always know quite who guarded prisoners and what the likely regime would have been.

The case studies of ill-treatment of prisoners in the Channel Islands show very clearly how the type of offence dictated how prisoners were treated by German guards. The length of the resulting prison sentence also dictated whether a prisoner was deported. The resistance-related offences carried out in the Channel Islands were predominantly non-violent, and although young men were caught with weapons in Jersey and sentenced harshly, they never used their firearms, nor carried out acts of military sabotage, nor killed any occupying soldiers, unlike their French counterparts. The lack of these most serious of offences alone is also likely to have had an impact on the treatment of prisoners in the Channel Islands. This is not to say, however, that islanders who committed non-violent offences such as attempting to escape from the island with information about gun emplacements, or systematic theft of food from the occupiers or spreading the BBC news were not treated with violence and deportation after their arrest in the Channel Islands.[2]

The greatest difference between the prisoner experience in the Channel Islands and on the continent would have been the treatment of the prisoners by their guards. This is likely to have been dictated by factors such as the behaviour, offences and nationality of the prisoners, and the personalities of the individual German guards. The nature of the military occupation in that territory and the instructions given to the occupiers about how to treat occupied peoples would also have played a role.

In order to learn about the regime in continental prisons in more detail, it is useful to hear from Channel Islanders who were incarcerated in such places. Kingston Bailey was in Caen Prison, the institution geographically closest to the Channel Islands' prisons. He described the cell in which he was held in 1942 as follows:

> The room was a large, stone, dirty, whitewashed affair with three wooden tables and forms. The prisoners could, if they wished, walk in the court-yard adjoining the room. There was one lavatory and a long galvanised bin for washing . . . the cubicles and bed frame were full of bugs which were, indeed, as hungry as ourselves. Sleep was practically impossible and many of the prisoners were covered from head to foot with lumps, caused by bites . . . The food was terrible, consisting mainly of cabbage soup, with about three- quarters of a pound of bread each day. For those who had

money in the canteen fund, there were dishes of cabbage and sour milk for sale. Many of the prisoners suffered from a mild form of dysentery, probably caused by too much cabbage water.[3]

Imprisoned in 1941, Channel Islander Eugene Le Lievre gave this description of Fort d'Hauteville Prison in Dijon:

> We were herded into large underground barrack rooms with 80 other men already imprisoned there. There was no lighting, no beds & no bedding. We just all huddled together on the floor, which was a concrete one. Many of our inmates were Jews & many of them had very little clothing or footwear. The food and conditions were of the worst possible order. What little water available had to be brought in by watercart, & with no washing facilities we were even more verminous than at Caen. Bugs were cooked in the soup we received once daily. This was fought for, as was the bread ration thrown through a hole in the door at 11am daily, the weaker having to put up with the smaller portion. I did on one occasion count 55 flies in a cellmate's soup, which he was most reluctant to remove, as this left him with a considerable waste & he was, as we all, most ravenous. Most of us could not walk as we were so weak, and at no time did we receive any Red + [Cross] parcels.[4]

Frederick Short was held in Fort de Villeneuve-Saint-Georges in Paris in 1942. His living conditions were atrocious:

> Conditions and treatment were deplorable for the 400 prisoners (approx.) which included French, Belgian, Italians etc., many of which were of Jewish religion, awaiting transport to Germany. We slept 50 to a room on beds of straw. Vermin was at its height (lice, bugs, fleas) and the sanitation and washing facilities were practically nil. A galvanised dustbin with a wooden plank for use as a W.C. was issued to each room for sanitation purposes and was emptied twice daily (morning and night) so the smell in the room as you can imagine was terrible. Washing facilities consisted of four small taps running out of a wall where one had to cup one's hands in order to gather enough water to swill your face. No baths or showers, so being impossible to wash one's body. Razors were forbidden, there being no facilities whatsoever for haircutting and shaving so you can imagine what a sorry mess we all looked . . . Food consisted of a semi starvation diet, two small cups of watery soup daily with two slices of dry bread and one thin slice of meat or cheese fortnightly and finally for good measure

the Nazi guards would raid and search the rooms on an average twice weekly (day or night) and each of us in turn would get a beating up by getting struck with their rifles and kicked.[5]

These three examples show that even in the earlier stages of the war, prisons in occupied France were even worse than those in the Channel Islands, although it is unclear whether the same could also have been said of these institutions before the war. We cannot realistically generalise about French prisons any more than we can about prisons elsewhere, although prisoners in Germany were used for forced labour, which made their experience much harsher than for those held in France. Although prisoners of the Germans in Guernsey carried out forced labour, they were not ill-treated, starved or abused as part of the experience.

Writing later about his experiences in Bernau Prison and forced labour camp, Guernseyman Thomas Gaudion stated that:

> Prisoners worked in groups of approx. 50 or 60, although Bailey was in the same building, we were in a different group at work, working on the ground in summer and making canals in winter. The guard in my group had a vicious dog, and besides beating the prisoners with his fists, boots and rifle butt, would set the dog on them. I suffered many of these atrocities. Being scantily clad (pants, jacket, shirt, boots, and rags for our feet), we suffered terribly with the cold. When winter came, snow was on the ground from Nov. to April, freezing hard every night. We were taken to work in the fields in all weathers with no extra clothing. Many times one was soaked through even before arriving on the work, but it made no difference, one had to carry on irrespective of the conditions. Clothing got soaked and dried on one's back, sometimes frozen stiff. Many times I have been to the prison soaked through, after work in the fields. Arrived in our rooms, one had to undress, and wrap up in the only blanket to try and get warm. There was no heat in the rooms, the only heat was the pint of hot water with perhaps a cabbage leaf, or a few grains of corn in a bowl before going to bed. One had to get into bed immediately after drinking what was called soup, otherwise one couldn't sleep at all with the cold. Next morning one had to be up at six o'clock and dressed in soaking wet clothes as there was no means of drying. In consequence of beatings, bad food, and conditions, many prisoners died. I was reduced to skin and bones, and so weak that I couldn't get up when I fell down. I had to be assisted by my prison comrades, some who I am very sorry to say collapsed later and died.[6]

At Frankfurt Preungesheim Prison, where prisoners were used for clearing bomb rubble and were also executed by guillotine, Frank Falla later wrote that:

> It was here, too, that I had my initial introduction into what was to become commonplace: the beating-up of prisoners, especially when they became too noisy; and the noisiest were the French. After coming into their cells for the night from working-parties they would try to talk to their compatriots by shouting out of their shuttered windows . . . The warders went from cell door to cell door trying to catch them in the act and when they did three or four of them would go into the cell and beat hell out of the hapless victims until their yells echoed through the whole prison.[7]

Norman Dexter's experience of Frankfurt was no less complimentary of the German prison system:

> In Frankfurt I was in a prison for political offenders against the Reich, manned by soldiers, some partially disabled, and all under the supervision of the Gestapo. I had to work for 11 hours a day and most of the time was spent in solitary confinement in my own cell where we were forced to stay during air-raids which were very frequent. The prison officers and staff had air-raid shelters in the yards, exclusively for themselves. Food, which was gradually reduced, consisted of a small round of bread morning and evening and a not very large dish of soup at midday. Frequently, Summer or Winter, we were made to stand completely nude in our cells while and clothes and cells were searched by prison chiefs. I witnessed the carrying from cells of several prisoners who could endure it no more and had committed suicide.[8]

These selected testimonies from French and German prisons lead us to the conclusion that Channel Islanders were in a much better position in their Island prisons. This position is further cemented by a document, now residing in the Imperial War Museum, which gives us an insight into the instructions for the treatment of prisoners in the Channel Islands by their occupiers. Among the papers of intelligence officer Captain Dening of Force 135, about whose documents we have already heard, is a brief typed history of the *GFP* in the Channel Islands. Within this document is a quote from a certain General Viebahn, who came to the Island to receive a report on the work of the *GFP* in November 1941. Viebahn is quoted as saying that 'It is the Fuhrer's express wish to deal with the Channel Islands population with the utmost tact and leniency and a distinct differentiation should be observed in regard to people of Northern France and Channel Islands'.[9]

This document constitutes the only evidence that the occupiers were ordered to treat the Channel Islanders more leniently than their closest occupied neighbours. We can only speculate whether Viebahn was giving an accurate representation of the Fuhrer's wishes, and whether these orders were obeyed to the letter, but we have no reason to disbelieve the statement itself. Those reading this book will form their own opinion about the severity or otherwise of treatment of prisoners in the Channel Islands, most especially during interrogation. The treatment of prisoners such as Peter Hassall, Frank Keiller and Joe Mière in Jersey, and that of the Guernsey police in the sister island, make it clear that not all Channel Islanders were treated with the 'utmost tact and leniency', although this might well have been a relative statement.

None of the Channel Islanders suffered permanent physical damage from their beatings carried out in the islands, even if the mental trauma stayed with them. The beatings of prisoners and psychological torture was of the sort that did not leave a permanent visible trace, which was not always the case in continental prisons. Neither was any Channel Islander shot by firing squad within the islands. These facts would seem to back up the reported instructions verbalised by Viebahn, even if they did not prevent the far worse ill-treatment that awaited islanders who were deported to the continent, as reported in the compensation claims of victims of Nazi persecution of the mid-1960s from which several of the quotes above were taken.

Our fundamental problem remains the lack of extant material. The record is rife with missing German documents and logbooks and a lack of diaries and memoirs, most especially from Guernsey. We cannot know whether the extent or range of both good and ill-treatment of prisoners is fully accounted for in the handful of Occupation memoirs which survive. We also do not know whether 'tact and leniency' were fully defined for the *GFP* or whether these were relative terms and able to be interpreted as the individual officer desired. What we can say is that not everyone was as fortunate to be treated as well as John Hayes, who tellingly observed that, for him, 'the Germans' lackadaisical attitude in so much of prison life could well have been deliberate policy'.[10]

What we do know is that islanders were very keen, and wisely so, to spend their prison sentences locally rather than being deported to the continent. While some prisoners were deported if their sentence was longer than three months, a sentence of six months or more virtually guaranteed deportation to a continental prison. Hayes' memoir is again of use here: he remarked that the Germans themselves said that 'my being allowed to serve my sentence in the Island was a special favour, implying that they knew prison life would be harder elsewhere'.[11] Indeed, it was for almost all islanders who had anything other than a very short sojourn in a prison in France before being returned to the islands. Those deported later in the war were at risk of being moved from prison to prison across Europe, sometimes ending up in a labour or concentration camp.

Paul Sanders has questioned whether the regime in the Channel Islands really amounted to the kind of 'model occupation' after which Guernsey's authorities, in particular, strived from the earliest days of the Occupation. He argues that, compared with France, the 'differential treatment of islanders on issues such as the death penalty could not have been the product of coincidence, or a result of the lack of armed resistance'.[12] In France, 200 death sentences were executed by January 1942 for offences similarly 'trivial' to those committed in the Channel Islands, which illustrates his point. However, he argues that there was no 'velvet glove policy' in the Channel Islands; the German stance was more 'carrot and stick', as those whose experiences are recounted in this book testify.

We cannot help but conclude that the better experience for prisoners in the Channel Islands (while a relative observation), was indeed not, as Sanders argues, 'coincidence'. It seems clear that the *GFP* took their instructions seriously and obeyed them, but interpreted them in their own way. Channel Islanders were indeed harshly and sometimes violently interrogated by the *GFP*. They were imprisoned in old, dark cells and given poor rations in both islands. In Guernsey they were compelled to carry out forced labour to 'occupy their time'. But this experience, for many, proved to be a gentle introduction to life in continental prisons, where prisoner neglect, semi-starvation and general violence was the very best for which they could hope. The reality was often a great deal worse, and led to the death of twenty-eight Channel Islanders.

Postscript: The 1946 Hilton Report

We associate the name Hilton with the most luxurious of hotels, and so it is ironic to note that a Mr N.R. Hilton, Senior Assistant Commissioner of Prisons, was sent to the Channel Islands in April 1946 to write a report on the 'Gloucester Hotel' and the 'St James Hotel', as the prisoners nicknamed Jersey and Guernsey prisons. These dirty and decrepit Victorian buildings were not, however, about to be invited to join the Hilton chain.

Mr Hilton's remit was to 'discuss and advise on the prison rules and administration' of the two prisons with the aim of writing a report to enable the islands' authorities to 'bring them into line with more modern prison standards'. His tour of both prisons paints a vivid picture, very much in line with prisoners' Occupation memoirs.

The cells in Jersey Prison, he wrote, were:

> Large, ventilated by a window high up in the wall, the inside walls of cells are rough hewn granite, lime-washed from floor to ceiling. In the old or 'debtors' block, the lighting is poor. The furniture consists of a table fixed to a wall, drinking mug, tin or aluminium plate and a chair. The door to each cell is of enormous thickness, studded with large-headed bolts or nails and secured from outside by a heavy lock and two bolts the width of the door. Both these bolts are shot and the heavy door locked for the safe custody of the prisoner . . . The prison and cells were spotlessly clean, nevertheless the prison had a most depressing atmosphere. The men, individually, were dull, uninterested and gave the impression of being extremely depressed, no doubt partly the result of their long daily period of confinement to cell and lack of any mental occupation.[1]

In Guernsey Prison, the situation was not very different. The lack of toilets in cells meant that a 'small tin pail is used instead; these are emptied into an adjacent

WC by the men in the morning; there is no water tap to rinse these small pails and they soon become dirty and objectionable'.[2] Frank Falla, whose eyes were no doubt still smarting at the memory of the pails during his wartime incarceration, would have agreed with this observation.

Hilton also found that the furniture and amenities in the cells for prisoners was poor and inadequate. There were no mirrors, hairbrushes or combs, prisoners shaved just twice a week and their uniform was in a bad state and supplemented by their own clothes from home. Their only industry was making fruit and vegetable packing boxes in Guernsey, and two of the prisoners had scabies. Presumably the wartime outbreak had not yet been eliminated. There was also no prison laundry and no provision for education. One prisoner could not read or write. There was no provision for exercise for convicted prisoners. Hilton also noticed a lack of prisoner association: in both prisons, prisoners ate alone and passed the time in their cells. In this respect, at least, prisoners were better off during the Occupation, when they were allowed daily exercise. Shared cells had at least meant that they received some stimulation and company while incarcerated.

Hilton was not impressed by what he saw in the Channel Islands. He believed that the prison buildings were 'ill-suited for the detention of prisoners under present day standards' and expressed doubts whether 'new methods and conditions can be introduced in the present buildings'. He recommended that the rough-hewn granite walls be plastered, decorated and painted, and that more furniture brought into the cells; that prisoners be provided with toiletries; that they be allowed exercise, outdoor games, association with each other and education.

As for employment – or what, during the Occupation, might have been called 'forced labour' – prisoners in Jersey carried out stone-breaking in the prison yard, just as they had before the war. 'This is unprofitable work', wrote Hilton, 'and not far removed from the monotony of the tread wheel'. The poor conditions also adversely affected the staff. As no prisoner training of any kind took place in the prison, the staff were 'more or less . . . mere turnkeys'.

It is worth reminding ourselves of the words of Eric Pleasants, who we might recall was a former inmate of Jersey Prison and various Nazi prisons on the continent, as well as a Russian Gulag. He wrote in his memoirs that 'conditions in Gloucester Street Prison were among the worst I have experienced, not merely from a physical point of view – the mediaeval cells, the meagre and disgusting food – but also because of the attitude of the warders in general'.[3] We might have been inclined earlier to take Pleasants' words with a pinch of salt; having volunteered to join the SS, he hardly endears himself to us as a reliable witness. It seems, however, that Mr Hilton might have agreed with Pleasants' assessment, even though he had only English prisons with which to compare those in the Channel Islands.

A memorandum in the file notes, probably written by Hilton, states that, 'having seen these prisons, I am sure the only thing to do is to blow them up or at any rate to discontinue their use. I should like to have a modern joint prison for Jersey and Guernsey but I think the numbers may be too few for this purpose – to say nothing of inter-insular jealousy.' After all, which Channel Island would host the new prison? As is often the case, it was the informal private notes rather than the formal reports that reveal the true assessment of the situation. An anonymous note in the file written by a Home Office official documented the private opinion that 'only radical remedies will cure what is evidently an intolerable situation'.

The Secretary of State responded to the Hilton report by recommending that:

> All convicted prisoners with sentences of three months or over should be sent to serve their sentences in England, as are already persons sentenced in the Islands to Penal Servitude and Borstal Detention. It is abundantly clear not only that the prison system in the Islands is not such as should be tolerated today in any part of His Majesty's dominions, but that there is no prospect that it could be made tolerable without great and unjustifiable expense and after a considerable lapse of time, and even so it would be no more than tolerable.' The existing buildings, it was stated, 'ought not to be retained for any purpose a day longer than is strictly necessary.[4]

This advice was not followed; Jersey's prison was used until the mid-1970s, and Guernsey's last prisoner left the old prison in 1989.

A Resistance Memorial was unveiled by the harbour in Guernsey in 2015, naming eight prisoners who passed through Guernsey Prison but who did not survive their career behind bars after deportation. Unlike in Jersey, the site of Guernsey Prison itself has no plaque today to commemorate its wartime function. Only a weed-covered parking lot marks the spot where once prisoners exercised during the German Occupation.

The remains of the exercise yard of the former prison today. (Copyright: Gilly Carr)

Notes

Prologue

1. P. Sanders (2018 (3rd edn)), *The Ultimate Sacrifice* (Jersey: Jersey Heritage Trust and Holocaust Memorial Day Committee), 5–6.
2. Ibid., 6.
3. Testimony written by Eileen Tierney inside her claim for compensation written on behalf of her husband; The National Archives, ref. FO 950/1254.
4. Letter from Albert Koch to Eileen Tierney, sent by the British Red Cross, 14 August 1947, in private ownership.
5. Czech National Archive, collection KT OVS, board/card 163; newspaper article, 28 June 1945, *Lidová demokracie*, I/42, 28 June 1945.

Chapter 1

1. For example, P. Gray, 'Island of Beauty, Island of Secrets', manuscript in private ownership; L. Harris (2004 [2000]), *A Boy Remembers* (Jersey: Channel Island Publishing [Apache]); Harris (2002), *A Boy Remembers More* (Jersey: Apache Guides Ltd); F. Keiller (2000), *Prison Without Bars* (Bradford on Avon: Seaflower Books Ltd); K. Le Cocq (2011), *My Favourite Occupation* (Jersey: Channel Island Publishing); F. Le Sueur (1990), *Shadow of the Swastika* (Jersey: Starlight Imports); J. Mière (2004), *Never to be Forgotten* (Jersey: Channel Island Publishing); R. Wiethley (2007 [2001]), *So It Was* (Jersey: Channel Island Publishing).
2. Letter from Francis Harris to author, 6 September 2010, emphasised that 'we all saw ourselves as patriots and we were proud that we had "done something"'.
3. E. Pleasants (2003), *Hitler's Bastard* (Edinburgh and London: Mainstream Publishing).
4. E. Chapman (1966), *The Real Eddie Chapman Story: I Lived to Kill* (London: Tandem Books Ltd).
5. A. Faramus (1990), *Journey into Darkness* (London: Grafton Books).
6. *Nacht und Nebel*, or 'Night and Fog' (NN), prisoners were part of a secret hostage programme devised by the Nazis as a means of controlling potential resistance in occupied territory.
7. P. Hassall, 'Night and Fog Prisoners', https://www.frankfallaarchive.org/wp-content/uploads/2016/08/Peter-Hassalls-memoirs.pdf.
8. L. Sinel (1945), *The German Occupation of Jersey, 1940–1945* (Jersey: Jersey Evening Post).
9. The author has found no living female political prisoners although, at the time of writing (May 2018), Mary Bird from Guernsey is still alive. She was deported to Cherche-Midi Prison in Paris for her role in sheltering commandos in 1940. However, although her memory of that period is now failing, it would not be correct to class her as somebody who perceived themselves as a political prisoner.

188   Nazi Prisons in the British Isles

10. The Bailiffs of Guernsey and Jersey preside over the Royal Courts in their respective Bailiwicks; they are the heads of their islands as regards to legal and civic matters. During the Occupation, the Bailiff of Guernsey was Victor Carey and the Bailiff of Jersey was Alexander Coutanche.
11. Jersey Archives, ref. D/AG/B1/4.
12. D/AG/B7/7.
13. Estimate made by Linda Romeril, Director of Jersey Archive, to author.
14. Dr P.G. Bentlif (n.d.), 'Newgate Street Prison', Unpublished memoirs, copy on file.

Chapter 2

1. Faramus, *Journey Into Darkness*, p. 36.
2. The Viscount is the chief executive officer of the Royal Court of Jersey. Their principal function is the execution of the orders of the island's courts.
3. This information was given in 1936 by Captain H. Le Seelleur, Governor of the prison at that time, to Clarence John Piquet. Unpublished manuscript, states of Jersey Library Service, ref. J365.
4. 'Seen for the first time behind Jersey's prison walls', *Jersey Evening Post*, 7 March 1964, pp. 1, 6 and 7.
5. Jersey Archives, ref. B/A/W40/8/30, letters between *Feldkommandant* Knackfuss and the Bailiff, 7 November 1941 and 19 March 1942.
6. Chapman, *The Real Eddie Chapman Story*, p. 48.
7. Joe Mière collection, in the possession of Michael Mière; a letter from Francis Harris to the author of 27 April 2013 notes that the civilian prisoners wore a white canvas jacket and trousers covered in arrows, and that they tended the prison vegetable garden.
8. War army prison facility.
9. Garrison prison facility.
10. Letter from Lucy Schwob to J.H. L'Amy, J.H. L'Amy, 'The German Occupation of Jersey', Société Jersiaise Lord Coutanche Library, *OCC 942, pp. 13–15.
11. Claude Cahun, 'Lettre à Paul Levy' (1950, 2002), pp. 709–57, in *Claude Cahun Écrits*, ed. François Leperlier (Paris: Jean-Michel Place), trans. Alex Stuart, p. 743; Keiller, *Prison Without Bars*, p. 125.
12. Letter from Lucy Schwob to J.H. L'Amy, L'Amy, 'The German Occupation of Jersey', p. 16.
13. Keiller, *Prison Without Bars*, p. 144
14. Mière, *Never to be Forgotten*, p. 228.
15. Interview with Mickey Neil, 14 August 2010.
16. Diary of George Le Marquand, entry for 20 December 1944 and 7 February 1945, unpublished diary, in private ownership.
17. Faramus, *Journey into Darkness*, p. 36.
18. Chapman, *The Real Eddie Chapman Story*, p. 35.
19. Faramus, *Journey into Darkness*, p. 38.
20. Different prisoners give different dimensions.
21. C. Cahun, Unpublished papers, Jersey Archives, ref. JHT/1995/00045/1, p. 37, account written by Claude Cahun about her time in prison.
22. Weithley, *So It Was*, p. 118; Keiller, *Prison Without Bars*, p. 124; Gray, 'Island of Beauty, Island of Secrets', p. 21.

23. Letter from Lucy Schwob to J.H. L'Amy quoted in L'Amy, 'The German Occupation of Jersey', p. 14.
24. Miére, *Never to be Forgotten*, p. 228.
25. G. Haas (1997), *Against All Odds* (New York: Sherpa Publishing), p. 44.
26. Weithley, *So It Was*, p. 132.
27. A.A. Chardine, 'Reminiscences', Société Jersiaise Lord Coutanche Library *OCC 942 CHA, p. 15.
28. Le Cocq, *My Favourite Occupation*, p. 93; Keiller, *Prison Without Bars*, p. 140; 'Seen for the first time behind Jersey's prison walls', *Jersey Evening Post*, 7 March 1964, pp. 1, 6 and 7.
29. Keiller, *Prison Without Bars*, p. 140.
30. E. Le Quesne (1999), *The Occupation of Jersey Day by Day* (Jersey: La Haule Books Ltd), entry for 9 October 1944.
31. Pleasants, *Hitler's Bastard*, p. 46.
32. Such shootings of Channel Islanders in the prison did not take place; however, the Germans were known to execute their own soldiers, although this did not take place regularly. It has been suggested that only five such executions took place; R. Le Tissier (2010), 'Newgate Street Prison – 1944–1945', *Newgate Club Gazette*, 1 (issue 2), p. 10. This statistic has not been confirmed.
33. Testimony of Stanley Coombs, 10 September 1964, The National Archives, ref. FO 950/1180.
34. Letter from Dora Hacquoil to her mother dated 20 May 1945. My thanks to Pauline Hacquoil for allowing me to quote from this letter.
35. W. Janvrin-Tipping (2015), *Any Day Now* (London: Austin Macauley Publishers Ltd), p. 117.
36. Le Quesne, *The Occupation of Jersey Day by Day*, entry for 20 October 1944.
37. Keiller, *Prison Without Bars*, p. 125.
38. Janvrin-Tipping, *Any Day Now*, p. 116.
39. Keiller, *Prison Without Bars*, p. 125.
40. Le Quesne, *The Occupation of Jersey Day by Day*, entry for 9 and 10 October 1944.
41. Le Cocq, *My Favourite Occupation*, p. 94; Weithley, *So It Was*, p. 119.
42. Le Cocq, *My Favourite Occupation*, p. 93.
43. Le Quesne, *The Occupation of Jersey Day by Day*, entry for 19 October 1944.
44. Letter from Lucy Schwob to J.H. L'Amy, quoted in L'Amy, 'The German Occupation of Jersey', p. 14.
45. Cahun, Jersey Archives, ref. JHT/1995/00045/2, p. 15, partial translation of account written by Claude Cahun.
46. Le Quesne, *The Occupation of Jersey Day by Day*, entry for 15 October 1944.
47. Ibid., entry for 10 October 1944; map drawn for author by Francis Harris, 27 April 2013.
48. Le Cocq, *My Favourite Occupation*, p. 94.
49. Weithley, *So It Was*, p. 125.
50. Haas, *Against All Odds*, p. 45.
51. Le Cocq, *My Favourite Occupation*, p. 95.
52. Keiller, *Prison Without Bars*, p. 143; Weithley, *So It Was*, p. 132; letter from Lucy Schwob to J.H. L'Amy, L'Amy, 'The German Occupation of Jersey', p. 15.
53. Le Quesne, *The Occupation of Jersey Day by Day*, entry for 9 October 1944; Le Sueur, *Shadow of the Swastika*, p. 79.
54. Haas, *Against All Odds*, p. 45; Miére, *Never to Be Forgotten*, p. 228.

55. Letter from Francis Harris to author, 6 September 2010.
56. Le Quesne, *The Occupation of Jersey Day by Day*, entries for 9–21 October 1944.
57. Keiller, *Prison Without Bars*, p. 142.
58. Weithley, *So It Was*, p. 119; Cahun, Jersey Archives, ref. JHT/1995/00045/1, p. 33; Harris, *Boys Remember More*, p. 90.
59. Letter from Lucy Schwob to J.H. L'Amy, L'Amy, 'The German Occupation of Jersey', pp. 11–12.
60. Le Sueur, *Shadow of the Swastika*, p. 69; Mière, *Never to be Forgotten*, p. 234; Cahun, Jersey Archives, ref. JHT/1995/00045/, pp. 37 and 39.
61. Cahun, Jersey Archives, ref. JHT/1995/00045/1, pp. 38–9; letter from Lucy Schwob to J.H. L'Amy, L'Amy, 'The German Occupation of Jersey', p. 12; reference to these men sleeping in the cells with other prisoners is suggested by entries in the autograph book, in which these men precis their life stories; they are also mentioned in memoirs, e.g. Keiller, *Prison Without Bars*, p. 129, but whether these are the same men as those who cleaned the military block for the Germans is unknown.
62. C. Cahun (2002 [1948]), 'Le Muet dans la Mêlée', in *Claude Cahun Écrits*, ed. François Leperlier (Paris: Jean-Michel Place), trans. Alex Stuart, p. 632.
63. Mière, *Never to be Forgotten*, pp. 234–5.
64. Cahun, Jersey Archives, ref. JHT/1995/00045/1, p. 45.

Chapter 3

1. P. Le Sauteur (1961), *Jersey Under the* Swastika (London: Streamline Publications Ltd), p. 129.
2. Jersey Archives, ref. D/AG/B7/1, logbook of names of political prisoners.
3. See G. Carr, P. Saunders and L. Willmot (2014), *Protest, Defiance and Resistance in the Channel Islands: German Occupation 1940–1945* (London: Bloomsbury Academic), p. 347.
4. Carr et al., *Protest, Defiance and Resistance in the Channel Islands*.
5. Keiller, *Prison Without Bars*, p. 137; Le Sauteur, *Jersey under the Swastika*, p. 105; Sinel, *The German Occupation of Jersey*, 11 January 1945.
6. Keiller, *Prison Without Bars*, p. 137.
7. Ibid., p. 137.
8. Jersey Archives, ref. D/AG/B1/4.
9. Jersey Archives, ref. B/A/W81/11.
10. Jersey Archives, ref. B/A/W50/183. Bailiff Alexander Coutanche to Platzkommandant, 22 November 1944.
11. Jersey Archives, ref. D/Z/H6/9. Sentences and Prosecutions by the Field Command and Troop Courts.

Chapter 4

1. The records of the Maison d'Arrêt in Caen (kept in Calvados Archives in Caen) show that fifty-two islanders had been sent to this prison by summer 1942. A further twenty-one islanders were sent to Beaulieu Prison in Caen. Some of these were later deported to Dijon or Paris.
2. Le Quesne, *The Occupation of Jersey Day by Day*, entry for 9 October 1944.

3. Harris, *Boys Remember More*, p. 89; Le Quesne, *The Occupation of Jersey Day by Day*, entry for 9 October 1944; Gray, 'Island of Beauty, Island of Secrets', p. 21.
4. My thanks to Barbara Greene, daughter of Belza Turner, for giving her permission for her mother to be publicly named here.
5. Letter to Joe Mière, name withheld, 3 November 2003. Joe Mière collection, courtesy of Mick Mière.
6. Email to author from Barbara Greene, daughter of Belza Turner, 22 January 2019.
7. Letter from Francis Harris to author, 27 April 2013; Gray, 'Island of Beauty, Island of Secrets', p. 21.
8. Le Quesne, *The Occupation of Jersey Day by Day*, entry for 9 October 1944; Keiller, *Prison Without Bars*, pp. 124–5.
9. Keiller, *Prison Without Bars*, p. 126; Le Sueur, *Shadow of the Swastika*, p. 64.
10. M. Ginns (2009), *Jersey Occupied: the German Armed Forces in Jersey 1940–1945* (Jersey: Channel Island Publishing), pp. 50–1.
11. Le Cocq, *My Favourite Occupation*, p. 89; Le Sueur, *Shadow of the Swastika*, pp. 60–1; Keiller, *Prison Without Bars*, pp. 79–80, 122, 132; Mière, *Never to be Forgotten*, p. 196; Weithley, *So It Was*, p. 111; Harris, *Boys Remember More*, p. 90.
12. Weithley, *So It Was*, p. 119.
13. Ronald Beer, Compensation claim for Nazi persecution, The National Archives, ref. FO 950/1767, 20 January 1965.
14. Hassall, 'Night and Fog Prisoners', p. 59, https://www.frankfallaarchive.org/wp-content/uploads/2016/08/Peter-Hassalls-memoirs.pdf.
15. Ibid., p. 61.
16. Keiller, *Prison Without Bars*, p. 125.
17. Ibid., pp. 81 and 137—9; Le Sueur, *Shadow of the Swastika*, pp. 74–6; Le Cocq, *My Favourite Occupation*, pp. 96–7; Mière, *Never to be Forgotten*, p. 202.
18. Letter from Lucy Schwob to J.H. L'Amy, L'Amy, 'The German Occupation of Jersey', p. 16.

Chapter 5

1. Carr et al., *Protest, Defiance and Resistance*, p. 345.
2. Cahun, 'Le Muet dans la Mêlée', trans. Alex Stuart, p. 632.
3. A description of fellow prisoners noted in Cahun, 'Le Muet dans la Mêlée', trans. Alex Stuart, pp. 632–3.
4. Ibid., trans. Alex Stuart, p. 633.
5. Haas, *Against All Odds*, p. 44.
6. Letter written by Peter Gray to his mother, 24 December 1944.
7. Cahun, 'Le Muet dans la Mêlée', trans. Alex Stuart p. 633.
8. Undated letter from Joseph Tierney to Eileen Tierney, in private ownership.
9. Keiller, *Prison Without Bars*, p. 129.
10. Le Quesne, *The Occupation of Jersey Day by Day*, entry for 17 October 1944; Haas, *Against All Odds*, p. 45; Jersey Archives, ref. JHT/1995/00045/2, partial translation of Lucy Schwob's experience in prison.
11. Weithley, *So It Was*, p. 132.
12. Janvrin-Tipping, *Any Day Now*, p. 80.

13. Ibid., p. 81.
14. Cahun, 'Lettre à Paul Levy', trans. Alex Stuart, p. 723, n. 8.
15. Keiller, *Prison Without Bars*, pp. 125 and 143; Le Sueur, *Shadow of the Swastika*, p. 72; Weithley, *So It Was*, p. 120; letter from Francis Harris to author, 6 October 2010.
16. Weithley, *So It Was*, pp. 120 and 127; Le Sueur, *Shadow of the Swastika*, p.73; Harris, *Boys Remember More*, p. 97; Mière, *Never to be Forgotten*, p. 215; letter from Francis Harris to author, 27 April 2013.
17. Weithley, *So It Was*, p. 126.
18. Cahun, 'Lettre à Paul Levy', trans. Alex Stuart, pp. 721–2.
19. Weithley, *So It Was*, p. 139.
20. Harris, *Boys Remember More*, pp. 90 and 93; Cahun, Jersey Archives, ref. JHT/1995/00045/2, pp. 6, 9 and 10, partial translation of account written by Claude Cahun about her time in prison; letter from Francis Harris to author, 6 October 2010.
21. Mière, *Never To Be Forgotten*, p. 214.
22. Letter from Lucy Schwob to J.H. L'Amy, L'Amy, 'The German Occupation of Jersey', p. 12.
23. Haas, *Against All Odds*, p. 46.
24. Harris, *Boys Remember More*, p. 97.
25. Haas, *Against All Odds*, p. 46.
26. Cahun, 'Lettre à Paul Levy', trans. Alex Stuart, p. 723.
27. Faramus, *Journey into Darkness*, p. 39.
28. Interview with Angela O'Connor, daughter of prison warder Sidney Jordan, 20 August 2014.
29. Keiller, *Prison Without Bars*, p. 140; Le Cocq, *My Favourite Occupation*, p. 94; letters from Francis Harris to author, 6 October 2010 and 27 April 2013.
30. Letter from Francis Harris to author, 27 April 2013.
31. My thanks to Paulette de la Haye for allowing me to examine the autograph book of Pauline Lamy, her mother.
32. Le Tissier, 'Newgate Street Prison', p. 12; however, an examination of the prison book which lists punishment and offences inside Jersey Prison (Jersey Archives, ref. D/AG/B9/1) lists more than eight surnames of warders who had made entries in the book, indicating either some staff turnover or expansion, or else more than eight warders. The surnames listed are: Fisher, Le Huquet, Hescott, Wakefield, Le Gros, M. Ozouf, E(mile) Ozouf, Vasselin, Quarry, Lee, Newingstone and Payne. Joe Mière recalled that Mr Packer was the head warder and that other 'civilian warders' included Frank Vernon, Marcel and Frank Ozouf, and a Mr Vibert (letter from Joe Mière to Michael Ginns, 1 July 2005). There were therefore more than eight warders, or else there was a turnover of staff during the Occupation.
33. Chapman, *The Real Eddie Chapman Story*, p. 46.
34. Keiller, *Prison Without Bars*, p. 140; letter from Peter Gray to author, 28 February 2012.
35. Le Tissier, 'Newgate Street Prison, p. 12.
36. Le Cocq, *My Favourite Occupation*, p. 94.
37. Le Quesne, *The Occupation of Jersey Day by Day*, entry for 14 October 1944.
38. Keiller, *Prison Without Bars*, pp. 141–2.
39. Le Quesne, *The Occupation of Jersey Day by Day*, entry for 20 October 1944.
40. The inability of prison warders on the civilian side to prevent contraband from entering the prison is exemplified by an entry in George Le Marquand's diary for 16 December 1944, which reads 'Runner up in darts tournament. Presented with set of knives.'

Notes   193

41. Mière, *Never to be Forgotten*, pp. 229–31.
42. Book of Offences and Punishments, Jersey Archives, ref. B/AG/B9/1.
43. Keiller, *Prison Without Bars*, p. 140.

Chapter 6
1. Faramus, *Journey Into Darkness*, p. 39.
2. Chapman, *The Real Eddie Chapman Story*, p. 47.
3. Faramus, *Journey Into Darkness*, p. 39.
4. Mière, *Never to be Forgotten*, p. 274.
5. Le Quesne, *The Occupation of Jersey Day by Day*, entry for 25 October 1944.
6. H.M. Von Aufsess (1985), *The von Aufsess Occupation Diary* (Chichester: Phillimore and Co. Ltd), p. 42.
7. Ibid., p. 66.
8. Le Quesne, *The Occupation of Jersey Day by Day*, entry for 13 October 1944.
9. Ibid., entry for 21 October 1944.
10. Jersey Archives, ref. B/A/W81/5/2.
11. Jersey Archives, ref. B/A/W80/1. Resolution of the Superior Council of the States of Jersey, signed by Alexander Coutanche, 21 September 1942.
12. Jersey Archives, ref. B/A/W81/7, handwritten document by Alexander Coutanche dated 19 February 1945.
13. Mière, *Never to be* Forgotten, pp. 211–12 and 274.
14. Jersey Archives, ref. B/A/W81/7, handwritten document by Alexander Coutanche dated 19 February 1945.
15. Jersey Archives, ref. B/A/W81/7, handwritten document by Alexander Coutanche dated 19 February 1945.
16. Mière, *Never to be Forgotten*, pp. 212–13 and 274.
17. Jersey Archives, ref. B/A/W81/9, report on inspection of prison dated 26 February 1945.
18. Ibid.
19. Jersey Archives ref. B/A/W81/9, letter from R.N. McKinstry, Medical Officer of Health, to C.S. Le Gros, President of the Jersey Prison Board, 18 April 1945.
20. Jersey Archives, ref. B/A/W81/11.
21. Ibid.
22. Jersey Archives, ref. B/A/W81/10, letter from Captain von Cleve, Platzkommandant, to Alexander Coutanche, 7 April 1945.
23. Leslie Sinel's diary, entry for 3 May 1945.
24. Le Cocq, *My Favourite Occupation*, p. 129.
25. Le Quesne, *The Occupation of Jersey Day by Day*, entry for 11 and 19 October 1944; Cahun, Jersey Archives, ref. JHT/1995/00045/1, account written by Claude Cahun about her time in prison, p. 48.
26. Keiller, *Prison Without Bars*, p. 141.
27. Le Quesne, *The Occupation of Jersey Day by Day*, entry for 14 October 1944.
28. Cahun, 'Lettre à Paul Levy', trans. Alex Stuart, p. 722.
29. Le Quesne, *The Occupation of Jersey Day by Day*, entry for 18 October 1944; Keiller, *Prison Without Bars*, pp. 141 and 147.
30. Keiller, *Prison Without Bars*, pp. 125 and 136.

31. Ibid., p. 124 and 146; Le Sueur, *Shadow of the Swastika*, p. 62; Le Cocq, *My Favourite Occupation*, p. 93.
32. Le Sueur, *Shadow of the Swastika*, p. 71.
33. Janvrin-Tipping, *Any Day Now*, p. 82.
34. JHT/1995/00045/4; notes written by Suzanne Malherbe about a communication with Kurt Gunther, detained in March–April 1945.
35. Keiller, *Prison Without Bars*, pp. 133–4; Haas, *Against All Odds*, p. 44; Cahun, Jersey Archives, ref. JHT/1995/00045/1 account written by Claude Cahun about her time in prison, pp. 38–9.
36. Le Cocq, *My Favourite Occupation*, p. 95; Haas, *Against All Odds*, p. 47.
37. Le Sueur, *Shadow of the Swastika*, p. 74; Wiethley, *So It Was*, p. 133.
38. Keiller, *Prison Without Bars*, p. 129.
39. Janvrin-Tipping, *Any Day Now*, p. 89; Alice Thaureux's entry in a political prisoner autograph book strongly suggests that she was informed upon.
40. Janvrin-Tipping, *Any Time Now*, pp. 86–7; Mière, *Never to be Forgotten*, pp. 234–5; Jersey Archives, ref. B/A/W50/20/1, letter from Bailiff Alexander Coutanche to Platzkommandantm 25 April 1945.
41. Cahun, Jersey Archives, ref. JHT/1995/00045/1, p. 43.
42. Weithley, *So It Was*, p. 121.
43. Letter from Francis Harris to author, 27 April 2013.
44. Mière, *Never to be Forgotten*, p. 215.
45. Box GO3 (prisoners), item 1, Société Jersiaise Library.
46. Cahun, 'Lettre à Paul Levy', trans. Alex Stuart, p. 736.
47. Letter from Peter Gray to his mother, 11 March 1945.
48. Letter from Peter Gray to his mother, 24 December 1944.
49. Gray, 'Island of Beauty, Island of Secrets', p. 22; letter from Peter Gray in prison to his mother, 19 March 1945.
50. Jersey Archives, ref. L/F/54/A/D/2, Richard Mayne's unpublished notes on prison.
51. Diary of George Le Marquand, entry for 31 January and 10 February 1945. Unpublished document in private ownership.
52. Letter from Peter Gray to his mother, November 1944.
53. Cahun, 'Letter à Paul Levy', trans. Alex Stuart, p. 734.
54. Keiller, *Prison Without Bars*, pp. 140 and 143; Harris, *Boys Remember More*, p. 141; letter from Francis Harris to author, 6 October 2010; unpublished letters from Peter Gray to his mother while in prison, 1944–5.
55. Letter from Peter Gray to his mother, 18 March 1945.
56. Diary of George Le Marquand, 9 February 1945. Unpublished document in private ownership.
57. Letter from Francis Harris to author, 28 October 2010.
58. Le Quesne, *The Occupation of Jersey Day by Day*, entry for 14 October 1944; Harris, *Boys Remember More*, pp. 96–7; Keiller, *Prison Without Bars*, p. 130; Le Sueur, *Shadow of the Swastika*, p. 63.
59. Janvrin-Tipping, *Any Day Now*, p. 67.
60. Cahun, Jersey Archives, ref. JHT/1995/00045/2, partial translation of account written by Claude Cahun about her time in prison, p. 8.
61. Letter from Lucy Schwob to J.H. L'Amy, L'Amy, 'The German Occupation of Jersey', pp. 15–16.

62. Harris, *Boys Remember More*, p. 96.
63. Chapman, *The Real Eddie Chapman Story*, p. 38.
64. Le Sueur, *Shadow of the Swastika*, p. 73.
65. Weithley, *So It Was*, pp. 124–5.
66. Diary of George Le Marquand, 27 January 1944.
67. Weithley, *So It Was*, pp. 133–4.
68. Diary of George Le Marquand, entries made in March 1945.
69. Letter from Francis Harris to author, 6 October 2010.
70. Keiller, *Prison Without Bars*, p. 128.
71. Letter from Francis Harris to author, 6 October 2010.
72. Keiller, *Prison Without Bars*, p. 130.
73. Ibid., p. 152.
74. Weithley, *So It Was*, pp. 122–3.
75. Harris, *Boys Remember More*, p. 92; Harris, *A Boy Remembers*, pp. 119–20.
76. Jersey Archives, ref. B/A/W81/3. Letter from Dr McKinstry to the Bailiff, 11 March 1944.

Chapter 7

1. Clarence John Piquet, 'Background to Newgate prison', unpublished MS, States of Jersey Library, ref. J365.
2. Keiller, *Prison Without Bars*, p. 124.
3. Le Sueur, *Shadow of the Swastika*, pp. 69–70.
4. Chapman, *The Real Eddie Chapman Story*, p. 47.
5. Cahun, Jersey Archives, ref. JHT/1995/00045/1, pp. 47–8.
6. L'Amy, 'The German Occupation of Jersey', p. 15; Cahun, Jersey Archives, ref. JHT/1995/00045/1, pp. 47–8.
7. Undated letter from Joseph Tierney to his wife, Eileen, in private ownership.
8. Cahun, Jersey Archives, ref. JHT/1995/00045/1, p. 48.
9. Cahun, 'Lettre à Paul Levy', trans. Alex Stuart, p. 737.
10. Letter from Francis Harris to author, 6 September 2010.

Chapter 8

1. Janvrin-Tipping, *Any Day Now*, p. 52.
2. Letter from Francis Harris to author, 6 October 2010.
3. Peter Gray's autograph book, in private ownership.
4. Janvrin-Tipping, *Any Day Now*.
5. For example, political prisoner certificates of Joe Mière and Bernard Hassall, copies of which were held at Jersey War Tunnels.
6. The author wishes to thank Wendy Tipping for letting her examine Muriel Costard's autograph book.
7. Société Jersiaise, ref. GO3 12, Renée Griffin's autograph book.
8. Ibid.
9. L. Willmot (2014), 'Sabotage, intelligence gathering and escape', pp. 213–42 in Carr et al., *Protest, Defiance and Resistance in the Channel Islands: German Occupation 1940–1945* (London: Bloomsbury Academic).
10. Société Jersiaise, ref. GO3 12, Renée Griffin's autograph book.

11. Ibid.
12. Ibid.
13. Peter Gray's autograph book, with thanks to Mr Gray for lending it to the author for study.
14. Société Jersiaise, ref. GO3 12, Renée Griffin's autograph book.
15. Muriel Costard's autograph book; the author wishes to thank Wendy Tipping for letting her examine this book.
16. The author wishes to thank Wendy Tipping for letting her examine Evelyn Janvrin's autograph book.
17. Autograph sheet of Allan Costard; Wendy Tipping archive.
18. Poem written by prisoner no. 12181 (Edward Osborne), autograph book of Pauline Lamy, cited by kind permission of Paulette de la Haye.
19. Société Jersiaise, ref. GO3 12, Renée Griffin's autograph book.
20. The author wishes to thank Wendy Tipping for letting her examine Muriel Costard's autograph book.
21. The author wishes to thank Wendy Tipping for letting her examine Muriel Costard's autograph book.
22. Evelyn Janvrin's autograph book.
23. Ibid.
24. Ibid.

Chapter 9

1. H.R.S. Pocock, *The Memoirs of Lord Coutanche: A Jerseyman Looks Back* (London and Chichester: Phillimore and Co. Ltd), p. 47.
2. Le Quesne, *The Occupation of Jersey Day by Day*, p. 284.
3. Leslie Sinel's diary, entry for 7 and 8 May 1945.
4. Harris, *Boys Remember More*, p. 98.
5. Document from the Feldkommantur, dated 7 May 1945 signed by the Heeresjustizinspektor. Document from Joe Mière collection.
6. Cahun, 'Lettre à Paul Levy', trans. Alex Stuart, p. 742.
7. Letter from Joe Mière to Michael Ginns, 1 July 2005, Joe Mière archive, courtesy of the family of Michael Mière.
8. Mière, *Never To Be Forgotten*, p. 260.
9. Cahun, 'Lettre à Paul Levy', trans. Alex Stuart, p. 743. Later in life, Francis Harris found out (although from what source is unknown) that all prisoners who the *Geheime Feldpolizei* classified as dangerous because of their firearms offences were, as part of the German surrender agreement, to be kept in custody until the Allied forces were in full control in order to protect the Germans (letter from Francis Harris to author, 6 October 2010). I have been unable to verify this statement.
10. Peter Gray, 'Island of Beauty, Island of Secrets', p. 57.
11. Undated document in Joe Mière archive, courtesy of Michael Mière.
12. Sinel, *The German Occupation of Jersey*, entry for 8 May 1945.
13. Cahun, 'Lettre à Paul Levy', trans. Alex Stuart, p. 742.
14. Ibid., p. 743.
15. Harris, *A Boy Remembers*, p. 159.
16. Weithley, *So it Was*, p. 142.

17. In his diary, Deputy Edward Le Quesne noted that the 'chiefs of the infamous Gestapo' were taken to prison at bayonet point on 11 May. Leslie Sinel also records this event on 11 May, writing that 'the crowd which saw them in a lorry surrounded by Tommies with fixed bayonets contained many who had suffered mental or physical strain through their activities'.
18. Miére, *Never to be Forgotten*, p. 214; Lucy Schwob also records giving her testimony to British intelligence officers, Cahun, 'Lettre à Paul Levy', trans. Alex Stuart, p. 742.
19. Weithley, *So It Was*, p. 143.
20. Miére, *Never to be Forgotten*, p. 245.
21. Letter from Bailiff Alexander Coutanche to J.B. Howard, 21 June 1945, Jersey Archives, ref. D/Z/H5/456.
22. Letter from Charles Markbreiter (Home Office) to Duret Aubin, 16 July 1945, Jersey Archives, ref. D/Z/H5/456.
23. Jersey Archives, ref. D/Z/H5/456.
24. Cahun, 'Le Muet dans la Mêlée', trans. Alex Stuart, pp. 632–3.
25. Leslie Sinel's diary, entry for 31 March 1945.
26. It is unknown which of the Jersey 21 were not included on this list.
27. 'Ex-convicts meet in Lyric Hall', *Jersey Evening Post*, 12 December 1945.
28. Jersey Archives, ref. B/A/W21/1.
29. Jersey Archives, ref. D/Z/H9/8.
30. The Jersey 21 started life as the Jersey 20, as we have seen. When the Lighthouse Memorial was erected in their memory in 1996, it was dedicated to the Jersey 22. Since then, one of this number, Walter Dauny, was found to have survived.
31. The reader interested in the subject of political opposition to Joe Miére's work and campaign for a memorial to political prisoners is referred to in Chapter 11 (2014), Gilly Carr, 'Heritage, Memory and Resistance', pp. 307, in G. Carr, P. Saunders and L. Willmot, *Protest, Defiance and Resistance in the Channel Islands: German Occupation 1940–1945* (London: Bloomsbury Academic).
32. 'Bailiff unveils plaque to the prisoners of the Occupation', *Jersey Evening Post*, 28 April 1995.

Chapter 10

1. Food supplies for civilian prisoners under German arrest, undated document. Island Archives, Guernsey, ref. BA 52-04.
2. *Feldkommandantur* 515 (FK 515) was the German military administration in the Channel Islands.
3. The Controlling Committee in Guernsey was a streamlined emergency war cabinet of nine men.
4. Letter from Major Kratzer to President of the Controlling Committee, 9 December 1943. Island Archives, Guernsey, ref. CC 1-15/16.
5. Island Archives, Guernsey, ref. HA/P 03-02.
6. Letter from H.J. Blampied to Fuerst von Oettingen, 28 February 1942. Island Archives, Guernsey, ref. FK 04-09.
7. Island Archives, Guernsey, ref. FK 04-09.
8. J. Hayes, 'A Sojourn in Guernsey', Unpublished manuscript, no longer available online.
9. The author knows of only one person who experienced Guernsey Prison and who is still alive at the time of writing.

10. Admissions logbook, Island Archives, Guernsey, ref. HA P, 19-01.
11. F. Falla, Unpublished prison diary, in private ownership, entry for 3 April 1944.
12. Ibid., entry for 12 April 1944.

Chapter 11

1. A. Westman, J. Godfrey, A. Brodie and J. Renouf (2003), 'The Old Prison Site, St James Street, St Peter Port, Guernsey: A record of the building and site' (London: Museum of London Archaeology Service; Island Archives, Guernsey), ref. AQ 750/1-4, i.
2. The Gaoler (chief warder) was a specific title or rank in the island and always spelled with a capital G in the archival records.
3. Westman et al., 'The Old Prison Site'.
4. Ibid., pp. 41–2.
5. Ibid., pp. ii and 13.
6. Ibid., p. 50.
7. Report on Guernsey Prison during the Occupation, The National Archives, ref. T161/1415/1.
8. A.P. L'Amy, Chief Officer Guernsey Police, 'Policing during the Occupation, 1940–1945'.
9. Report on Guernsey Prison during the Occupation, The National Archives, ref. T161/1415/1.
10. Letter from John Leale to Dr Brosch, 9 September 1940. Island Archives, Guernsey, ref. CC 1-15/1.
11. Report by Mr Mainguy, Receiver-General of Guernsey, to Mr Cook, Treasury Office, 18 August 1945. The National Archives, ref. T161/1415/1.
12. L'Amy, 'Policing during the Occupation'.
13. Letter from Dr Brosch to President of Controlling Committee, 27 December 1941. Island Archives, Guernsey, ref. CC 1-15/12.
14. Westman et al., 'The Old Prison Site', p. 55.
15. Admissions logbook, Island Archives, Guernsey, ref. HA P, 19-01.
16. Ibid.
17. Letter from the Receiver-General's Office to the Sheriff, 8 December 1943. Island Archives, Guernsey, ref. BA 52-04.
18. R. MacCulloch (1856), *Recueil d'Ordannances de la Cour Royale*, Vol. 2, *1801–1840* (Guernsey), pp. 217–21, cited in Westman et al., 'The Old Prison Site', p. 27.
19. Westman et al., 'The Old Prison Site', p. 55.
20. Admissions logbook, Island Archives, Guernsey, ref. HA P, 19-01.
21. Ibid.
22. Ibid.
23. R. Durand (2018 [1946]), *Guernsey under German Rule* (Guernsey: Guernsey Society), p. 228.
24. Ibid., p. 238.
25. Letter from H. Blampied, Sheriff, to John Leale, 22 February 1944. Island Archives, Guernsey, ref. CC 1-15.
26. Ibid.
27. Island Archives, Guernsey, ref. HA/P 03-02.
28. The prison provisions logbook indicates that this probably began in February 1944. Island Archives, Guernsey, ref. HA/P 17-05.
29. In the Channel Islands, a jurat is a lay magistrate.
30. Note of 24 February 1944, admissions logbook, Island Archives, Guernsey, ref. HA P, 19-01.

31. Letter from Schneberger to the Bailiff of Guernsey, 21 January 1945. Island Archives, Guernsey, ref. CC 1-15/28.
32. Extract from letter from Sutcliffe, medical officer to HM's Prison, Guernsey, to the Bailiff, 22 January 1945, in 'Imprisonment and Crime in Guernsey: extracts and transcripts', Priaulx Library, ref. LOC 365 Gue.
33. Admissions logbook, Island Archives, Guernsey, ref. HA P, 19-01.
34. List of prisoners in prison and annexe as on 19 March 1945, Island Archives, Guernsey, ref. PR 3-7.
35. Durand, *Guernsey under German Rule*, p. 301.
36. Admissions logbook, Island Archives, Guernsey, ref. HA P, 19-01.
37. Annual report of Medical Officer Dr Sutcliffe, 20 January 1946, Island Archives, Guernsey, ref. PR 3-7.
38. Admissions logbook, Island Archives, Guernsey, ref. HA P, 19-01.
39. Channel Islands Property Rehabilitation Scheme, statement made by H.J. Blampied. Island Archives, Guernsey, ref. PR 3-7.

Chapter 12

1. These can be consulted at the Island Archives Guernsey, ref. CC EC 06-02.
2. Island Archives Guernsey, ref. HA/P 08-03.
3. Island Archives Guernsey, ref. HA/P 19-01.
4. Island Archives Guernsey, ref. HA/P 5/1.
5. For a discussion of this point, see G. Carr (2019), *Victims of Nazism in the Channel Islands: A Legitimate Heritage?* (London: Bloomsbury Academic).
6. Harold Ira Gallienne was imprisoned for getting into an altercation with a German soldier which was, before we learned of his nickname, assumed to have been only verbal.
7. Falla, Unpublished prison diary, entry for 19 April 1944.
8. https://www.frankfallaarchive.org/people/evelina-kathleen-garland-nee-weston/, accessed 25 July 2019.
9. Hayes, 'A Sojourn in Guernsey', p. 58.
10. Falla, Unpublished prison diary, entry for 24 April 1944.
11. Ibid., entry for 13 May 1944.
12. G. Domaille, Unpublished memoirs, https://www.frankfallaarchive.org/people/gerald-charles-domaille/, accessed 25 July 2019.
13. Island Archives Guernsey, ref. HA/P 03-02, Prison correspondence.
14. Prison provisions logbook, Island Archives, Guernsey, HA/P 17-05.
15. For example, note for 26 April 1944, prison logbook, Island Archives, Guernsey, ref. HA P / 19-01.
16. Provisions logbook, Island Archives, Guernsey, ref. HA/P 17-05.
17. Carr et al., *Protest, Defiance and Resistance in the Channel Islands*.
18. Files of J.R. Dening, Imperial War Museum, ref. 13409.

Chapter 13

1. List of admissions logbook, Island Archives, Guernsey, ref. HA P/19-01.
2. Entry for 9 November 1940, diary of H.E. Marquand, in private ownership.
3. Letters and diary of H.E. Marquand, in private ownership.

4. Ibid.
5. Ibid.
6. Hayes, 'A Sojourn in Guernsey', p. 46.
7. F. Stroobant (1997 [1967]), *One Man's War* (Guernsey: Burbridge Ltd [Corgi]), p. 54.
8. Hayes, 'A Sojourn in Guernsey', p. 46.
9. Ibid., p. 47.
10. C. Duquemin, Unpublished memoirs, https://www.frankfallaarchive.org/people/cecil-oliver-duquemin/, accessed 24 July 2019.
11. Domaille, Unpublished memoirs, available on https://www.frankfallaarchive.org/people/gerald-charles-domaille/, accessed 25 July 2019.
12. Hubert Lanyon, Unpublished memoirs. Manuscript in private ownership.
13. Letter from the Feldkriegsgerichtsrat to Agnew WG Giffard, Dean of Guernsey, 23 August 1941. Island Archives, Guernsey, ref. CC 1-15/8.
14. Letter from H.J. Blampied, Sheriff, to Victor Carey, Bailiff, 11 December 1943. Island Archives, Guernsey, ref. BA 52-04.
15. Falla, Unpublished prison diary, entry for 4 and 5 April 1944.
16. Ibid., entry for 9 April 1944.
17. Ibid., entry for 8 April 1944.
18. F. Falla (1981 [1967]), *The Silent War* (Guernsey: Burbridge Ltd [London: Leslie Frewin]), p. 110.
19. Falla, Unpublished prison diary, entry for 22 April 1944.
20. Ibid., entry for 6 April 1944.
21. Ibid., entry for 21 April 1944.
22. Ibid., entry for 28 April 1944.
23. Hayes, 'A Sojourn in Guernsey', p. 64.
24. Ibid.
25. Ibid., p. 65.
26. Ibid., p. 66.
27. Stroobant, *One Man's War*, p. 55.
28. Ibid.
29. Ibid., p. 59.
30. Hayes, 'A Sojourn in Guernsey', p. 64.
31. M. Ozanne, Unpublished diary, entry for 11 September 1942. Island Archives, ref. AQ 1139/21.
32. She was accused of having '*openly abused the German forces or maliciously and with intent thrown the same into suspicion*' and of having '*offered gifts to a member of the Armed Forces in order to incite him to commit an act contrary to his duty and insulting another in the same way*'. Priaulx Library, documents and memorabilia, German Occupation of the Channel Islands miscellea 1940-1945, Box 3.
33. Ozanne, Unpublished diary, 29 September 1942.
34. Ibid., 4 and 7 October 1942.
35. Ibid.
36. Ibid., 27 September 1942.
37. Ibid., 17 October 1942.
38. Ibid., 28 September 1942.

39. Compensation testimony for Nazi persecution, Julia Brichta, The National Archives, ref. FO 950/999.
40. O. Frampton, Unpublished memoirs. In private ownership.
41. Falla, *The Silent War*, p. 105.
42. Ibid.

Chapter 14

1. Westman et al., 'The Old Prison Site', p. 48.
2. Report on Channel Islands' prisons in the 1930s. The National Archives, ref. HO 45/17032.
3. For example, Falla, *The Silent War*, p. 105.
4. For example, entry for 14 December 1943, prison logbook, Island Archives, Guernsey, ref. HA P/19-01.
5. Letter from John Leale to *Feldkommandantur* 515, 3 August 1941. Island Archives, Guernsey, ref. CC 1-15/4.
6. Letter from H.J. Blampied, HM's Sheriff, to G.J.P. Ridgeway, HM's Comptroller, 1 August 1941 and 26 July 1941. Island Archives, Guernsey, ref. CC 1-15/3 and CC 1-15/1A.
7. Hayes, 'A Sojourn in Guernsey', pp. 49–50.
8. Ibid., p. 50.
9. Ibid.
10. Ibid., p. 49.
11. Ibid., p. 52.
12. Domaille, Unpublished memoirs, https://www.frankfallaarchive.org/people/gerald-charles-domaille/, accessed 25 July 2019.
13. Duquemin, Unpublished memoirs, https://www.frankfallaarchive.org/people/cecil-oliver-duquemin/, accessed 24 July 2019.
14. Falla, *The Silent War*, p. 109.
15. Hayes, 'A Sojourn in Guernsey', p. 51.
16. Domaille, Unpublished memoirs, https://www.frankfallaarchive.org/people/gerald-charles-domaille/, accessed 25 July 2019.
17. Falla, Unpublished prison diary, entry for 11 May 1944.
18. Ibid., entry for 15 May 1944.
19. Ibid., entry for 22 and 23 May 1944.
20. Lanyon, Unpublished memoirs.
21. Hayes, 'A Sojourn in Guernsey', p. 51.
22. Ibid., p. 52.
23. Ibid., p. 53.
24. Lanyon, Unpublished memoirs.
25. Hayes, 'A Sojourn in Guernsey', p. 67.

Chapter 15

1. Hayes, 'A Sojourn in Guernsey', p. 3.
2. Ibid.
3. Falla, *The Silent War*, p. 102.
4. Ibid., p. 104.

5. Domaille, Unpublished memoirs, https://www.frankfallaarchive.org/people/gerald-charles-domaille/, accessed 1 August 2019.
6. Hayes, 'A Sojourn in Guernsey', p. 55.
7. L'Amy, 'Policing during the Occupation'.
8. Lanyon, Unpublished memoirs.
9. Hayes, 'A Sojourn in Guernsey', p. 56.
10. Police logbook listing charges against local civilians, Guernsey police station.
11. Sanders, *The Ultimate Sacrifice*, pp. 30 and 33.
12. Hayes, 'A Sojourn in Guernsey', p. 16.
13. Ibid., p. 56.
14. Falla, Unpublished prison diary, entry for 26 April 1944.
15. Falla, *The Silent War*, pp. 106–7.

Chapter 16

1. K.G. Bailey (1958), *Dachau* (Guernsey: CI Marine Ld), p. 22.
2. According to the logbook listing admissions, the policemen arrived in Guernsey Prison between 5 and 10 March 1942. Island Archives, ref. HA/P 08-03.
3. Jack Harper, Nazi persecution compensation testimony, The National Archives, ref. FO 950/2187.
4. Bailey, *Dachau*, p. 24.
5. Photographs of *GFP* men in Dening 10, files of J.R. Dening, Imperial War Museum ref.13409.
6. Bailey, *Dachau*, p. 24.
7. Ibid.
8. Jack Harper, Nazi persecution compensation testimony, The National Archives, ref. FO 950/2187.
9. This is believed to be Sergeant Major Oeser, of the German *Feldgendarmerie*.
10. Affidavit by Alfred Howlett, 15 May 1945. The National Archives, ref. WO 311/11.
11. Frederick Short, Nazi persecution compensation testimony, The National Archives, ref. FO 950/962.
12. W. Bell (1995), *I Beg to Report: Policing in Guernsey during the German Occupation* (Guernsey: The Guernsey Press), p. 142.
13. Ibid., p. 153.
14. Bailey, *Dachau*, p. 24.
15. Stroobant, *One Man's War*, p. 55.
16. Bailey, *Dachau*, p. 25.
17. Ibid.
18. Bell, *I Beg to Report*, p. 155.
19. Ibid., p. 156.
20. Ibid., pp. 156–8.
21. Bailey, *Dachau*, p. 27.
22. Note in margin for 26 March 1942, admissions logbook, Island Archives, ref. HA P/19-01.
23. Bailey, *Dachau*, p. 27.
24. Bell, *I Beg to Report*, p. 179.
25. Durand, *Guernsey under German Rule*, p. 139.

Notes 203

26. Ralph Durand tells us that this was a one-off occasion, as at no other time were members of the public allowed to be present at German trials; ibid., p. 141.
27. Bailey was getting his dates mixed up here. The trial was around seven weeks after his initial imprisonment. In total, the men were held for just shy of three-and-a-half months before their deportation.
28. Bailey, *Dachau*, p. 29.
29. Ibid.
30. Bell, *I Beg to Report*, p. 160.
31. Note for 13 June 1942, admissions logbook, Island Archives, Guernsey, ref. HA P/19-01.
32. Ibid., p. 30.
33. Bailiff Victor Carey's speech reproduced in Bell, *I Beg to Report*, p. 188.
34. Durand, *Guernsey under German Rule*, p. 140.
35. See P. Sanders (2014), 'Economic resistance and sabotage', pp. 277–306; Carr, *Victims of Nazism in the Channel Islands*. It seems likely that the reputations of the policemen had to be the scapegoats in this episode of the wartime narrative so that no blame is allowed to fall on the memory of Bailiff Victor Carey for allowing the abuse and deportation of the men.

Chapter 17

1. Westman et al., 'The Old Prison Site', p. 82.
2. Further information about resistance in the Channel Islands can be found in Carr et al., *Protest, Defiance and Resistance in the Channel Islands*.
3. Bailey, *Dachau*, p. 40.
4. Eugene Le Lievre, Nazi persecution testimony. The National Archives, ref. FO 950/2992.
5. Frederick Short, Nazi persecution testimony. The National Archives, ref. FO 950/1224.
6. Thomas Gaudion, Nazi persecution testimony. The National Archives, ref. FO 950/1373.
7. Falla, *The Silent War*, p. 114.
8. Norman Dexter, Nazi persecution testimony. The National Archives, ref. FO 950/2064.
9. 'History of the GFP in the Channel Islands', Captain J.R. Dening, JRD 9, Imperial War Museum ref. 13409.
10. Hayes, 'A Sojourn in Guernsey', p. 68.
11. Ibid.
12. Sanders, *The Ultimate Sacrifice*, pp. 137–8.

Postscript

1. Report on Jersey Prison by N.R. Hilton, April 1946. The National Archives, ref. PCOM 9/436.
2. Report on Guernsey Prison by N.R. Hilton, April 1946. The National Archives, ref. PCOM 9/436.
3. Pleasants, *Hitler's Bastard*, p. 46.
4. Statement of 23 May 1946 by Secretary of State to the Prisons Commission, response to Mr Hilton's report on Jersey and Guernsey Prisons of April 1946. The National Archives, ref. PCOM 9/436.

Bibliography

Published works

Bailey, K.G. 1958. *Dachau*. Guernsey: CI Marine Ltd.
Bell, W. 1995. *I Beg to Report: Policing in Guernsey during the German Occupation*. Guernsey: The Guernsey Press Ltd.
Cahun, C. 'Le Muet dans la Mêlée' (1948), pp. 626–48, in *Claude Cahun Écrits*, ed. François Leperlier. 2002. Paris: Jean-Michel Place.
Cahun, C. 'Lettre à Paul Levy' (1950), pp. 709–57, in *Claude Cahun Écrits*, ed. François Leperlier. 2002. Paris: Jean-Michel Place.
Carr, G. 2019. *Victims of Nazism in the Channel Islands: A Legitimate Heritage?* London: Bloomsbury Academic.
Carr, G., Sanders, P. and Willmot, L. 2014. *Protest, Defiance and Resistance in the Channel Islands: German Occupation 1940–1945*. London: Bloomsbury Academic.
Chapman, E. 1957. *I Lived to Kill: The Story of Eric Pleasants as told to Eddie Chapman*. London: Cassell and Company Ltd.
Chapman, E. 1966. *The Real Eddie Chapman Story: I Lived to Kill*. London: Tandem Books Ltd.
Durand, R. 2018 [1946]. *Guernsey under German Rule*. Guernsey: Guernsey Society.
Falla, F. 1981 [1967]. *The Silent War*. Guernsey: Burbridge Ltd [London: Leslie Frewin].
Faramus, A. 1990. *Journey into Darkness*. London: Grafton Books.
Ginns, M. 2009. *Jersey Occupied: the German Armed Forces in Jersey 1940–1945*. Jersey: Channel Island Publishing.
Haas, G. 1997. *Against All Odds*. New York: Sherpa Publishing.
Harris, L. 2002. *Boys Remember More*. Jersey: Apache Guides Ltd.
Harris, L. 2004 [2000]. *A Boy Remembers*. Jersey: Channel Island Publishing [Apache].
Janvrin-Tipping, W. 2015. *Any Day Now*. London: Austin Macauley Publishers Ltd.
Keiller, F. 2000. *Prison Without Bars*. Bradford on Avon: Seaflower Books Ltd.
Le Cocq, K. 2011. *My Favourite Occupation*. Jersey: Channel Island Publishing.
Le Quesne, E. 1999. *The Occupation of Jersey Day by Day*. Jersey: La Haule Books Ltd.
Le Sauteur, P. 1961. *Jersey under the Swastika*. London: Streamline Publications Ltd.
Le Sueur, F. 1990. *Shadow of the Swastika*. Jersey: Starlight Imports.
Le Tissier, R. 2010. 'Newgate Street Prison – 1944–1945', *Newgate Club Gazette*, 1 (issue 2): pp. 6–13.
MacCulloch, R. 1856. *Recueil d'Ordannances de la Cour Royale*, Vol. 2, *1801–1840*. Guernsey.
Mière, J. 2004. *Never to be Forgotten*. Jersey: Channel Island Publishing.
Pleasants, E. 2003. *Hitler's Bastard*. Edinburgh and London: Mainstream Publishing.
Pocock, H.R.S. 1975. *The Memoirs of Lord Coutanche: A Jerseyman looks back*. London and Chichester: Phillimore and Co. Ltd.
Sanders, P. 2014. 'Economic resistance and sabotage', pp. 277–306, in G. Carr, P. Sanders and L. Willmot. 2014. *Protest, Defiance and Resistance in the Channel Islands: German Occupation 1940–1945*. London: Bloomsbury Academic.

Sanders, P. 2018 (3rd edn). *The Ultimate Sacrifice*. Jersey: Jersey Heritage Trust and Holocaust Memorial Day Committee.
Sinel, L. 1945. *The German Occupation of Jersey, 1940–1945*. Jersey: Jersey Evening Post.
Stroobant, F. 1997 [1967]. *One Man's War*. Guernsey: Burbridge Ltd [Corgi].
Von Aufsess, H.M. 1985. *The von Aufsess Occupation Diary*. Chichester: Phillimore and Co. Ltd.
Wiethley, R. 2007 [2001]. *So It Was*. Jersey: Channel Island Publishing.
Willmot, L. 2014. 'Humanitarian resistance: help to Jews and OT workers', pp. 97–126, in G. Carr, P. Sanders and L. Willmot. 2014. *Protest, Defiance and Resistance in the Channel Islands: German Occupation 1940–1945*. London: Bloomsbury Academic.
Willmot, L. 2014. 'Sabotage, intelligence gathering and escape', pp. 213–42 in G. Carr, P. Sanders and L. Willmot, *Protest, Defiance and Resistance in the Channel Islands: German Occupation 1940–1945*. London: Bloomsbury Academic.

Unpublished works

Bentlif, P.G. n.d. 'Newgate Street Prison'. Unpublished memoirs, copy on file.
Cahun, C. Unpublished papers. Jersey Archives ref. JHT/1995/00045/1, account written by Claude Cahun about her time in prison.
Chardine, A.A. 'Reminiscences'. Société Jersiaise Lord Coutanche Library, *OCC 942 CHA.
Dening, J.R. Private Papers of Captain J.R. Dening. JRD 9, Imperial War Museum Ref. 13409.
Domaille, G. Unpublished memoirs. https://www.frankfallaarchive.org/people/gerald-charles-domaille/; accessed 15 July 2019.
Duquemin, C. Unpublished memoirs. https://www.frankfallaarchive.org/people/cecil-oliver-duquemin/; accessed 15 July 2019.
Falla, F. Unpublished prison diary. In private ownership.
Frampton, O. Unpublished memoirs. In private ownership.
Gray, P. 'Island of Beauty, Island of Secrets'. Manuscript in private ownership.
Hassall, P. 'Night and Fog Prisoners'.
https://www.frankfallaarchive.org/wp-content/uploads/2016/08/Peter-Hassalls-memoirs.pdf; accessed 15 July 2019.
Hayes, J. 'A Sojourn in Guernsey'. Unpublished manuscript, no longer available online; accessed July 2014.
'Imprisonment and Crime in Guernsey: extracts and transcripts'. Priaulx Library ref. LOC 365 Gue.
L'Amy, A.P., Chief Officer Guernsey Police. 'Policing during the Occupation, 1940–1945'.
L'Amy, J.H. 'The German Occupation of Jersey'. Société Jersiaise Lord Coutanche Library, *OCC 942 L'AM.
Lanyon, H. Unpublished memoirs. Manuscript in private ownership.
Le Marquand, G. Unpublished diary. In private ownership.
Le Seelleur, Captain H. Unpublished manuscript. States of Jersey Library Service, ref. J365.
Marquand, H.E. Unpublished diary. In private ownership.
Ozanne, M. Unpublished diary. Island Archives, Guernsey.
Piquet, Clarence John. 'Background to Newgate prison'. Unpublished MS, States of Jersey Library, ref. J365.
Westman, A., Godfrey, J., Brodie, A., and Renouf, J. 2003. 'The Old Prison Site, St James Street, St Peter Port, Guernsey: A record of the building and site'. London: Museum of London Archaeology Service. Island Archives, Guernsey, ref. AQ 750/1-4.

Index

Aune, André 69, 74
autograph books xvi, xx, 9, 12, 15, 42, 46, 57, 59, 60, 76, 77, 83–97

Bagatelle House 48
Bailey, Kingston 163–5, 167–9, 171–2, 177, 179
Bailhache, Philip 104–5
Baudains, Alexandrine 101
beatings *see* violence
Beer, Ronald 49
Bennett, Arnold 88–9
Bentlif, Philip 16–17
Bernau forced labour camp 172, 179
Blampied, Harold 110, 120, 122
Bode, *Hauptmann* 48, 50
Briard, Ernest 33, 58, 59, 60–1, 64, 66, 70, 78
Brichta, Julia 149
Brideaux, Laura 33–4
Buesnel, Philip 92–3
'bungalow', the 26–7, 60, 76
Burton, Bill 168

Caen Prison 139, 172, 175, 177–8
Cahun, Claude *see* Schwob, Lucy
Canivet, Ernest 92
Carey, Victor 172
Chapman, Eddie 64, 75, 80
Chelsea Hotel 69, 100
Cherche-Midi Prison, Paris 139, 176
Cohu, Clifford 1
Collins, Kenneth 90
Coombs, Stanley 32–4
Costard, Muriel 72, 85, 87, 93, 95–6
Coutanche, Alexander 43, 65, 67–8, 99–100, 102

Dening, Captain 136, 165, 180
deportations (from Channel Islands) 1–2, 8–9, 13, 31–2, 41, 45, 67, 133, 135–6, 149, 172, 177, 181, 185
Dexter, Norman 140–1, 180
Domaille, Gerald 114, 134, 143, 154–5, 158, 161
Dorey, Arthur 127
Duquemin, Cecil 114–15, 143, 154, 157, 161
Durand, Ralph 126–8, 171
Durtnall, Harry 83–4

Einert (GFP) 144, 158

Falla, Frank 3, 10, 12–13, 112–16, 131–4, 144–6, 150, 154–8, 161–2, 169, 180, 184
Faramus, Anthony 11, 19, 27, 59, 64, 153
Feldgendarmerie 48, 124, 136, 149, 159, 162
Ferbrache, William 120, 122, 134
Folie Inn 48
Forster, Ivy 33
Fort George, Guernsey 169–72
Fort d'Hauteville, Dijon 175, 178
Fort de Villeneuve-Saint-Georges, Paris 172, 175, 178
Frampton, Olive 116, 117, 124, 147, 149–50
Frank Falla Archive website 13, 131–2
Friend, Charles 168

Gaudion, Thomas 179
Gavey, Alice 33
Geheime Feld Polizei (*GFP*) 2, 17, 46, 48–50, 56, 57, 70, 101, 140, 142, 144, 150, 154, 157–9, 163–70, 176, 180–2
German prisoners 37, 35, 39, 72, 104
Giffard, Agnew 144
Giffard, John (Major) 42, 67–8

Gillingham, Joseph 4, 161
Gould, Louisa 33
Gould, Maurice 51
graffiti 28, 64, 79–82, 97, 111
Grange Lodge 164–6, 168–9
Gray, Peter 54, 73, 83–4, 88–91, 100
Griffin, Renée 76–7, 83–4, 88, 90–4
Guards (German) 36, 38, 46, 55–8, 70, 72–5, 80–2, 124, 147–50, 156, 163, 167, 172, 177, 179
GUNS 112, 114, 134, 143, 157, 162

Haas, George 54, 57, 74
Hacquoil, Dora 33, 34
Harper, Jack 164–5, 168, 171
Harris, Francis 37, 42, 74, 77, 82–3, 92, 100–1
Hassall, Bernard 88–9, 91, 93
Hassall, Peter 11, 49, 51, 181
Haut-Clos Prison, Troyes 175
Hayes, John Crossley 112, 114, 133, 141, 143, 144, 146–7, 154–62, 169, 181
Howlett, Alfred 165–6

interrogation 32, 46–7, 49, 139–40, 142

Janvrin, Evelyn 72, 85, 93, 96
Jourablo, Michael 95

Keil, Georg 71
Keiller, Frank 27, 34, 41, 51, 72, 75–6, 79, 93–4, 103, 181
Koster, Siebe 92–3

Lainé, Sir Abraham 127
L'Amy, Albert 123–4, 159
Lanyon, Hubert 114–15, 143–4, 150–1, 155–6, 159
Leale, John 127, 153
Le Cocq, Kevin 35, 69
Le Gros, Charles 42, 68
Le Lievre, Eugene 178
Le Marchand, Douglas 90
Le Marquand, George 43–4, 74–5, 90–1
Le Pennec, Frank 67

Le Quesne, Edward 11, 34–5, 45, 60, 65–6, 69–70, 99–100, 103
Le Sueur, Francis 79–80
Lohse, Karl 48, 50

Machon, Charles 134, 157–8, 161
McKinstry, Noel 68, 76–8
McLinton, Denis 87
Malherbe, Suzanne 12, 38, 42–3, 53–4, 58, 81–2, 93, 99, 101
Marquand, Henry 139–40, 141, 176
Mière, Joe 7–8, 26–7, 46, 57, 60, 65, 67–8, 99–101, 104, 181
Mylne, Clement 103

Neil, Mickey 27
Neuoffingen forced labour camp 172
Nicolle, John 1
Nicolle, Marie Louise 147
Noel, Peter 74, 87
North Clifton annexe 126, 128, 130

Old Glostonians 103
Ozanne, Marie 116, 117, 124, 147–50

Pike, Albert 120, 122, 148
Pike, Lizzie 120
Pleasants, Eric 11, 31, 184–5
PTSD 31, 173

Quarrie, Reverend 35
Quin, William 168, 171

radios 1–2, 11, 43, 45, 53–4, 57, 59, 74, 83, 89, 92, 96, 103, 112, 115, 140, 142, 150, 157–8, 160
Red Cross parcels 33, 35, 57, 67
Russian prison servants 38, 79, 82, 103, 147, 150–1
Rutherford, Edward 92

St-Lô Prison 133, 175
St Saviour's wireless case 1
Sanderson, Roy 93
Saunders, Claude 88

Schmitz, Nikolaus 39, 72, 104
Schwob, Lucy 12, 29, 34, 38, 42–3, 46, 53–4, 57, 72, 74, 80–2, 95–6, 99–102
Scornet, François 64, 72–3, 80
Sherwill, Ambrose 123, 171
Short, Frederick 166–7, 169, 178
Silvertide 32, 47
Smith, Herbert 170–1, 173
Stroobant, Frank 114, 142, 146, 167

Terres, The 142, 157, 159
Thaureux, Alice 72
Thelland, James 34, 96
Tierney, Eileen 2–3
Tierney, Joseph vii, 1–4, 9, 54, 80–1
trial 1–2, 39, 112, 115, 131, 145, 157, 159–63, 168–72

Tuck, Frank 163, 164, 167, 170
Tudor Lodge 48
Turner, Belza 46, 86

Underground Retaliation Movement 88–90

violence 2, 32, 49, 51, 61, 67, 149, 157–8, 163–4, 167–8, 170, 176–7, 179–82
Von Aufsess, Baron 65–6, 68

warders (Jersey) 14, 23, 26, 28, 31, 35, 49, 58–9, 61, 70, 73, 75, 77, 90, 112, 122, 126–7, 130, 135, 139, 145, 148, 150, 176, 185
Webb, Denis 92
Webb, Victor 89–90
Weithley, Richard 75–6, 101
Wölfle, Heinz-Carl 48, 50, 139, 140, 165